Publishing
Political Science

Stephen Yoder
editor

AMERICAN POLITICAL SCIENCE ASSOCIATION
STATE OF THE PROFESSION SERIES

ISBN 1-878147-50-1

TABLE OF CONTENTS

III. TOPICS IN PUBLISHING 195

CONTRIBUTORS 255

STEPHEN YODER, UNIVERSITY OF MARYLAND, COLLEGE PARK

PUBLISHING POLITICAL SCIENCE: INTRODUCTION

For the past several years, the sessions hosted by the American Political Science Association at their annual meetings on successfully publishing in political science—one on book and one on journal publishing—were amongst the meetings' best attended. The persistent high demand for these sessions reveals that most political scientists are eager to learn the intricacies of getting published; this book guides political scientists on the fine points of writing and publishing successfully. This collection combines the sage writing advice of established political science authors with the insider knowledge of publishing professionals; it explains how to improve your writing for, and get published in, a variety of venues. It is the first edited volume on writing and publishing to target political scientists, and as such it offers advice not found elsewhere. Political scientists at all levels of the profession will find something new and useful here, but this book is particularly essential for graduate students and junior scholars.

This book gives firsthand accounts of the current layout of the publishing marketplace for political scientists (Part I), of what works (and what doesn't) in writing very specific types of articles or books (Part II), and of how to work with a publisher to get your work into print (Part III).

THE ACADEMIC PUBLISHING MARKETPLACE

Technological advances over the past 10 years alone, foremost amongst them the incredible growth and spread of the Internet, have revolutionized how books are produced and sold. Web printers have made small, on-demand print runs economically feasible, a welcome development indeed for scholarly publishing in particular, which has always taken a bath on small-print-run academic monographs. Academia has responded to these advances, Sandy Thatcher notes in Chapter 3, in a predictable way: by targeting even smaller audiences and thereby selling even less. This is truer in some subdisciplines than in others, but this change, among others Thatcher introduces, shrinks the marketplace for publishing political science as a whole. The most-telling proof being that many academic presses now insist on scholarship that has never before been published—including in electronic databases or on the Internet. Many academic presses will no longer publish revised dissertations as much of the original work therein has already been "published" through the ProQuest database. This change alone will affect how departments make hiring, promotion, and tenure decisions.

All presses have had to adapt to the advent of digital technology, though different types of presses have managed in different ways. Large university presses have generally consolidated or have limited their support of less lucrative fields. Those small university presses that have survived have found ways to outsource their distribution or production, often to larger academic presses. Institutional presses, as Chris Kelaher notes in Chapter 2, often find themselves somewhere in-between—being only an arm of a larger organization shields them from the full brunt of the free market, but this protection comes with certain restrictions, foremost being that the good of the institution trumps the good of the press.

Yes, despite the prognostications of doomsday books with harrowing titles,[1] presses still exist. Someday perhaps the rumors of the death of the book will not be greatly exaggerated, but that day is not today. Society as a whole has grown path dependent on books. Like for the internal-combustion engine, DVDs, and coal power, technologies better than the book exist. My recently purchased, used copy of E. E. Schattschneider's *Semi-Sovereign People* cannot seamlessly hyperlink to the universe of citations and refutations it beget; I cannot take notes in the text (at least not without substantially downgrading its $3.00 resale value); I cannot instantly send copies of it to an entire class. But I can easily carry it with me. I can bend it, drop it, and dog-ear its pages. I can read it anywhere where there is sufficient light. I like the (meager) weight of it. And I am still in the vast majority. Despite the advances that online databases such as Jstor, e-Gutenberg, or Google Scholar have wrought, or the increasing sophistication of the e-readers now on sale at your local bookstore, society remains committed to the old, in many ways inferior, technology of the book. This, I argue, comes from the tangible permanence people associate with the media of ink, paper, and binding; these give not just the book but the writing contained therein a certain comfortable heft.

WRITING FOR DIFFERENT PURPOSES

I've never had difficulty writing; it's in sharing my work, which hinges on producing writing that meets a certain standard, that the difficulty enters. This is made more difficult when I set the bar for quality high by writing for my ideal audience—my wife, family, and friends. This drive to perfect for our ideal audience, when combined with a good, healthy, idealistic belief in the eternal importance of our work, inhibits so many young writers, academics, and academic writers, young and old. This inhibition can be overcome, as many of the contributors to this collection note, through practice. Writing for an hour a day will give you a better feel for your writing and for the audience you hope it reaches. But practice is time-consuming and takes a great deal of devotion. Many scholars choose a faster, easier route. They neglect that holy grail of publisher's audiences, the "general, educated reader," to write to the narrowest audience possible. Political science journals are rife with articles whose authors, in their quest to find a perfect niche where their expertise goes unchallenged, chose words not to communicate ideas but to protect their egos and reputations. Subtle shifts between the meanings of synonyms intended to elide greater clarity are sacrificed for the words the author believes the most erudite, and often the least familiar. In the process, words lose their meaning, authors lose their audience, and jargon spews forth with ease. But, then, what is the point?

Scientists of all ilk are beholden to two tasks: study fascinating cases of interaction, and report the learned results for the benefit of the broader good. To whom we address our work is as important as the work itself, and as Beth Luey notes in Chapter 1, political science is unique among the social sciences and humanities in the sheer variety of the audiences to which it speaks, from scholars in other academic fields to members of the general public to the very practitioners of government themselves. This is an advantage that political scientists should not take for granted, yet many do so when they refuse to meet their audiences half way by explaining their data, methods, and findings in accessible prose. Perhaps it is inevitable that young scholars will continue to write for the audience for which their first major scholarly work was intended, the smallest, most esoteric grouping imaginable—a Ph.D. dissertation committee. Fortunately, academic careers are long enough to unlearn such habits and to relearn how to write for the myriad publishing audiences with which political science is blessed. Re-education of this sort has to start with the basics of good writing.

Writing is an extremely personal exercise that is difficult to take advice on from others and even more difficult to change. In Chapter 4, Tom Cronin sets forth sound advice on the foundations of good writing for authors at every academic level. Integrating just a few of his suggestions, say on bringing writing to life through sentence variation and usage of the active voice, will pay immediate dividends for authors and their audiences. Further, Cronin extols two rules on the process of writing. The first is to revise, revise, revise. The second is to set a specific number of times to revise, say five, then let whatever you're working on go.

This advice assumes, of course, that you have already started writing, whereas for many writers beginning is itself a chore. This is as it should be, Jennifer Hochschild notes in Chapter 5, for the first paragraph sets the tone for the rest of the paper. Her advice here lays out how successful articles in specific subfields introduce their argument. In Chapter 6, Jeffrey W. Knopf and Iain McMenamin move this advice forward to include writing literature reviews. If a solid introduction sets the tone for a piece of scholarship, then a thorough literature review "informs a focused setting of the scene for the argument developed in the text." They provide a detailed plan for acknowledging, evaluating, and building upon the work of others to frame the proposed research's contribution to knowledge.

Many political scientists write only monographs and journal articles. Though these comprise the profession's bread-and-butter, political scientists can supplement their diet (and their income) by writing for textbooks and reference books and by editing multi-authored books. When asked, I suspect that most political scientists would jump at the opportunity to write a textbook; they provide a larger audience and potential for fiscal rewards beyond that generally available to authors of academic monographs. But sufficient enthusiasm and a thorough knowledge of the subject matter, Karen O'Connor explains in Chapter 7, are not enough. Successful textbook authors must be extremely organized and disciplined to keep up with the daunting workload; much of a textbook's success depends on the quality of the press and its editors; and textbooks are often frowned upon by departments for the amount of an academic's time they take from other scholarly and pedagogic activities.

Academics who write for reference works and who edit multi-authored books can see their efforts similarly slighted when their portfolios come up for promotion or tenure. Reference books, Andrea Pedolsky, Doug Goldenberg-Hart, and Marc Segers explain in Chapter 8, are very different products than monographs, with the according benefit that your work may very well reach those outside of the discipline, and maybe even those outside of academia. Clive Thomas and Ronald Hrebenar's advice on editing multi-authored books in Chapter 9 speaks directly to the production of this book. Their advice is backed by academic editors everywhere, several of whom have mentioned to me that they assign the original 1992 *PS* article to academics thinking about taking on an edited volume. This version brings the process of editing multi-authored books current with the technological changes of the past 15 years. Editing a multi-authored book is intrinsically rewarding, but it is not for everyone. This chapter lets those considering such a project assess its rewards and pitfalls.

Mark Miller's contribution, Chapter 10, lays out the costs and benefits of reaching out in your written work to audiences in different academic fields. The rewards clearly echo what should be the academic creed: to dispense knowledge broadly. The actual costs, advancement and tenure, may exceed the value of even that lofty a goal. Blogging, Dan Drezner writes in Chapter 11, can extract a similar or greater cost. The risks of being passed over for or losing a job are high enough to lead many academics to blog anonymously or pseudonymously. But the rewards, disseminating academic knowledge across an immense, *general* audience, are even larger.

PUBLISHING POLITICAL SCIENCE

I served as managing editor for *PS: Political Science and Politics* for the past five years and have worked for various scholarly journals prior. During that time, I was constantly surprised at how little academics know about the peer-review process, especially in light of how pervasive peer-review is for scholarly books and journals and how many academics participate in some aspect of it. I edited Andrew Polsky's 2007 *PS* article on the peer-review process at scholarly journals, and have chosen (with his permission) to reprint it here in its entirety as Chapter 12 because it is the best explanation of the process I have read.

Alex Holzman's insights into the standards and practices of book publishing as a regular discussant in the APSA publishing sessions made him a natural choice to write Chapter 13 on query letters. These introduce and pitch a potential author's book idea to a publisher. Publishers notice the care that a potential author puts into the query letter, and see that level as representative of what an author will put into their project. Jennifer Knerr carries this good advice forward to negotiating the book contract. Her contribution, Chapter 14, is unprecedented in that it uses a publisher's insight to break down every facet of negotiating a book contract for the benefit of authors. A chapter of this sort is long overdue, and armed with it perhaps authors can begin to dissipate much of the acrimony that seems to exist in author/publisher relations. Leanne Anderson's conclusion, Chapter 15, speaks to how authors can reach for the still higher goal of author/ publisher understanding, and how doing so will directly benefit authors. Both parties are, after all, intent upon the same goal: publishing innovative scholarship that reaches its targeted audience.

ACKNOWLEDGEMENTS

This book could never have been published without the support of Rob Hauck, deputy director of the APSA. His belief in the need for just such a book, and in my ability to construct it, was unwavering, and no doubt steeped in his overarching and selfless goal of constantly improving the profession. Polly Karpowicz, APSA director of publications, ably handled all details of production. Rich Pottern created the attractive cover and page designs. I have worked on the editing and production of several different journals, and assumed that compiling an edited volume would be much the same. I was wrong; it is both more difficult and more rewarding. While my inexperience receives the blame for the former, the contributing authors receive the praise for the latter. They were as flexible with their schedules as they were dedicated to this book's concept, and they have produced truly well-researched and well-written chapters. It is my belief and hope that political scientists of all stages of career will find it reliable, well-written, and, most important, useful. Finally, this book owes a debt of gratitude to my wife, Alyssa, whose good humor, thoughtful advice, and steadfast belief saw this project through from its conception several years ago to its publication several months from now.

Stephen Yoder
University of Maryland, College Park
February 8, 2008

NOTE

[1] Of which 1995's *The Gutenberg Elegies* is my favorite title.

I

STATE OF PUBLISHING

BETH LUEY, EDITORIAL CONSULTANT

SHARING WHAT YOU KNOW

1

Most scholars choose their careers because they want to spend a lifetime learning things that other people do not know, and then let others in on the secret. The technical terms for these activities are, of course, research and publishing. Although all successful academics publish their research findings, political scientists have a great advantage over those in the humanities and even the hard sciences: their work and their audiences are so varied that a wide range of publishing opportunities is open to them. Other political scientists are interested in their work, of course, but so are scholars in other fields, including history, economics, and sociology. In addition, members of the public find political science both interesting and important; they form another audience for work in the discipline. Finally, people in government at all levels, political activists, lobbyists, and other policy makers find the research of political scientists relevant to their work. Each of these audiences may be addressed in a different way. To take advantage of these opportunities, academic writers need to know about the audiences and the media that reach them most efficiently. They should also recognize that research with more than one audience may need to be published in a variety of ways.

MEDIA

Like all academics, political scientists communicate with one another through journal articles and monographs. Unlike other scholars, though, political scientists have options for their academic books beyond university presses and commercial scholarly publishers because research institutes interested in politics or in specific geographic areas welcome their submissions. Monographs are something of an endangered species, as Sandy Thatcher points out in chapter 3, but they remain an important medium for communicating complex arguments that cannot be encompassed within an article. They also remain a tenure requirement in some fields.

Another medium that political scientists share with colleagues in other departments is the textbook, as Karen O'Connor explains in chapter 7. Although textbooks may be adding—or shifting to—electronic media, they remain crucial to college teaching. Textbook authorship is difficult, and it becomes an ongoing commitment because a successful book must be revised every two or three years. Unfortunately, textbooks often fail to impress tenure and promotion committees, so their authorship is generally reserved for senior scholars. (Senior scholars' reputations and names help to sell the books as well.) A successful textbook, particularly one for a survey class, can be extremely lucrative. Equally important, though, it is perhaps one of the best ways to promote one's view of the discipline to future scholars and citizens. A faculty member may reach dozens or possibly hundreds of students each year in the classroom, but tens of thousands each year through a textbook. And there are no exams to grade. Textbook authorship is also thought to be a good way to recruit graduate students to a doctoral program, though I have never seen any data to support this bit of folk wisdom.

One area where political scientists have a great advantage over scholars in every discipline except perhaps history is popular nonfiction. Foreign policy, domestic politics, elections, policy issues ranging from arms to the environment to welfare—all of these are of great interest to the intelligent reading public. Scholarly publishers will pursue these titles, but so will some of the trade houses (commercial publishers) whose wares range beyond sensational fiction and celebrity memoirs. Houses like Basic Books, W. W. Norton, John Wiley, and many others are all possible publishers for works in political science that address an audience beyond the academy.[1] There is a publisher to fit every point on the political spectrum, as well as those that are politically neutral. University administrators do not always give full credit for books published by trade houses. They reason, erroneously, that because such books may not have undergone the thorough peer review that university presses employ they are not as good.[2] Like textbooks, then, trade books are often written by senior scholars whose reputations also help to sell their books.

Senior scholars are also more likely to have developed the writing skills needed to communicate with educated but nonacademic readers. Making complex ideas accessible to nonspecialists is a challenge. Trade books require authors to provide context and explain theory and background that would be familiar to peers but not to others who will find their work valuable. They also require writing without resort to jargon and other linguistic shortcuts. They can be financially rewarding (though almost always less so than textbooks), but they are also rewarding because they allow authors to get their ideas out to the public, where perhaps they will make a difference outside academe.

Making a difference suggests writing for yet another audience: policy makers and practitioners. If research has implications for policy, its author will want to make sure that the relevant politicians and administrators are aware of it. If research suggests better ways for practitioners to do their job, the author will want to reach them. This does not necessarily require writing a book. Sometimes media attention to a paper given at a national or international conference, or to an article in an influential journal, is all that is needed. A researcher will probably get more attention from an interview on NPR than from a scholarly monograph. Consulting is also an efficient way to influence policy and practice. If people hire a political scientist to give them advice, they are likely to listen. But sometimes a book will help. If nothing else, having published a book may make it more likely that the author will be interviewed on NPR or hired as a consultant. In these cases, university presses, research institutions, or trade publishers may be the appropriate publisher, but houses like Jossey-Bass, often referred to as professional publishers, specialize in books for professionals in specific areas. If they publish a book on educational policy, for example, they will target an audience of education officials, advisors, and administrators.[3]

Reference books, discussed in chapter 8, are another relevant medium for political scientists. Specialized encyclopedias, dictionaries, handbooks, almanacs, yearbooks, and the like provide up-to-date information relevant to elections, international relations, and many other topics. Because they need to be updated frequently, and because users consult them rather than read them cover to cover, many reference publications are now appearing in electronic formats.

So much debate today is centered on electronic publication that it is worth a few words. Both journals and books are being made available in electronic formats, with or without a print equivalent. The shift in medium makes less real difference than you might think. First, the cost savings is small if it exists at all. The major costs of publishing—overhead, editing, design, and marketing—remain the same. If there is no paper-and-ink product, then printing costs are eliminated, but these are not large for books published in only a few hundred copies, as is true of specialized monographs. In addition, the cost of creating and maintaining a site where the book is available is significant. Perhaps more important, users of electronic products have high expectations for searchability, documentation, illustration, and so forth. Meeting these expectations adds to the cost of the book and means more work for the author. For example, the data sets that an author would never include in a printed book might be expected in an online version. Finally, the assumption that if you post it they will come is erroneous. Without marketing and publicity, no one will find an electronic publication. If you don't believe this, see how many copies of your dissertation UMI has sold, or simply post a new site on the Web without publicity and see how many hits you get. Publishers are experimenting with business models for electronic publications, and they will undoubtedly find some that work well, but—with the exception of reference books—we aren't there yet.

The other question about electronic media is whether the committees that hire or grant tenure and promotion will be receptive to them and know how to evaluate them. The central question should not be the medium: it should be the quality of the work. Quality may be recognized by readers, it may be certified by peer review and the publisher's imprint, or it may be attested to by citation counts. In all of these matters, electronic publication has not caught up. It will, and probably soon, but perceptions may lag behind.

Authors who choose to publish in an online-only journal, or to publish an e-book without a print equivalent, need to ensure that certain things happen. The publication should appear with the imprimatur of a respectable publisher. It should be peer reviewed, and this fact should be readily apparent to evaluators. The publisher should guarantee that the work will be properly edited and should describe an effective marketing plan. (The point of the marketing plan is not to make the work a bestseller. It is to make sure that the people who should read it, no matter their number, will know that it is available.) Finally, authors should be sure that their institution, from the department chair to the president, is receptive to online publication.[4]

MATERIAL

Scholarly books are the product of research. In the past, it was common for authors to publish articles based on their research as they went along and then collect these, with some introductory material and connective tissue, into a book. This is no longer possible. Most book publishers will ask how much of the material in a manuscript has appeared in print, and if it is more than 20 or 25%, they will not be interested. As library budgets have tightened, librarians have little interest in paying twice for the same information. This does not mean that research results must be hoarded for years until there is enough for a book. It does mean that authors must be careful about how they use their work as they go along. In all likelihood, articles can be published from material that will be tangential to the book. For example, an innovative methodology can be written up as an article. When it's time to write the book, the methodology can be described with merciful brevity plus a note citing the article.

The possibility of using work more than once is enhanced if the writing will be addressed to more than one audience. Fellow political scientists want more detail and less background than politicians or educated general readers, so the articles addressed to the former will be quite different from the books or articles for general periodicals addressed to the latter. Although both are based on the same research, there is really no duplication.

And duplication is to be avoided. Scientists are especially attuned to the dangers of redundant publication, or publishing the same work, perhaps thinly disguised, more than once. Political scientists should be equally wary of the practice. Science publishers use a term that illustrates the dishonesty and futility of duplicate publication: salami publishing. Imagine the outcome of a research project as a one-pound salami. You may slice it very, very thin (in slices sometimes referred to as LPUs, or least publishable units) and add many lines to your CV, or you may publish it in larger, meatier chunks. If you choose the thin-slice method, your readers (and possibly the peer reviewers) will get the feeling that they've seen this before somewhere, and they will consider the work trivial or outdated. When the time for tenure or promotion rolls around, the reviewers who look at your entire record will not be fooled: a pound of salami is still only a pound. Productivity should reflect the quantity of actual research performed, not the ability to pad a CV.

With that said, however, authors should get as much legitimate mileage as possible from their work. This requires being thoughtful about the possibility of going off on a productive tangent to generate an article, or thinking about how part of the work might interest a different set of readers. For example, might something in the research be useful to people who teach in high school or freshman surveys? If so, a journal addressed to teachers is a possible venue for part of the work that might otherwise go unpublished. If historical material was part of the research, might some of the findings be of interest to historians in their disciplinary journals? Does the work have possible applications that might be of interest to practitioners? Waste not, want not.

Publishing material from a dissertation, or developing a dissertation into a book, is a similar but somewhat special case. As Sandy Thatcher notes in chapter 3, publishing a dissertation as a book, even if it has been revised, is becoming extremely difficult. To be honest, not all dissertations deserve to become books. A dissertation is an academic exercise with a limited purpose: to allow the candidate to demonstrate knowledge of the discipline, its literature, and its research methods; the ability to carry out independent research; and the writing skill to communicate findings. When the candidate is wise enough—and lucky enough—to choose a subject that generates interesting new knowledge, the results are publishable. But these results may be published most productively as one or more journal articles. After all, major parts of the dissertation— the literature review and bibliography and the methodology—are not usually publishable. The more defensive prose, in which the candidate defends the thesis against everyone who might possibly attack it, is not of interest. The balance can usually be written up more briefly. A strong article published in an excellent journal is often the best result.

If, however, book publication is necessary, the dissertation is the obvious source, but it will require extensive revision. The key is deciding on the audience. The audience for the dissertation was the committee— hardly a large enough group to interest a publisher. Expanding the audience will probably require expanding the topic geographically, temporally, or theoretically; and that will require expanding the research. It is probably best to think of the book as an entirely new project based loosely on the dissertation. The first step, then, is for the author to evaluate objectively whether the subject of the dissertation is worth the additional work, in terms of his or her own interests and its publishability. If it is worth the work, is the work possible? If the author no longer has access to the necessary sources, or if there *are* no sources, or if tapping those sources will take too long, the answer is no. Let us suppose, though, that the author's interest in the project is still keen, that others will be interested, and that the resources are available to do the additional research needed. Let us assume, too, that accessible secondary sources can fill in some of the gaps. Then the author can go ahead and get to work, planning the tasks and time according to the schedule the tenure clock imposes. (A postdoctoral fellowship is a considerable help here.) Along the way, as the focus of the book becomes clear, material that will not be needed in the book can be used as the basis of journal articles. These serve a dual purpose: they make the tenure committee happy, and they get the author's name and work into the public view—and into the consciousness of book editors. When the manuscript is complete, editors will be eager to see it. When the book comes out, the author's name will be known and potential readers will be eager to read—and buy—the book.[5]

WRITING AND PUBLISHING

Dozens of books have been written about how to write, and I have taken a solemn oath not to add to them. Because writing is the core of academic life, being a successful and happy scholar requires learning to write clearly and easily. Any scholar who adds up the conference papers, articles, books, recommendation letters, grant applications, progress reports, and committee reports generated over a lifetime has used more reams of paper than any of us really want to think about. The best way to learn to write is to read good books and to write every day. The more you write, the easier it gets. After five or ten years, it should get pretty easy. After ten or twenty, it may even get to be fun. But it takes practice. Spending at least an hour a day, every day, will do the trick.

Another pair of eyes is always helpful. Colleagues who are good critical readers can be asked to read either early work or polished drafts. Tactful readers are easier on the ego, but insight is more important than diplomacy. Some people find it helpful to form a writing group that meets regularly to review one another's writing, to help when someone has gotten stuck, and to celebrate completed work and publishing contracts.

Publishing efficiently requires that you become familiar with the journals and book publishers in your field. All researchers naturally keep up with the literature. All that needs to be added is a bit of attention to the media along with the message. Every journal has a statement of editorial policy, published at least once a year in its pages and probably on its web site. Wise authors have a collection of these, kept up to date, for all the journals that are possible venues for their work. These statements generally explain the kind of work the editor is looking for, the refereeing process, and the physical requirements for submissions. It is important, however, to look beyond the published statements.

Those who read a journal attentively will quickly become attuned to what the editor is looking for. Any bias that exists toward a particular ideology, methodology, or subdisciplinary area will be apparent. A preference for controversy over consensus, or vice versa, will be detectable. Does a journal seem to publish mostly established scholars, or does it give considerable space to new researchers? Is policy-oriented research welcome or frowned upon? Does highly quantitative research dominate? Editorial statements may not answer these questions, but regular reading will. And, of course, the answers may change when the editorship moves.

Before submitting an article, it is essential to look carefully at the physical requirements. Does the editor want a query letter? Should submissions be electronic or hard copy and, if the latter, how many copies are requested? Should the author's name appear only on a cover page, simplifying blind review? What documentation style is preferred? Journal editors are busy, and failure to meet the mechanical requirements they impose may abort the review process before anyone can tell how interesting or important the content is.

The same is true of book publication. Close attention to a press's mission statement, backlist, and current publications will shorten the list of possible publishers and prevent wasting time. Query letters and prospectuses will also rule out publishers who are not right for the manuscript. Following instructions about the physical preparation of the manuscript and the number of copies to be submitted will save time both in the review process and in the production of the book.[6]

The key to successful authorship is to write about interesting, important work in a manner that will appeal to the audience being addressed. Not an easy task—and certainly not one for which there is a magic formula. Fortunately, opportunities abound, and anyone who has survived graduate school has all the basic tools close at hand.

NOTES

1. On writing for this audience see Susan Rabiner and Alfred Fortunato, *Thinking Like Your Editor: How to Write Great Serious Nonfiction . . . And Get It Published* (New York: Norton, 2002).

2. Beth Luey, "Are Fame and Fortune the Kiss of Death?" *Publishing Research Quarterly* 19 (Winter 2003): 36–47.

3. For a thorough discussion of the various types of publisher, see my *Handbook for Academic Authors*, 4th ed. (New York: Cambridge University Press, 2002), chap. 4.
4. Ibid., chap. 12.
5. Two recent books on revising dissertations are Beth Luey, ed., *Revising Your Dissertation: Advice from Leading Editors*, rev. ed. (Berkeley and Los Angeles: University of California Press, 2007), and William Germano, *From Dissertation to Book* (Chicago: University of Chicago Press, 2005).
6. The three most popular advice books for academic authors are my *Handbook for Academic Authors;* Robin Derricourt, *An Author's Guide to Scholarly Publishing* (Princeton: Princeton University Press, 1996); and William Germano, *Getting It Published: A Guide for Scholars and Anyone Else Serious about Serious Books* (Chicago: University of Chicago Press, 2001).

CHRISTOPHER J. KELAHER, BROOKINGS INSTITUTION PRESS

2

INSTITUTIONAL PUBLISHING AND POLITICAL SCIENCE

Perhaps the most difficult aspect of institutional publishing is the recurring battle between institutional priorities and common publishing practice. When the two come into conflict—a fairly common occurrence—institutional needs typically come out on top. It is important for the author and publisher to keep that in mind while planning, to keep expectations reasonable and to avoid at least some potholes rather than driving through them. Given that disadvantage, it becomes doubly important to make good use of any comparative advantages your publishing program might have as a result of its institutional status—in other words, you use the good and deal with the bad. Presumably, every institution has some comparative strengths. (If yours does not, maybe you should go cash your paycheck now.)

I am fortunate to work for the Brookings Institution, an organization with a long and rich tradition of book publishing. Our first book was released in 1918, and we currently have nearly 1,000 books in print. Our signature economics journal, *Brookings Papers on Economic Activity*, was first published in 1970. Our bestselling title still in print, Arthur Okun's *Equality and Efficiency: The Big Tradeoff*, was published in 1975 and has now sold 172,000 copies. (Still no movie, though. Go figure.) So we definitely have a strong brand and a big backlist, giving us more clout in acquisitions, marketing, and fulfillment than many other institutional publishers. But we still need to overcome many of the same obstacles.

INSTITUTIONAL PUBLISHING

Generalizing about institutional publishing is a little dicey since the category covers such a wide range of organizations, audiences, missions, financial structures, and publishing programs. It includes, but is not limited to, the work of think tanks, professional membership groups, trade associations, scholarly societies, and advocacy groups. When I first started looking for a publishing job in Washington, I was amazed to find that one of the biggest, most vibrant book programs was at the American Association of Blood Banks. Blood banks—who knew? But all institutional publishing operations are subject to at least some of the challenges encountered by all independent or scholarly book publishers in these uncertain times:

- declining library sales;
- increased paper costs;
- increasing postal rates;
- consolidation of the book industry, including the decline of independent bookstores, the difficulty of selling scholarly or mid-list titles, the intense (and expensive) fight for bookstore shelf space, etc.;
- the need to provide authors with sufficient incentive;
- the insatiable desire for instant and up-to-date information; and
- competition from other modes of communication.

An institution's publishing program is a function of several different factors, including the institution's mission, leadership, history, clientele, author pool, and available resources. The book publishing operation is typically just one arm of an outreach or communications strategy. Although the shape of these operations and the degree of independence within divisions varies greatly, they face many of the same issues.

Electronic publishing

Every institutional and scholarly publisher worth its salt has been assessing and reassessing its electronic communication strategy over the past several years. Since all public policy authors think that their work is time-sensitive and thus needs to be "fast tracked," electronic dissemination (e.g., PDFs, email, web sites, podcasts) has obvious appeal. In some cases, this is the most logical distribution strategy. It is especially reasonable for organizations that give away most of their material, rather than trying to sell it. For one thing, it saves the cost and time needed for printing and delivery. For operations that need to bring in money as well as spend it, however, things get a bit more complicated. The Brookings Institution Press is a good example.

Although electronic dissemination can save some money, as shown above, many of the publishing costs remain. Take for example a fairly typical Brookings book—an edited volume on American politics—published in jacketed hardback and paperback editions simultaneously. Print and freight account for about 40% of the direct costs—a significant amount, but not much more than the projected combined costs of editing, proofreading, and indexing. In order for the publication to look presentable and be readable, it needs to be typeset, and that costs money too—in this case, we projected freelance composition costs of $3,400. So while e-publishing can certainly save some money, it is far from free. We tell people that all the time, but I have a hunch that some of them aren't listening.

If a publishing operation is expected to be self-sufficient or at least recover a large portion of its costs, ease and speed of delivery are not the only considerations. One also needs to consider the market: what people will actually buy, and in what format. We do currently produce "e-books"—essentially PDFs of final pages—and sell them through a handful of vendors such as Net Library and Ebrary. But they account for only a very small fraction of our overall sales, not nearly enough to cover the costs of producing them. We still rely on selling bound books for most of our income.

For a scholarly publisher such as Brookings, the costs of developing the manuscript need to be taken into account and recovered, as well. With our in-house projects, the author's time must be paid for somehow, and external acquisitions sometimes call for royalties to be paid. And in either case, a Brookings book manuscript typically goes through an extensive vetting process. (More on that later.) All of this takes time and money, thus making it important to recover costs through book sales and related revenue (e.g., reprint permissions, translation rights).

Incentives

Writing a book is hard work—writing a good one is an especially arduous task. Someone needs to have a good reason to invest the time and energy necessary. In most cases, money is at least one factor, though it typically is not the key issue for institutional or scholarly authors.

In our case, in-house authors often produce book manuscripts as part of their salaried position. Occasionally, our research directors will actually commission books by outside authors, typically for a fee. Other authors, however, come to us via our external acquisitions program, in which case the money they stand to earn through royalties is often modest. In order to produce and sell enough books to make real money for an author, a publisher needs to invest considerable resources not only into development and production, but into marketing and promotion as well. Many institutions don't have those resources to spare, or they don't look at book publishing as the best use of limited capacity.

Other author incentives are professional. Most scholarly authors, for example, don't expect to pay the mortgage with their first few books, but those titles are very helpful in the Great Tenure Quest. Not all publishers count equally when a tenure committee makes its decision, however. Authors need to consider their own needs, especially when they have a choice of publishers. I have lost some great manuscripts because a young author was advised that his or her tenure committee would rather see a "more traditional" university press on the CV even if that meant a slower production time, less marketing, and less exposure outside academia. On the other hand, some academic departments like our "applied" focus and encourage (and reward) their faculty for publishing with us.

Most organizations have a stated mission, and contributing to that mission can be the most important incentive of all for an author. For example, many folks who choose to publish with us do so because they know we will promote the book in policy circles and that we are plugged into those debates, on Capitol Hill or elsewhere. These authors share the Brookings mission to inform and improve public policy. They want their work to matter, and access to their desired audience becomes the most important incentive of all.

MY INSTITUTION, MY PRESS

According to our web site:

> The Brookings Institution is a private nonprofit organization devoted to independent research and innovative policy solutions. For more than 90 years, Brookings has analyzed current and emerging issues and produced new ideas that matter—for the nation and the world. For policymakers and the media, Brookings scholars provide the highest quality research, policy recommendations, and analysis on the full range of public policy issues.

> Research at the Brookings Institution is conducted to inform the public debate, not advance a political agenda. Our scholars are drawn from the United States and abroad—with experience in government and academia—and hold diverse points of view. Brookings's goal is to provide high-quality analysis and recommendations for decision-makers in the U.S. and abroad on the full range of challenges facing an increasingly interdependent world.

The key to publishing successfully *within* an organization is to stay relevant to its overall mission while remaining economically viable. The current mantra in our headquarters is: "Quality. Independence. Impact." So we at the Brookings Press need to keep honing our ability to produce books of high quality, free of undue influence or political baggage, that have the potential to improve public policy and politics. And we need to produce them quickly enough to keep on top of current events. That can be a challenge in the era of instant news cycles, the Internet, blogging, podcasting, and RSS feeds. And of course we also need to do all of this efficiently enough to keep the operation financially sustainable.

Despite the need for speed, we still need to maintain high quality not only in our content, but in our presentation and manufacturing as well. In my mind, there are real differences between a book and a report, a white paper, or a policy brief. Those differences help define the distinction between being a "publisher" and a "publications department," and they help justify having a full-fledged scholarly press as part of the institution's structure. There is a reason we are called the Brookings Institution *Press*, and to me, at least, the distinction is very important.

Scale

Our operation is large enough to provide us with economy of scale over many smaller publishing operations. Thus we are able to market and distribute books published by several other policy groups with similar audiences but smaller publishing operations. Our distributed presses include reputable organizations such as the Century Foundation, the Carnegie Endowment for International Peace, and the Center for Global Development. These partner presses help fill out our list and give us additional heft in the marketplace, while our existing structure allows them to swim in the same marketing and fulfillment streams as Brookings books. Both sides win.

On the other hand, we are also one of several scholarly publishers now farming out its warehousing and order fulfillment to Hopkins Fulfillment Services, hoping to capitalize on *their* greater economy of scale. This type of partnership helps make it possible for institutional publishers to survive in a challenging environment. As with everything in life, there are tradeoffs, which can include some reduction of autonomy or flexibility. But if that's what it takes to stay in the game, it's probably worth it.

Manuscript acquisition

Over the past couple of decades, the Brookings Institution Press has built a successful program of external acquisitions, through which we publish manuscripts that do not originate with our scholars but that do fit our profile. This program has been important in a number of ways. It adds both depth and breadth to our catalog, allowing us to fill gaps in our in-house list and helping us get through occasional fallow periods in our research divisions. Since we theoretically have more options open to us than our research divisions do, we can choose projects that might actually turn a profit. The idea is that the acquisitions program can help float the press operation, ensuring our ability to keep publishing important but relatively narrow research that might not find a large buying audience. (Some university presses use their journals in a similar way, and others use textbook programs to support their scholarly monographs.)

Once again, economy of scale comes into play—we believe that a larger list gives us greater market presence and makes us more attractive in the eyes of media, reviewers, and the entire book trade. Ideally, that will help us attract more strong authors, and the whole happy cycle continues.

Establishing an external acquisitions program has placed us in a competitive arena. Prospective acquired authors presumably have options on where to publish, so we stress to them our comparative advantages, particularly in terms of what we can do for them and their work. We have many strong points, of course, but two of our most effective recruiting tools are our speed of publication and access to the public policy community. Brookings is an ideal home for manuscripts designed to bridge the gap between academics and practitioners of public policy, and many prospective authors look to us in order to reach a broader audience than the typical monograph would find. I also stress our continuing commitment to high-quality editing and production standards, which often suffer when a press finds itself in a money crunch. We don't cut those corners, and that's one reason we have many repeat customers, i.e., authors that publish more than one book with us.

We find new manuscripts in a number of ways, many of which mirror other publishers. Some projects or tips come to us through Brookings scholars who hear of interesting work being done elsewhere. We read through political science journals and conference papers to see who is working on what, and follow up on that with direct contact (usually starting with email). And then there is the ideal case, where we target a hot topic and an author to address it, and we then find that the author either is working on something relevant already or is interested in taking on the topic. All editors would like to be more proactive than reactive, but that is easier said than done, given the volume of proposals we receive and the attention they need.

We also work very hard at making ourselves known to—and seen by—outside scholars. We attend key academic meetings and meet with authors. For example, we took three booths and two pages of advertising at the recent APSA conference, where we exhibited our newest books while meeting with a number of potential authors. We never miss visiting the Palmer House for Midwest PSA, and we usually exhibit at the APPAM and International Studies Association conventions. One good approach for a political scientist hoping to publish with Brookings is to contact me or my colleague Mary Kwak well in advance of a convention that he or she plans to attend. If we have time enough before the conference to read and react to a proposal, a subsequent face-to-face at the convention can be fruitful.

We read and consider many proposals that come to us unannounced, or "over the transom." In such cases, we ask for a synopsis of the project, a table of contents, a list of contributors if the book is a collection, a sample chapter or two, and the author's CV. We need to know the intended audiences, and who will buy the book. As with most good publishers, a relatively high percentage of these unsolicited proposals don't get very far, but some do get off the ground. (One small hint to prospective authors: don't *ever* send a blind query—address it to a specific person. If you can't be bothered to learn my name, we aren't going to get along very well.)

INSTITUTIONAL CHALLENGES

Our acquisitions program helps illustrate how being an institutional press can make life easier as a publisher, and how it can sometimes work in the opposite direction.

Preconceptions

Brookings has a well-earned and longstanding reputation for high-quality policy analysis and other scholarly research. We are especially adept at bridging the gaps between theory and practice, and between academia and government. Thus, we are very attractive to potential authors who want to inject their work directly into policy debates. Authors tell me, "I want my book to be read and used, rather than just sit on a shelf." Amen to that. However, over the years I have had to turn down some potentially excellent work that was deemed by colleagues in our research divisions (my *de facto* editorial board) to be insufficiently policy-centric. I am happy to report that we've improved our ability to push through books that merit publication even if they don't precisely fit a preconceived Brookings "mold," but it remains the case that I cannot publish a manuscript without some stamp of approval from the most relevant research division. In this way, Brookings's traditional emphasis on applied public policy actually works against me in the search for new projects. So a strength can become a weakness in certain contexts.

Quality control

The most powerful asset I have as an acquisitions editor, by far, is the strong reputation of Brookings. That was true when I arrived in 1999, and it will be true when they wheel me out the door. It certainly makes acquiring outside projects much easier. But there is a price.

When my predecessor (Nancy Davidson) and Director Bob Faherty started the acquisitions program, they met with some resistance. In order to assure our scholars that enlarging the list would not dilute it, the Press agreed to follow essentially the same vetting process that applied to in-house research projects. That means I usually need in-house approval of an initial proposal; the manuscript needs to pass muster with the relevant research director; then we need three peer reviews, despite my annual pleading that we reduce this number to two.

In addition to confirming the quality and originality of a manuscript, we must be able to project a profit when all is said and done, even taking into consideration our overhead costs. After all, we can lose money with our own people—no one is paying me to go out and find new ways to build a deficit. (Too bad—I would be really good at that job.) So as you can see, getting a manuscript over all the hurdles and across the finish line is very challenging. It is the price to be paid for the Brookings imprimatur that goes so far in many circles, and it is another case where the needs of the institution establish the parameters of my work.

As an acquisitions editor, I benefit from the reputation of unofficial scouts within the ranks of our scholars. Several of our most successful acquisitions were first pitched to Brookings scholars, who then put the prospective author in touch with me. That is a great help to us, because while many political scientists know me by now, I'm no Tom Mann. I need to be wary of competing with in-house work, however, and that occasionally can limit what I can acquire. Thus while the existent program can help bring in strong new titles, it can also make it harder to build a list. Allow me to illustrate.

Competition and turf

Several years ago I established a relationship with a well-known scholar who was working on terrorism *before* everyone was working on terrorism. I took the book proposal to our scholars but was warned off of it because our foreign policy program already had a terrorism book in the pipeline, and there was a concern that my project would compete with it. I understood the rationale and didn't push the envelope but still disagreed with that approach to a topic so important (and so wide open, at least at the time). Our book *Terrorism in U.S. Foreign Policy* was released in early 2001. Needless to say, after September 11 we could barely keep up with demand. I'm certainly glad we had that book available at the time, but no one will ever convince me that having another authoritative book on terrorism available at the same time would have been a bad thing. (Witness the number of books on terrorism that have been published *since* 2001.) But my autonomy is limited, and the perceived needs of the institution won out over my needs as a book publisher.

Situations such as these amplify the importance of maximizing and utilizing whatever comparative advantage your institutional context provides, because that context will also present obstacles that competitors may not face.

MARKETING

Marketing institutional publishing can be a lot more difficult than one might think. It comes with its own inherent challenges, as any type of publishing does. And there are times when the wants and needs of the press clash with those of the institution as a whole.

Perceptions

While Brookings's brand recognition is a major asset to our operation overall, it can sometimes work against us. Although we stress our independence and non-partisan status, people have their own preconceived notions about most "think tanks." At least once in every major exhibit I attend, someone comes up and asks me, "Are you the liberal one, or the conservative place?" Or they ask which political party we represent. That mindset colors the lens through which they see us and interpret our work, and it can make both acquisitions and marketing more difficult. We operate in a competitive environment, and most university presses and commercial presses don't carry that kind of baggage. In contrast to the common misperception that we are all slightly left-of-center Democrats, we publish plenty of work that could appeal to the other side of the aisle, too: witness recent titles such as *Work over Welfare: The Inside Story of the 1996 Welfare Reform Law.* Still, I suspect that some right-leaning authors might not think to submit their work to us, and some potential customers might tune us out too quickly because of their preconceived notions. We are making inroads here, I'm pleased to say, but we have a lot more work to do. Hopefully, we will find more authors willing to help us make our case.

Timing

Our authors have a nasty habit of being late with manuscripts. (I suspect we are not alone in this.) In addition to the usual litany of excuses about homework-eating cocker spaniels, our rigorous vetting process sometimes slows things down. The need to participate in real-time policy debates (e.g., Capitol Hill testimony, op-eds, and media calls) often takes precedence, too. So a project with a longer lead time can get pushed back, back, back. Books that come in well beyond their announced dates cause havoc in sales, and I worry that they cost us some credibility with customers and potential reviewers. However, it's just another example of having to take the bad with the good in institutional publishing.

Many of our prospective authors do not understand the calendar of publishing, or they choose to ignore it. Given that publishing is only one of the institution's activities rather than its sole purpose, this is understandable, but it can certainly make our job tougher. Sometimes we have a hard time getting necessary information from our research divisions in a timely fashion, yet we often can't go very far without it. And at least twice a season we need to bring out a book before it has ever appeared in a catalog, in order to keep up with events. That makes it difficult to promote, sell, and distribute the work through booktrade channels effectively, but that often is of less importance to our authors than quickly getting the book into the hands of key audiences such as legislators and media. Once again, the research needs and bureaucratic organization of the institution win out over the needs of book publishing.

For years, our seasonal catalog process ran behind that of other presses so that we could give our most time-sensitive (or late-arriving) policy books a chance to be included. I just recently changed our schedule, however, to make new title information available earlier—time will tell how much it helps, and how much cooperation we get. But in this case, the market spoke. As a publisher, we had to answer.

DISSEMINATION

Brookings generates all sorts of written outreach material. Pamphlets, brochures, catalogs, email blasts, web sites—you name it. And like many think tanks, it produces a passel of policy briefs, op-eds, congressional testimony, and media appearances. All of these vehicles have their purposes, their strong and weak points.

Why books?

Books serve many purposes better than shorter, more ephemeral pieces can. They allow for more depth of analysis, more complete citation to buttress arguments, fuller fleshing out of details, and better use of examples. Plus they have a greater permanence, and I would argue that a printed book is as good a user interface as you'll find anywhere. I also believe that books convey greater gravitas in general, although some people would argue that is untrue or beside the point, and that I'm woefully out of date. (I don't have an iPod, what could I possibly know?) But books also take longer and cost more to produce; they are heavier and cost more to mail. An institution needs to take those things into consideration when deciding how to publish and disseminate its work.

Give it? Or sell it?

Many of our authors want their book to be distributed and read on Capitol Hill and in other branches or levels of government. Legislators and their staffers often expect to get the books for free, however. Since a primary goal of our work is to inform policymakers and help them do *their* job, it is in Brookings' interest to get books into their hands. But it is a financial loss. In those cases, the research divisions are assessed a unit price for each copy they give away, thus providing some cost control, but the assessed cost is nowhere near the list price or even the heavily discounted price we get from wholesalers. In the case of some esoteric material, the research divisions distribute enough free copies to hamper our sales efforts—a healthy percentage of the people who might be expected to buy the book get it for free. That's fine—it serves the needs of the institution, which is what matters most. But in some cases it can hurt the Press' bottom line, and it is incumbent upon us to remind the powers that be why sales are low in a case like that. Since we are held accountable for the bottom line, we need to keep people cognizant of the things that influence it. Fortunately, our administration is pretty savvy to these factors by now.

Many institutions are member-based. (Brookings is not.) In some cases, the cost of membership includes free receipt of the organization's key publications. Either the membership fees adequately cover the costs of producing and distributing those free copies, or the net loss is considered affordable and a worthwhile tradeoff. For example, as an APSA member I receive *PS*, *APSR*, and *Perspectives*. The subscriptions alone more than justify my membership fees, and I do use the publications, but I'm not sure I would think to seek out and buy those publications if they weren't sent to my house. So direct mailing of them to members increases the chances that political scientists will use these important publications, and it thus advances the mission of APSA.

I won't pretend I know a great deal about association publisher operations, since I've never worked for one. But I have enough friends that do to say that many of the challenges presented above pertain to most or all institutional publishers. They are nearly always under financial pressure, for several reasons:

- They have limited budgets, often constrained by the limits of membership, fundraising, or sales.
- Since the nature of what and how they publish often narrows their buying audience, sales revenues are often (though not always) modest.
- They are often pressured to be generous with free or discounted copies, making it difficult to recoup costs.
- Every organization has many different modes of constituent communication from which to choose. In many cases, book publishing needs to compete with other forms of outreach and dissemination for limited resources.

Of course, some institutional publishers are abundantly well funded, in which case they actually have more freedom to produce the long-term, in-depth, tightly focused work that so many scholars would like to do. Heck, they might not even be in a hurry. Every press is different, after all. But I have a feeling that those publishers are the exceptions, not the rule. In order to compete with other forms of communication, many institutional publishers are pressured to improve speed, widen distribution, and increase accessibility, all while keeping costs manageable. And oh yes, they need to make their books available, especially since each author has an aunt in Peoria who searched and searched for his or her new book in Borders but just couldn't find it *anywhere*. It is not an easy proposition, but you might be surprised at how many organizations are giving it a go, and doing a great job. Long may they continue.

Sanford G. Thatcher, Penn State University Press

Scholarly Book Publishing in Political Science: A Hazardous Business

3

Scholarly book publishing has been a hazardous business at the best of times. One of its most famous practitioners, Chester Kerr of Yale University Press, admitted as much in 1949 when he authored a major report on the state of the industry at that time: "We publish the smallest editions at the greatest cost, and on these we place the highest prices and then we try to market them to people who can least afford them. This is madness." A contemporary of Kerr's who directed Harvard University Press, Thomas Wilson, had a similar view: "A university press exists to publish as many good scholarly books as possible short of bankruptcy," the implication being that presses operate very close to the margin, if they do not actually operate on life support most of the time through subsidies from their parent universities. More recently, a close observer of the business, Cathy Davidson, vice provost for interdisciplinary studies at Duke University, even questioned whether it could be properly called a business at all: "The bottom line is that scholarly publishing isn't financially feasible as a business model—never was, never was intended to be, and should not be. If scholarship paid, we wouldn't need university presses. Without a subsidy of one kind or another, scholarly publishing cannot exist" (Davidson 2003).

That is an exaggeration, of course, because we do have plenty of commercial academic presses that publish books indistinguishable from those issued by university presses. Their names are familiar to political scientists: Blackwell, Lynne Rienner, Palgrave/Macmillan, Rowman and Littlefield, Sage, Taylor & Francis (including Routledge), Westview. While these companies do include in their lists some titles that are more like standard anthologies and textbooks than anything university presses publish, the bulk of their publishing programs nevertheless consist of the same types of scholarly monographs that university presses are mandated to publish. They manage to survive, and even sustain levels of profit sufficient to satisfy their owners, despite requirements like having to pay taxes and having to keep close control of inventories (because of the 1979 *Thor* ruling) from which university presses as non-profit institutions are exempt. Collectively, they undoubtedly publish many more books in political science than do all university presses combined, and that is one of the secrets to their success: high-volume publishing that benefits from economies of scale. As a broad generalization, it is probably also true to say that they do not lavish as much money on copyediting, design, and production as do university presses, nor are they obliged to maintain an expensive peer-review process as are university presses. Still, it is to their credit that they remain vigorous players in the space of monograph publishing, and without them the profession of political science would be hard pressed to maintain anything close to its current level of scholarly output. Not being privy to the financial details of their operations, I will refrain from saying more about commercial publishers in this article, though most of the changes that have affected the way university presses conduct their business in the last 40 years have equally affected commercial publishers.

The golden age for scholarly book publishing was the 1960s. Research funding was plentiful, many countries welcomed scholars from the United States doing studies in comparative politics, libraries had large budgets for buying books, and university presses could count on sales of books in the field averaging around 3,000 copies in hardback. But as the decade wore on, clouds began appearing on the horizon. Notably, an NSF report on library purchasing found that, for the period 1969–1973, the ratio of book to journal expenditures in the largest academic libraries had dropped over that five-year period from better than 2 to 1 to 1.16 to 1 (Fry and White 1975, 61), with every expectation that this trend would only get worse. The report's prognosis for university presses was particularly gloomy: their situation "can be described, without exaggeration, as disastrous. Already heavily encumbered by operating deficits ..., university presses appear ... to be sliding even more rapidly toward financial imbalance" (11).

This precarious situation was viewed with alarm by university presses themselves at the time. A series of articles appeared in the journal *Scholarly Publishing* in April 1972, July 1973, and April 1974 based on successive surveys of presses covering the years 1970–1974. "The Impending Crisis in University Publishing," the first article in this series, "clearly indicated that presses were in the midst of a period of extraordinary financial stress, which posed a serious threat to the continuing survival of many of them" (Becker 1974, 195). The next two articles bore the titles "The Crisis—One Year Later" and "The Crisis— Is It Over?" The somewhat encouraging conclusion of the last article in this series was that, "except for the smaller ones, presses for the most part have managed to survive their financial difficulties quite well by making a host of adjustments, including radically increased book prices, substantially lower discounts, economies achieved in book production costs, slashing staffs, publishing more books with sales potential and fewer which cannot pay their own way, special inventory sales, and so forth." But, the author wondered, how much more can such methods be used without becoming at some point self-defeating. Ominously and—as we can now see with the wisdom of hindsight—presciently, he ended by pointing to "the increasing danger that presses will turn more and more to publishing books on the basis of saleability rather than scholarly merit." And, while noting the temporary mitigating effects that a generous grant from the Mellon Foundation to presses for publishing books in the humanities might have, he asked: "But what then?" (Becker 1974, 202)

What then, indeed? William Becker, the chief financial officer of Princeton University Press who co-authored the first of these articles with the press's director, Herbert Bailey, and wrote the other two articles himself, had reason to be concerned. I was an editor at Princeton then and began in the early 1970s to build a list in Latin American studies, with a strong focus in political science. Over time it became a very distinguished list, but the evidence became clearer with every passing year that it was a field fraught with economic pitfalls. As I wrote in an article I published in the LASA *Forum*, "back in the early 1970s . . . one could still count on selling between 1,000 and 1,500 copies of most new monographs in the field. By the early 1980s this average had dropped to less than 1,000, and by the end of the decade it was moving closer to 500" (Thatcher 1993). In that article I gave many examples of the sales of specific books to illustrate the trend, noting in particular the increasing divergence between scholarly value (as measured by book awards) and market value (as measured by sales) and also the growing inequities across subfields, with history being the lowest in sales and modern political economy the highest.

As a press director at Penn State beginning in 1989, I had to be even more concerned about "the bottom line" and therefore was compelled to make some tough decisions about what kinds of books to publish. In "The Crisis in Scholarly Communication" (Thatcher 1995) I announced that Penn State was obliged to cease publishing in the field of literary criticism. My analysis of 10 years of our sales experience in literature, further supported by a survey I did of our authors in this field, persuaded me that we couldn't viably continue our program despite the high recognition it had attained. Of the 150 books we had published since 1985, 91% had sold fewer than 800 copies and 65% had sold fewer than 500. Experience at Penn State again confirmed for me the sharp disjunction between market value and scholarly value.

In an article five years later for the newsletter of the APSA's Organized Section on Comparative Politics I gave some data specifically about declining sales in political science, drawing on the historical sales records first of Princeton University Press with regard to the field as a whole and then of Penn State University Press with regard to sales of books on Latin American politics:

> For political science as a whole [at Princeton], the average five-year total for books published in hardback only in the period 1960–1967 was 3,387. That average had already dropped to

1,889 for books published between 1971 and 1973. And for books
published in 1985–1987 it had slumped even farther to 764. . . .
Between Fall 1992 and Spring 2000 [at Penn State] we have so
far issued 20 titles on Latin American politics, all simultaneously
in cloth and paper editions. The average sales for this group of
books as a whole so far has been 213 cloth and 862 paper. If we
count only the 15 titles published before 1999 (so as not to bias
the numbers because of the lower sales of books, especially in
paper, in the first year of publication), the averages come out to
230 cloth and 1,054 paper. What is most ominous is the average
of 165 for sales of the hardback edition of the 11 titles published
since 1997, indicating yet a further significant erosion in library
purchases in the most recent period. (Thatcher 2000)

As the data given above reveal, a major shift in publishing strategy
occurred in the 1970s; though not noted by William Becker in his 1972
article, Princeton had already adapted its publishing strategy through
introduction of simultaneously published Limited Paperback Editions. It
did not take long before other publishers emulated this strategy. By the
mid-1970s, competition with other presses, not to mention expectations
from authors, made this the dominant approach in most fields of
scholarly publishing, especially in the social sciences but also in many
fields of the humanities. But by the 1990s, the numbers were already
beginning to suggest that this strategy had its limits, too. In a talk I gave
at the November 2006 meeting of the Association for Political Theory
I illustrated the problem by using data from sales of the 73 books in
political theory that Penn State had published from 1991 to 2006.

For convenience I'll group them into clusters, dividing them into
three five-year periods during which the Press published 29, 24,
and 20 titles respectively (reflecting the overall pattern of initial
growth of the Press's annual output to a maximum of 80 titles
in the mid-1990s and then a gradual retrenchment to about 50
titles a year currently). In the first two periods, 1991–1996 and
1996–2000, the Press published only 9 titles that were not dual

> editions and 44 that were, and of the 9 two were paperback
> reprints of books by Stephen Bronner and Jean Bethke Elshtain
> that commercial publishers had allowed to go out of print,
> leaving just 7 as books issued only in hardback. Excluding Chris
> Sciabarra's atypical *Ayn Rand: The Russian Radical* (1995),
> which enjoyed significant book club sales and total sales of
> 2,530 hardbacks and 7,385 paperbacks, the average total
> sales through June 2006 for the 43 remaining titles were 466
> hardbacks and 1,366 paperbacks for the 23 books published in
> 1991–1995 and 243 hardbacks and 931 paperbacks for the 20
> books published in 1996–2000. These represent declines of 48%
> and 32% respectively—sobering numbers for any publisher.
> (Thatcher 2007a)

I am deeply disturbed about what this evidence portends for the future of scholarship in a variety of such "endangered" fields or, as may happen, subfields within broader disciplines. In political science it has long been true that some subfields are more dependent on book publishing than others. If one were to construct a spectrum ranging from most to least dependent for political science (with a corresponding spectrum for article publishing being the mirror image), surely it would align the major subfields in this order: political theory, comparative politics, international relations, and American politics. Note that this also parallels the extent to which these subfields rely on quantitative analysis and formal modeling, and no doubt also the relative proportions of articles that appear in the *APSR* from these subfields. The careers of some scholars in political science are therefore more affected than those of others by the problems affecting academic book publishing and the "endangered" subfields they impact.

University presses have indeed, as William Becker long ago argued, survived by becoming more efficient and effective publishers, and they have also done so by strategically changing the "mix" of their lists, doing more regional books, paperbacks for the course-adoption market (which itself, however, has been significantly impacted by the popularity of coursepacks), reference books, the trade books that formerly constituted the "midlist" of commercial houses, even fiction. But therein lies another source of the problem. A study conducted by Herbert Bailey (1990) for the AAUP and ACLS on "The Rate of Publication of Scholarly Monographs in the Humanities and Social Sciences: 1978–1988" showed, contrary to expectation, that there had been no decline in the number of monographs published by presses during this period; in fact, the number had increased by 51%, principally because most presses had to grow significantly in annual title output in order to achieve operating economies of scale and other efficiencies. But that study came too early to pick up what by 1990 had become more noticeable, that presses were no longer expanding at that rate or—as I determined from a survey of the top largest presses in that year—planning to expand in the future, which meant that as the changes in commercial publishing continued to offer opportunities for presses to pick up "midlist" titles, their shifting priorities would inevitably lead to some erosion in publishing of monographs in fields where sales were known to be low (Thatcher 1990).

That erosion has now developed to the point where it has finally become noticeable to many junior and even senior scholars in these fields that outlets for their scholarly works are hard to find. And acquiring editors at presses, under pressure from their directors who are themselves concerned by declining subsidies from parent universities (or, what amounts to the same thing, increasing administrative levies), are ever more anxious to focus on getting the most saleable books, which are not necessarily the best contributions to scholarship (though we continue to hope against hope that there will be some correlation between the two). It is no accident—and, ironically, a comment on how publishers' priorities differ from academic administrators'—that editors fall all over themselves trying to acquire good books in women's studies; that is a field (witness the success of Routledge, for instance) whose book sales are consistently better, discipline by discipline, than fields whose books have no focus on gender issues. Probably this is at least in part because scholars in that field support each other by buying their colleagues' books. Patterns like this exist in other fields, too, such as in the classics and medieval studies and even to a degree still in philosophy, where aspirations to build personal libraries of all the core books in the field remain as strong as they traditionally have been.

If students planning academic careers were to take such evidence seriously, as "rational actors" doing expected utility calculations, then hardly any would want to take the risk of entering fields of scholarship that are becoming increasingly underserved by university presses. Within political science, such utility-maximizing would surely lead more students to major in American politics and international relations, reflecting the still relatively healthy market for scholarly journals in those areas and the greater weight placed on article publishing in those subfields. Not only is this not fair to individual scholars experiencing such difficulties today, but it augurs ill for the healthy and balanced development of scholarship in the future. Universities are accustomed to some departments and programs being less able than others to generate revenue and have made the necessary adjustments. I suggest it is time to figure out a way to make these adjustments for scholarly publishing, too.

A further problem exists for junior faculty who need to publish at least one or, at some universities, two books to have a good chance of being awarded tenure after six years. Given the constraints under which they operate, with many demands on their time and the tenure clock inexorably ticking, junior faculty almost invariably will try to get one book out of revising their dissertation. But they now face an obstacle that did not exist 10 years ago. Back then, University Microfilms (UMI) sold the dissertations it archived in a photocopied form with an ugly blue paper cover in a small and bulky format. If any of these sold more than a few copies, it was considered a best seller. Presses did not consider "publication" of dissertations by UMI any threat at all. But along came ProQuest, which gobbled up UMI and began introducing electronic storage of dissertations and then later licensed this growing dissertation database to academic libraries. Many libraries subscribed, especially the larger libraries that belonged to the Association of Research Libraries, which had all along constituted the core market for scholarly monographs. Rationally, from their own limited perspective, these libraries wondered why they should be buying books based on dissertations when they already had access to all of the original dissertations through the licensed ProQuest database.

And so it came about that many libraries that had previously purchased revised dissertations without question notified their approval plan vendors to inspect the front matter of all books and to exclude from their pre-approved purchase all that could be identified as having originated as dissertations. Authors, innocently enough, abetted the vendors' ability to make this identification by thanking their dissertation advisers and referring in other ways to the genealogy of their books in their acknowledgments. And sometimes the book titles were identical to the dissertation titles, too. Many libraries, concerned with saving money anywhere they could to put off cancelling journal subscriptions as long as possible, ceased ordering books that were revised dissertations. One of the main vendors, Yankee Book Peddler, has estimated that this practice resulted in a reduction of sales of these book by 20% to 25% compared with other monographs. A growing number of the larger universities, at the same time, joined the Networked Digital Library of Theses and Dissertations (NDLTD; www.ndltd.org), which cooperated in making dissertations available "open access" (before the term was invented). Presses, noticing the decline in sales of these titles and learning about librarians' new strategy and the growth of the NDLTD, have responded in kind: by instructing acquisitions editors to be more reluctant in inviting submission of such books or, at the very least, requiring authors to explain in detail how their books differ from their dissertations so that judgments about "value added" can be made and communicated to the presses' editorial boards, which often include a librarian among the members.

Well, one might ask, what really is lost if we don't publish any revised dissertations? Maybe the tenure-and-promotion system can be adjusted to put less emphasis on the monograph as the "gold standard" for career advancement, as a recent report from the Modern Language Association (2006) has recommended. At most research universities we have access to all of these dissertations anyway in electronic form through ProQuest and NDLTD, and, after the deal that ProQuest made in 2005, now they can even be readily purchased through Amazon.com. It seems a reasonable question: Does revising a dissertation add sufficient value to justify the cost to the presses which publish and the libraries which buy them? In a recent article (Thatcher 2007a) I answered the question in this way:

> As an editor who has spent nearly forty years working with authors on revised dissertations, I want to argue that the correct answer is yes. Although I could provide plenty of examples of dissertations that underwent very substantial revision to become books that have only a faint resemblance to the dissertations whence they originated, I do not want to base my argument on just that kind of evidence alone, for it is true that revisions vary a great deal in their extent and depth and it would be difficult for librarians to identify which dissertations have been only lightly revised and which have been heavily revised. Authors' acknowledgments, while they often give credit to inspiration and help they received from their dissertation advisers and other colleagues, rarely go into any detail about how much revision was undertaken and what it entailed. Only press editors are privy to such information. Rather, my main argument comes down to this: if libraries do not buy revised dissertations, and presses do not publish them, some outstanding books might never see the light of day and exert the influence on the fields they have the potential to advance in major ways. I doubt that the best of the dissertations will somehow, magically, come to be rescued from the mass of dissertations in the ProQuest database through Google searching and be recognized for the gems they are, with high rankings in citation indices to follow commensurate with their importance. Let me give you just a few examples of books I have edited over the years that got their start as dissertations and proved, in revised form, to become pioneering works in their respective fields and to catapult their authors into the forefront of their disciplines: Sonia Alvarez, *Engendering Democracy in Brazil* (1990), Charles Beitz, *Political Theory and International Relations*

(1979), Miguel Centeno's *Democracy within Reason* (1994), Susan Eckstein's *The Poverty of Revolution* (1977), Jean Bethke Elshtain's *Public Man, Private Woman* (1981), Peter Evans's *Dependent Development* (1979), Helen Milner's *Resisting Protectionism* (1988), Susan Moller Okin's *Women and Western Political Thought* (1979), and Iris Marion Young's *Justice and the Politics of Difference* (1990), Alvarez and Eckstein have both served as president of the Latin American Studies Association, Centeno is director of the Princeton Institute for International and Regional Studies, Beitz and Milner also teach at Princeton, Evans is Professor of Sociology at UC-Berkeley, and before their recent untimely deaths Okin and Young were on the faculty, respectively, of Stanford and Chicago. One wonders what would have happened with their careers if they had not published such influential first books. I wonder the same for another person whose revised dissertation I published at Princeton in 1984: Condoleezza Rice. Would she be where she is today without that important first book, which helped her get tenure at Stanford where she later became provost?

Until the late 1990s, university presses had little reason to feel optimistic about the future, and indeed for most presses the first few years in the new millennium proved among the most challenging financially they had ever experienced. But several developments began to lay the ground for better times to come. The most important changes came in technology. Already, from the early 1980s, presses had begun to take advantage of innovations and improvements in computer hardware and software to achieve considerable gains in efficiency and productivity, which helped keep the prices of books from rising more than they otherwise would have as a result of shrinking markets. These changes were internal to press operations for the most part, however, and the external environment of publishing remained pretty much the same as it had been for a century or more. But the advent of chain superstores like Barnes & Noble first, then online retailers like Amazon.com, and finally search engines like Google with everything else they brought in their wake changed the environment of publishing dramatically in a few short years. Publishing in 2005 was very different from what it had been in 1995.

Some of these changes proved to be mixed blessings. For example, while superstores provided a huge increase in shelf space for displaying new books and university presses benefited initially from the greater exposure their books got, the chains' discount and inventory turnover policies ended up financially squeezing many presses and producing a sharp increase in their returns. Amazon.com, too, while bringing university press books to the attention of a much wider potential audience worldwide and offering browsing capabilities through its innovative "Search Inside the Book" program, later on offered its own competition to presses by selling used books on its site. And Google, which was greeted enthusiastically by most presses when it set up its Google Print (later called Book Search) program, bit the hand that fed it when it teamed up with libraries to offer the Google project to scan massive numbers of books in library collections, including many from presses still in print and under copyright, without seeking permission under a dubious theory of "fair use," which is currently under challenge from publishers and authors in court (Thatcher 2006).

If you asked most press directors, though, I am confident that the majority would agree that, on balance, these changes have had more positive than negative effects. But even more important than any of these changes in the system for selling and distributing books was the technological revolution in printing. John Thompson, Cambridge sociologist and co-director of Polity Press, identified this as the "hidden revolution" in his insightful analysis of the academic publishing system in *Books in the Digital Age* (Thompson 2005). Not much known or discussed outside the hermetic community of scholarly publishing, this revolution introduced digital printing as the solution to one of the most nagging and financially disabling problems of the business: inventory management. Traditional offset printing created perverse incentives for publishers to be overly optimistic about potential sales: the unit cost of manufacturing dropped sharply as more copies of a book were printed. The result was warehouses full of unsold books—and also a whole new parasitical business of selling remainders. University presses felt the effects even more severely than did other publishers, since print runs for their monographs were declining to levels that made offset printing almost economically unfeasible. Then, just as presses began to wonder how they could continue to publish monographs at all, digital printing arrived as an outgrowth of the same technology that made Xerox a household name. Not only did digital printing allow for smaller print runs (in what the industry now calls short-run digital printing, or SRDP) than possible in offset printing, but it even made possible print-on-demand (POD) production, where a book can be printed one copy at a time as ordered by a customer. In the late 1990s, Lighting Print (later Lightning Source), a subsidiary of Ingram, the largest book wholesaler in the country, started providing just such a service and, even more crucial, integrated it into Ingram's entire book distribution system.

This innovation immediately solved two problems for university presses. Backlist titles that were about to go out of print and that could not be reprinted by offset in any financially feasible way thenceforth could remain in print indefinitely as POD titles through Lightning Source. They would thus continue to provide a small but steady stream of revenue and, with their existence made known through Google searching, collectively would create the "long tail" that has been identified as the secret of economic success for publishing and other industries in the future. At the same time, digital printing in the form of SRDP gave presses the ability to print small quantities economically, keeping supply more closely related to current demand and eliminating the speculation about long-term demand that had earlier led to large inventories, which ended up having to be written off and pulped or sold into the remainder market at prices often below unit cost. SRDP allowed presses to keep much smaller inventories on hand and hence decreased the need for ever-expanding warehouse space, which had been the bane of many presses for a century. Some publishers, like Chicago and Rowman and Littlefield, entered into agreements with SRDP vendors to operate digital printing machines right in their warehouses, resulting in even more savings as the freshly printed books did not have to be shipped to a distant location.

This was a complete solution for almost all political science monographs, very few of which contain the kinds of illustrations found in art books, which require the very high-quality reproduction that digital technology has not yet managed to provide in competition with traditional offset printing. Competition from SRDP vendors has, however, brought a decrease in prices for low runs from offset printers; it is now possible to print 400 copies of a monograph by offset, all while maintaining offset's higher-quality production capabilities. This further benefit of digital printing has led to a new model for scholarly publishing at some presses. Penn State University Press, for example, initially publishes monographs in hardback in runs of 400 or 500; paperbacks are issued later by SRDP in small runs of 200, 100, or even 50 iteratively; when the book's life-cycle reaches the point at which it makes sense, it is produced purely by POD through Lightning Source. This model was a rational response also to the trend of libraries, revealed in the data above, to order paperbacks instead of hardbacks whenever books were published in the dual formats; in that way, SRDP facilitated a new strategy for delayed publication of paperbacks that was becoming a necessity anyway. Not here yet, but coming soon, is the capability of digital printing to economically produce internal color reproductions of, for example, graphs and figures and maps; authors will not have to see the wonderfully colored illustrations they have produced on their computers converted to black and white in their books.

This "hidden revolution" has already transformed the business of scholarly publishing in major ways—and spared press directors from a long bout of depression. It has enabled university presses, and commercial academic publishers as well, to continue operating in a largely market-based economy. But change of an even more sweeping sort is on the horizon. "Open access" has become the new buzzword in some sectors of publishing, especially in journals in science, technology, and medicine (STM), which have been the source of librarians' nightmares as they have tried to figure out how to maintain subscriptions to expensive STM journals and subscribe to new ones while not completely eviscerating their book-buying budgets. Legislation introduced in Congress as the

Federal Research Public Access Act of 2006 has brought the issue to a head. It mandates that all articles whose research has been supported by grants from any agencies with budgets of over $100 million (which include the National Science Foundation, funder of much research in political science) be deposited in a federally maintained online repository within six months after publication. Many commercial STM journal publishers like Elsevier, but also many non-profit society publishers, are fighting this legislation tooth and nail, and the Association of American Publishers has hired a Washington lobbyist to generate support for its position opposing the legislation. The Association of American University Presses (AAUP), on the other hand, issued a statement on open access late in February 2007 (which I drafted for the AAUP as its president-elect) that takes a more balanced approach. But, significantly, the AAUP statement does not confine its attention to just journals but instead calls for experimentation and dialogue on open access for books, too. This is in part an affirmation of the basic mission of presses to "disseminate knowledge far and wide" using whatever business models can support this overriding goal; but it is also a reflection of experiments already under way at presses such as those at the University of California, the University of Michigan, Oxford University, and Penn State University. These presses are building on the pioneering approach of the National Academies Press, which has digitized its entire catalogue for free, full-text online browsing as an incentive to visit the press's web site, where visitors can order books in POD or PDF form. This type of open-access publishing is compatible with a market-based approach to publishing, but the AAUP is not opposed to models that would move toward a "gift economy" where funding would come not from sales, but from fees and subsidies up front, and where the books would be free to the end user and completely unrestricted technologically.

The "hidden revolution" of digital printing has bought time for university presses to engage in experiments with open access, both for the type that is compatible with a market economy and for the type that goes beyond to a full-fledged gift economy. Needless to say, it is difficult to predict what the future holds for commercial academic publishers as the open-access movement gains momentum. They could survive, presumably, with open access based on a market economy; it is less likely that universities and funding agencies would be willing to support their existence in a gift economy. And such a full-fledged gift economy for books may never come to pass. It would require system-wide changes within universities on a scale that has seldom been seen in this tradition-encrusted environment. Old habits die hard. On the other hand, the vision underlying this most fully developed form of open access may eventually prove irresistible as it embodies the ambition of scholars everywhere to engage in the fully unfettered, "free" exchange of ideas among themselves and beyond to the public at large—a noble vision indeed.

References

AAUP. 2007. "AAUP Statement on Open Access." February 27. New York: Association of American University Presses. Available at www.aaupnet.org/aboutup/issues/oa/statement.pdf.

Bailey, Herbert S., Jr. 1990. *The Rate of Publication of Scholarly Monographs in the Humanities and Social Sciences 1978–1988*. New York: Association of American University Presses.

Becker, William C. 1973. "The Crisis—One Year Later." *Scholarly Publishing* 4 (July): 291–302.

———. 1974. "The Crisis—Is It Over?" *Scholarly Publishing* 5 (April): 195–210.

Davidson, Cathy N. 2003. "Understanding the Economic Burden of Scholarly Publishing." *Chronicle of Higher Education*, October 3.

Fry, Bernard M., and Herbert S. White. 1975. *Economics and Interaction of the Publisher-Library Relationship in the Production and Use of Scholarly and Research Journals*. Washington, D.C.: National Science Foundation.

Harvey, William B., Herbert S. Bailey, Jr., William C. Becker, and John B. Putnam. 1972. "The Impending Crisis in University Publishing." *Scholarly Publishing* 3 (April): 195–207.

Kerr, Chester. 1949. *A Report on American University Presses*. Washington, D.C.: Association of American University Presses.

MLA. 2006. *Report of the MLA Task Force on Evaluating Scholarship for Tenure and Promotion*. New York: Modern Language Association. Available at www.mla.org/tenure_promotion.

Thatcher, Sanford G. 1990. "Scholarly Monographs May Be the Ultimate Victims of the Upheavals in Trade Publishing." *Chronicle of Higher Education*, October 10, B2–B3.

———. 1993. "Latin American Studies and the Crisis in Scholarly Communication." *LASA Forum* (winter): 10–4.

———. 1995. "The Crisis in Scholarly Communication." *Chronicle of Higher Education*, March 3, B1–B2.

———. 2000. "The Future of Scholarly Publishing in Comparative Politics." *APSA Organized Section on Comparative Politics Newsletter* (summer): 6–10.

———. 2006. "Fair Use in Theory and Practice: Reflections on Its History and the Google Case." *Journal of Scholarly Publishing* 37 (April): 215–29.

———. 2007a. "Dissertations into Books? The Lack of Logic in the System." *Against the Grain* 18 (April): 75–7.

———. 2007b. "The Future of Scholarly Book Publishing in Political Theory." *PS: Political Science and Politics* 40 (January): 129–32.

Thompson, John B. 2005. *Books in the Digital Age*. Cambridge, UK: Polity Press.

II

HOW TO WRITE—
SPECIFICS FOR DIFFERENT
AUDIENCES

THOMAS E. CRONIN, COLORADO COLLEGE

THE WRITE STUFF: WRITING AS A PERFORMING AND POLITICAL ART*

4

"Have something to say, and say it as clearly as you can."
MATTHEW ARNOLD

"The art of writing has for backbone some fierce attachment to an idea."
VIRGINIA WOOLF

"Writing and rewriting are a constant search for what it is one is saying."
JOHN UPDIKE

"The great enemy of clear writing is insincerity."
GEORGE ORWELL

"I have always felt that the first duty of a writer was to ascend—to make flights, carrying others along if he could manage it. To do this takes courage, even a certain conceit."
E. B. WHITE

"There is nothing to writing. All you do is sit down at the typewriter, open a vein, and bleed."
LEGENDARY SPORTS WRITER RED SMITH

INTRODUCTION

Writing well is a form of leadership. Good writing helps us think clearly, express ideas, heighten consciousness, promote community, inspire, or even outrage us. Writing can be an effective means of communicating, persuading, and changing how people think, dream, and behave. Plato, Machiavelli, Jefferson, Madison, Marx, Harriet Beecher Stowe, George Orwell, Rachel Carson, Martin Luther King, Jr., and Alexander Solzhenitsyn provide examples of this power.

Writers always have advice for aspiring writers: Read good writers and good writing. Use as many words as you must and as few as you can. Skip long words where short ones will do. Make every word count. Use the language of everyday life, yet don't substitute common words for distinctive words just to keep your writing simple. Say what you mean and sound like yourself. Strive for cadence, smoothness, and freshness. Clarity of writing flows from clarity of thought.

Direct your writing to a single reader, or at least to a distinct audience. Signal your voice, tone, and theme in your first two paragraphs. Write to inform, arouse, persuade. "Readers ... have a tough job to do," notes novelist Kurt Vonnegut, "and they need all the help they can get from writers."[1] After all, readers have to decipher thousands of little notations and make sense of them. Unlike symphony musicians, they have no conductor to lead them through a work. Few phrases signal how fast or slow, or loud or soft a text is to be read. Punctuation can help. "Punctuation marks," writes Pico Iyer, "are the road signs placed along the highways of our communication—to control speeds, provide directions and prevent head-on collisions."[2]

The difference between poor writing and good writing lies in *careful revising*. Edit, recast, and tighten your material. Have the guts to cut. Spare the reader windy generalizations, clichés, uncritical thought. Writers have to custom design their own rules and be prepared, more than occasionally, to break them rather than write barbarous prose.

Research, writing, rewriting, and editing are hard work. And the more you care about your writing, the harder it gets. Professional writers seldom boast about the easiness of their craft. To write well requires time, hard work, and intellectual self-discipline, the kind that seldom comes naturally. No matter how much they love it, and they usually love it more than anything else, it's lonely, demanding, and often painful.

Ernest Hemingway said writing, at its best, is exacting and often frustrating, in part because it is something you can never do as well as it can be done. Hemingway rewrote his ending of *A Farewell to Arms* 39 times before he was satisfied. "There's no rule on how it is to write. Sometimes it comes easily and perfectly. Sometimes it is like drilling rock and then blasting it out with charges," Hemingway remarked. "I love to write," he added, "but it has never gotten any easier to do and you can't expect it to if you keep trying for something better than you can do."[3]

Hemingway believed each writing project should be a new beginning—a time to try again for something never done before or for something others have tried to do and failed. One cannot, he said, be satisfied to write in another way what already has been well written. No, it is precisely because we have known such fine writers in the past that we who write are driven well beyond where we are comfortable, to where no one can help us.

The joy of research and writing comes from the challenge of being out there on your own, rethinking the explored realm of life and the human condition, and examining the unexplored. It is scary to be out there alone, yet, writing itself is one of the grand, free, human activities. Working back and forth between experiences and ideas, evidence and imagination, data and theory, a writer has more than space and time can offer. A writer with a sense of justice can remind us of what we ought to be, what might be, where we have failed. Writers can also help vanquish lies. Alexander Solzhenitsyn elaborates:

> What is the place and role of the writer? . . . A writer is no sideline judge of his fellow countrymen and contemporaries; he is equally guilty of all the evil done in his country or by his people. If his country's tanks spill blood on the streets of some alien capital, the brown stains are splashed forever on the writer's face. If, some fatal night, his trusting friend is choked to death while sleeping, the bruises from the rope are on the

> writer's hands. If his young fellow citizens in their easy going way declare the superiority of debauchery over frugal labor, abandon themselves to drugs or seize hostages, the stink of it mixes with the writer's breathing.[4]

As in the mastery of any skill, writing requires discipline. If you already know how to use time effectively, writing papers becomes easier, and even enjoyable. Most of us, however, are accomplished procrastinators. A research assignment can overwhelm you if you let it. Yet, if planned carefully, it can strengthen self-discipline and sharpen your ability to manage time. Effective time management is one of the most important gifts you can give yourself.

Be prepared to retreat to a quiet place and devote several hours a day for two or three weeks to uninterrupted, focused concentration. For extroverts, such a schedule is like being sentenced to solitary confinement. If you are going to take pride in your writing, however, you must resign yourself to devoting time to extensive reading and research, rigorous analysis, and intense thought, not to mention the hours of writing, rewriting, revising, and editing a first-rate research project requires.

SELECTING A TOPIC

Search for a worthy topic. Then state it simply in a sentence or two. Your paper must have a focus, a point of view, an answerable question or a fresh way of considering a compelling problem. Have a purpose: to inform, persuade, clarify, instruct, entertain.

Avoid the perfectionist inclination to tackle only those questions that are tidy or readily answered. Attacking a trivial problem is a waste of time. Any writing project, whether a senior thesis, an opinion essay, testimony before a legislature, or a treatise on a social or economic issue, is an opportunity to match your talents against a perplexing problem.

"Broadly speaking, academic writing is argumentative writing," write Gerald Graff and Cathy Birkenstein. "You need to enter a conversation, using what others say…as a launching pad or sounding board for your own ideas."[5]

They are right. Most writers write in response to other writers or points of view. Sometimes this involves agreeing with earlier writers or speakers. Yet it can also involve contending that previous thinking is wrong and needs reexamination. Thus writing often has much in common with debating. You might concede certain points, yet you try to shed new light—based on your research and analysis—that permits a fresh way of understanding a concept, a theory, or an explanatory model.

Hence, in selecting a topic you may start out seeking to confirm or disprove a particular point of view. This requires you to understand that point of view, engage it, summarize it, and present your findings in the context of what others have said about it.

Make sure your topic interests you enough that you will devote the time needed for research and writing. Although few purely original ideas exist, make sure your topic is researchable and that it has not already been so researched that little new territory remains. Take care not only that you don't bite off more than you can chew, but that you don't chew more than is worth chewing.

Simple curiosity spawns many writing projects: the urge to understand something better, to resolve or at least to grasp a paradox, dilemma, or set of previously unsolved, unanswered questions. To discover the way people live. My own research often springs from questions students or others ask me and from question-and-answer sessions on the lecture circuit. When I give an answer I am not wholly satisfied with, I say to myself, "That's a fine question, and it deserves a better answer."

Always have a pen and paper handy. Often inspiration hits when you are not directly searching for it. Any type of discussion, no matter how off topic of the paper, can inspire an idea not yet considered.

Perhaps something has been puzzling you, or a topic has been covered inadequately in an earlier course or in a speech you've recently heard or a book you've just read. Topics arise from discussions with friends, teachers, colleagues, or parents or from your own observations in a job, internship, or campaign experience. You may also be motivated by the search for truth or by an outrage at hypocrisy, lies, and injustice. Good writing is often telling the truth about things.

Refining and Researching Your Topic

As you decide on a research topic, ask yourself some questions about it. What do I want to say? What's the big idea? Or puzzle? Or confusion? What is it I want to discover, solve, learn more about? Why does X institution, or process, or leadership theory work in its own peculiar way? Could or should it be otherwise?

How, for example, is powerful leadership held accountable? Do we need politics and politicians? When are we well served by political leaders? How can we reconcile democracy and leadership? Are changes needed in our political system? Is one party better able to solve our problems than the other? Are our economic inequalities or our inability to prevent civil and inter-nation wars the fault of governmental structures, inadequate leadership, or deficiencies in vision?

You will obviously have to narrow your topic to accord with your time and talent. Then ask, What is the central question? Define it. Explore its origins and development. Explain its consequences. If it is a policy, process, or constitutional interpretation, you may want to analyze its effect on current and future political leaders. Try to discern the underlying assumptions, agendas, and incentives of groups advocating change or the status quo. In what ways do different schools of thought define the problem differently, and why?

You will want to clarify your topic by assimilating as much material, qualitative and quantitative, as possible. Search the library literature, the Internet, periodicals, and available documents. You will sometimes discover works that already have answered, or at least addressed, parts of your topic. Explore the availability of polling or survey data that may shed light on the problem. You may find, too, that interviewing knowledgeable leaders or experts, and current and former public officials, will be productive. Never underestimate the talent of local librarians, especially those who are specialists with reference works, computer search technologies, and government documents. They can be splendid allies.

Equally important is knowing when to stop researching and start writing. Saying you need more time for research often masks procrastination. "The temptation to read one more book or search another library shelf was always great," remarked a recent Ph.D. dissertation writer. "Investigation leads one to ask questions which demand answers. Those answers in turn breed new questions and so on until the process gets out of hand. I found it necessary to place strict time limits on my work. Sometimes this meant altering objectives to comply with a timetable. This was not to short change myself, but rather to avoid becoming paralyzed by perpetual analysis."[6] For many people, talking about their research and writing serves as a substitute for working on their project. Knowing when you have enough material to substantiate your claims, enlighten your reader, and put the problem in context is a skill writers need to develop. Remember the aphorism "Strive for excellence but not for perfection." Someone once said, too, "Don't get it right—just get it written," wise advice for many of us when we get bogged down.

Developing and Testing Hypotheses

Good writers don't just describe a problem and raise possible solutions offhand. Prepare a list of likely solutions or likely answers to your research question. Anticipate objections and contrary arguments. Experiment with competing or even opposing theoretical hypotheses. How does your hypothesis stand up to critical review? Ask yourself, What if... ? Be clear about cause-and-effect relationships. Clarify your dependent and independent variables. For example, were the leaders shaped by their group or situation, or were they the primary shapers of events?

Anticipate the arguments of those who might disagree with your analysis; then make their argument even more powerfully than they do. Then tear it apart.

Don't be constrained by the conventional wisdom of the day. Inventions, scientific breakthroughs, and better answers often come only when you step outside existing ways of thinking. Disregard prevailing wisdom, ask bold questions, pose fresh possibilities. Be imaginative.

Of course, this strategy for enumerating hypotheses is easier to suggest than to do. Write down everything relevant that comes to mind, or even sounds plausible. The trick is finding those bold questions and reframing them in a compelling way. Ask a lot of questions, and a few are likely to be bold. Still, we are, more than we appreciate, creatures of habit and cultural conditioning. Try to discern the mind-set shifts that are taking place or perhaps need to take place.[7]

Logical reasoning is important at this point. You will want to test, systematically, the plausible explanations you have posed. With a bit of ingenuity you can test solutions to difficult problems without making each particular test a two- or three-year enterprise. Appreciate, however, that empirical testing and the most rigorous forms of critical reasoning are indispensable to building the body of reliable knowledge needed to arrive at your conclusions.

Amassed information is not knowledge, merely a distant cousin. Information and findings are important only as intermediate phases of your research. You must make sense of what you have gathered. This step involves analysis. Writing a paper is ultimately an interpretive process. The skilled writer makes sense of the stories, aspirations, myths, and the symbolic as well as practical ideas that shape behavior.

Students of politics and leadership formulate theories about the "why" and the "so what" of political life and governance. Aristotle called the study of leadership and governance the "queen of sciences" and classified city-states according to their political structures, making predictions about how different structures would lead to different outcomes. Plato examined the need for enlightened leaders and the responsibilities of wise, informed leaders. Machiavelli, the famed author of *The Prince*, prescribed how rulers should best govern to maximize their own interests and how citizens should respond to different styles of leadership. Thomas Hobbes, John Locke, Jean-Jacques Rousseau, John Adams, Thomas Jefferson, and James Madison were all political theorists interested in formulating governance arrangements that would balance liberty and order, responsibility and leadership. Those who drafted the Constitution in the summer of 1787 in Philadelphia acted as both political philosophers and political architects as they merged experience and theory in the formation of practical political institutions.

Social scientists study patterns of politics, patterns of leadership, and the exercise of power and authority, just as physical scientists study atoms, genes, rocks, and stars. They describe things as a means of understanding. Understanding often leads to explanations; explanations can lead to predictive models; and predictions can generate sound theory.

We search for the predictable to discover, to describe, and, if possible, to verify the basic laws of politics, leadership, and governance. Although Plato's *Republic* and Aristotle's *Politics* showed the way, rigorous efforts to learn enough to predict have been essentially a modern-day development.

Just as money is viewed as the mother's milk of politics and campaigns, *evidence* is the well-spring of convincing writing. Evidence means furnishing proof, witness, manifest data. Readers will justifiably ask, Did the writer back up the thesis? Is there compelling evidence? Is the evidence clearly backed by logic, examples, data, or related supporting material? Evidence, evidence, evidence—this is what will ultimately convince your readers that you have made a strong case. Providing evidence is absolutely your responsibility when you are asking readers to think anew about an old problem.

Back to your challenge. Although most topics you will tackle already have been written about by one or more scholars, don't be put off by this fact. Your challenge is to examine the problem with a fresh eye. Approach it differently. Place it in a fresh context. Recombine, rethink, recontextualize. Try to find new linkages, put forth audacious new and relevant explanations. The challenge of research and writing is to raise new questions, to supply fresh data, evidence, or findings that point in promising new directions.

BEGINNING TO WRITE

Here are a number of concerns you should keep in mind as you research, outline, write, and edit an essay. My advice is subjective. Different styles and approaches work for different people. Novelist Somerset Maugham once joked that "there are three rules for writing a novel. Unfortunately, no one knows what they are."[8] What works for me may merely inhibit you. And what one professor likes another may not.

Retain what's useful, disregard the rest. Most of it is common sense. Much of it comes from standard writing and style books, from friends who teach composition and from editors who have criticized, corrected, and generally improved my writing over the years. My emphasis on certain uses and abuses also arises out of years of writing, and reading student papers.

The most important suggestions are:

- Prepare a paragraph or two to focus your objectives.
- Make an outline.
- Prepare a catchy and strong thesis.
- Write honestly.
- Write to convince.
- Adopt a working title.
- Revise, revise, revise.

Focus and Outline

It helps to have a map of where you're going. If you don't know where you're going, says an old aphorism, you just may end up there. The moral is important. In the past you may have sat down at your computer and produced a first draft you thought was a final product. Your essay may have been put together by cutting and pasting odd descriptions and definitions and tagging on a rough conclusion. This is unacceptable.

Write an outline to organize your argument in logical order. Prepare a simple one-page statement of purpose to clarify your objectives. What do you intend to do? Why are you writing on this topic? What's the problem? What is your main theme? Write in sentence form each major point needed to support your thesis. Jot down, under each sentence, the evidence you will use to support your central points. It's often best to do this before you turn on your computer.

You will want to ask yourself more questions as you review and revise your outline. What are my major points or most telling evidence? What are the weak points to my argument? Why do I really care about this topic? Will the conclusion flow smoothly from the body of the essay? Have I jumped to conclusions? In short, will my terms and concepts be clear, and will the essay persuade readers or offer a fresh way of seeing something?

An outline is merely a guide, a way of dividing a subject into its major points and subpoints. Your initial outline will change as you do more research and get into your writing. The best outlines grow and become more focused as the writer makes progress. Never let your outline limit or control you; alter it to serve your goals. Still, "to get anywhere, one first has to start. And a good way to start the outline is to jot down quickly . . . the ideas you have about your topic, asking what there is of interest that you want to pass along to the reader."[9] Your outline is in part a plan, in part a taking stock of information you have gathered, and a way of arranging your material and interpretive analysis in a logical order. Outlines are essential; they help avoid writer's block, affirm you have something to say, allow you to see how one idea logically leads to another, and organize your schedule.

Watch out for overwriting. Students nowadays are conditioned to writing in chatty, unstructured email style. Word processors encourage most people to write longer, but not necessarily better.

One reporter found "students submit essays that are longer but not better written than those in years past. Worse, many students do not revise or even proofread their work, relying instead on software to check spelling and grammar."[10]

But spell checkers are no substitute for careful proofreading. They don 't catch certain errors. For example, they don't catch punctuation mistakes or differences between such words as "principle" and "principal" or "capitol" and "capital." No word processor can make bad writing good.

If word processors help you overcome writer's block by making it easy to pour out ideas, remember editing then becomes all the more important.

Write Honestly, with Voice and Power

Once you have sketched an outline, sit down and start writing, or turn on your computer. Put your ideas into words, composing freely. Try "shotgun" writing (free-style brainstorming), thinking in terms of blocks or chunks of ideas. Your first inclination with words is usually what you really mean. Don't expect to get the vocabulary or flow exactly right on the first try. Concentrate on getting your ideas down in any way you can. Writing technically correct prose about irrelevant ideas is a waste of talent, time, and energy. Keep yourself focused on key concepts.

At this stage, it's okay to be sloppy. Make a mess. Who cares? Allow your ideas to begin to take shape. Serious thinking is far more important at this stage than error-free writing. Later you can get them in more concise and elegant form. "If you are like most people, you can't do much precise thinking until you have committed to paper at least a rough sketch of your initial ideas," writes Sylvan Barnet of Tufts University. "Later you can push and polish your ideas into shape, perhaps even deleting all of them and starting over, but it's a lot easier to improve your ideas once you see them in front of you, than it is to do the job in your head. On paper one word leads to another; in your head one word often blocks another."[11]

Each of us writes with a distinctive flavor and voice. Be yourself. Write from the heart. Good writing is about telling the truth as you understand it. Some stylists advise writers to place themselves in the background. They contend, with some justification, that writing and talking are separate modes of communication. A speaker, for example, has a rapport with listeners and takes into account what they already know. Formal writing and putting yourself in the background will work for many of you. It is absolutely required if you are writing for the *Yale Law Review* or the *New England Journal of Medicine*. But those who make political writing an art will write in their own voice with a compelling political purpose in mind; they draw attention to facts and argue for their views. Voice reveals a writer's character and passion.

When we were little, says Peter Elbow, we had no difficulty sounding the way we felt. Most children speak and write with real voice. But adults often have to work hard to achieve the same simple, direct honesty. Writing with no voice is lifeless, faceless, and wooden because it lacks sound, rhythm, and individuality. Elbow explains that

> Most people's writing lacks voice because they stop so often in mid-sentence and ponder, worry, or change their minds about which word to use or which direction to go in ....

> Writing *with voice* is writing into which someone has breathed. It has that fluency, rhythm, and liveliness that exist naturally in the speech of most people when they are enjoying a conversation ....
>
> Writing with *real voice* has the power to make you pay attention and understand—the words go deep.[12]

THEN REVISE, REVISE, REVISE

Starting to write is the most difficult part of writing for some people. For others, like me, rewriting, revising, and editing are more exacting. Rewriting is the essence of writing. If you are not already ruthless about editing, erasing, and discarding unnecessary words, get that way. Ask, Can I write it more concisely? If it is possible to cut a word, cut it.

The late James Michener wrote scores of best sellers about places such as Hawaii and the Chesapeake Bay yet described himself as less a gifted writer than a talented rewriter.

One technique for learning to revise and edit your work is to "use the knife" on other people's writings. It's easier to find the flaws and what doesn't work in a classmate's drafts. So exchange papers. Read a classmate's paper and ask them to proof and critique your work. You see more clearly what doesn't make sense or doesn't flow, and it is relatively painless to discard vigorously and mark up "their" prose. "Once you get comfortable wielding the knife and seeing blood on the floor, it turns out to be easier to wield it on yourself."[13]

Pulitzer Prize-winning poet Stanley Kunitz was asked if he had ever written a poem he thought perfect. He said he had deceived himself on occasion in thinking so. "But I no more expect a poem to be perfect than I expect a life to be perfect," he added. "The two are interwoven and inseparable. And if it's humans, the likeliness of perfection is so remote we might as well forget about it. One does the best one can and then one revises it. Then you revise it again. And then you publish it. And you see new flaws and then you try again. That's the life in art."[14] Kunitz also wonderfully observed, "Art is that chalice into which we pour the wine of transcendance."[15]

Begin the process of revising by reading your early efforts aloud to yourself, your friends, or anyone you can get to listen. When you read aloud, you invariably hear and see things you may be unable to discern in any other way. The ear catches errors of substance and style the eye often misses. Reading aloud also stresses what is important. An effective sentence is partly a matter of cadence and rhythm. Abraham Lincoln succeeded with precision and elegance but also with his uncommon vernacular ease and his rhythmical virtuosity.[16] Journalist James J. Kilpatrick urges us to "sound out" our sentences and suggests that if a sentence lacks cadence, it collapses like an overcooked soufflé. Essential to good writing is a good ear. Listen to your prose. Cultivate the inner ear. "The writer who learns the knack of balance or of deliberate imbalance; the writer who understands how to quicken his tempo with short words, quick darting words that smack and jab; the writer who learns to slow his composition with soft and languorous convolutions; the writer who practices the trick of sentence endings, striving deliberately for syllables that are accented in a particular way, for the long vowel sound or the short—such a writer is on his way toward mastery of a marvelous tool."[17]

Editing means figuring out what you want to say and saying it. Just as effective leaders avoid wasting people's time, effective writers avoid wordiness. After a draft or two or three, you'll want to get it clear in your head and then rewrite it in the most accurate way.

Here are additional editing suggestions.

Select Words Carefully

The most common writing deficiency is an overly casual approach to the use of words. "Use the right word," Mark Twain said, "not its distant cousin." Ask yourself, What is it I'm trying to say? Why am I using this word? Does it look right? Does it sound right? Is there a better, fresher way to say it? Is it clear, direct, brief, and bold? Can one word suffice for two or three now used?

"Vigorous writing is concise. A sentence should contain no unnecessary words, a paragraph no unnecessary sentences, for the same reason that a drawing should have no unnecessary lines and a machine no unnecessary parts," advise William Strunk, Jr., and E. B. White. "This requires not that the writer make all his sentences short, or that he avoid all detail and treat his subjects only in outline, but that every word tell."[18] In addition to using accurate words you will usually want to use familiar, simple, unadorned words. Simplicity increases readability. Complexity, unorthodox usages, needless adjectives, transitional adverbs, and abstract nouns diminish readability.

Strive for lean writing. Avoid jargon, pedantry, and "out-of-town" or foreign phrases designed to show off erudition. Arrogance pervades the work of certain scholars and professors. The greatest discovery in history is useless if no one understands what it means. One of my students summed up obfuscation perfectly: "It is a cardinal sin of so-called 'teachers' to write and talk so their students cannot understand them—I hate that." There is nothing wrong with using exotic or ten dollar words now and then if they are the best ones to describe what you're talking about; yet if your work is aimed at a lay audience, use words ordinary readers will understand.

Language, however, is a subjective matter. Substituting too many short, conventional words for unusual ones can devitalize your writing. A trade-off exists: simplicity on the one hand, the use of unusual words on the other. Excessive editing can make language drab, commonplace, and lifeless. Long paragraphs can work for gifted writers like William Faulkner, and long and unfamiliar words sometimes though rarely work as well. Occasionally they fit the meaning best or serve the rhythm of a sentence. In any case, editing should turn bland, imprecise writing into good writing.

An Associated Press handbook for writers states, "It's hard to see any advantage to long words such as these in the left-hand column," when the ones on the right can do the job:[19]

accommodations	rooms
ameliorate	improve
approximately	about
commence	begin
deactivate	close, shut off
endeavor	try

implement	carry out
in consequence of	because
initiate	begin
methodology	method
objective;	aim, goal
proliferation	spread
purchase	buy
remuneration	pay
replicate	repeat
socialize	mingle, meet
underprivileged	poor
utilize	use

Prize-winning economist John Kenneth Galbraith, author of several best-sellers, said clear writing, something his profession is not especially known for, comes from a commitment to revision. His simple formula: at least six drafts.

> To write accurately one must know, above all, how bad are one's first drafts. They are bad because the need to combine composition with thought, both in their own way taxing, leads initially to a questionable, even execrable result. With each revision the task eases, the product improves. Eventually there can be clarity and perhaps even grace . . . . My commitment is to not fewer than five revisions . . . .
>
> I have also been much helped in writing on economics by the conviction that there is no idea associated with the subject that cannot, with sufficient effort, be stated in clear English. The obscurity that characterizes professional economic prose does not derive from the difficulty of the subject. It is the result of incomplete thought; or it reflects a priestly desire to differentiate one's self from the plain world of the layman; or it stems from a fear of having one's inadequacies found out. Nothing so protects error as an absence of readers or understanding.[20]

Let Verbs and Nouns Do the Work

Use short words, short sentences, and short paragraphs; less is more. Carefully selected verbs and nouns seldom need a string of adjectives and adverbs to amplify their meaning.

Strong verbs (verbs that show action) infuse sentences with life-giving nectar. You can accomplish more with one carefully chosen, vivid verb than with a truckload of adjectives. A common verb offense is using the lame verb forms *there is, there are, it is,* and *it seems* where *it* is impersonal and has no referent. Good writers avoid the "to be" verbs when possible. People fall into the habit of using these out of pure laziness. They weaken most sentences and can almost always be replaced by more telling verbs. Further, using strong verbs rather than these flaccid forms contributes to word economy. Take the following simple yet universally applicable example: "There is one legislator who writes most of the committee's bills and reports." Remove three bland words: *there, is* and *who.* Now your sentence reads: "One legislator writes most of the committee's bills and reports." The new sentence is three words shorter and has a strong verb as its engine.

Active verbs make for vital sentences. An active verb has the person performing the action as its subject, as in "I am voting," or "She leads her team." A passive verb is a form of the "to be" family plus the past participle, as in "The group is being led by Heather," or "The election results have been counted." Try: "Heather leads her team," and "They tallied the votes."

The active voice verb provides pace and movement. It stresses the one doing something. It uses verbs to push, strike, carry, and persuade. "Joe led the discussion" is strong. "The discussion was led by Joe" is limp. The passive voice shifts the focus onto what's being done and makes for sluggish reading. It slows the pace and usually requires more words. "The active voice strikes like a boxer moving forward in attack," writes Theodore M. Bernstein. "The passive voice parries while backpedaling."[21] Remember Thoreau's famous advice: simplify, simplify, simplify.

Clear, lean thinking is usually the key to clear, lean writing. Keep complicated constructions to a minimum. The "secret of good writing is to strip every sentence to its cleanest components," writes William Zinsser. "Every word that serves no function, every word that could be a short word, every adverb which carries the same meaning that is already in the verb, every passive construction that leaves the reader unsure of who is doing what—these are the thousand and one adulterants that weaken the strength of a sentence."[22]

Use Qualifiers and Modifiers Sparingly

Be bold. Be definite. Say it in positive form. Take a stand. Be careful about using qualifiers: *it seems, it appears, very, quite, pretty, rather, usually, mostly, generally, a lot, all right, some, often, sort of, various, frequently, really, probably, basically, and essentially.* Banish: *somewhat unique, very unique,* or *almost unique.* Unique is an absolute adjective; *unique* is unique.

Avoid using *pretty, really, sort of* and similar words as qualifiers of intensity in formal writing. Be careful not to confuse qualifiers of size (huge, tremendous) with qualifiers of intensity (significant, important).

Also restrain the temptation to hedge with *possibly, if only, moreover, furthermore, the fact that, it is my understanding, it is believed that, it is sometimes said that, due to, on one hand, however, that which, notwithstanding,* and *to the contrary notwithstanding.* A qualifier is necessary, of course, if a statement or partial evidence is open to doubt; hence an occasional *perhaps* or *reportedly* or *on the whole* has to be used.

Good writers accentuate the positive and downplay the negative. Thus "Write in the affirmative" does the job for "Don't write in the negative." And while we can't convert every negative into an affirmative, consider these helpful translations:

not many	few
not the same	different
does not have	lacks
did not stay	left
did not consider	ignored
did not accept	rejected
not possible	impossible
not able	unable
not certain	uncertain[23]

Beware of Unnecessary Words and "Doubleheaders"

Edit out the clutter. Strike *of all* in *First of all*. Replace *end result* with *result*, *serious crisis* with *crisis*, *true facts* with *facts*, *personal beliefs* with *beliefs*, *free gift* with *gift*, *single-most* with *single*, and *new record* with *record*. Delete *together* in "The team gathered together." Delete the *very* in "Susan is a very strong leader." The word *very* weakens the word *strong*, just as the word *pretty* weakens the word *red* in "The brick building is pretty red." "He would claim that running is easier than swimming" is better written, "He claims running is easier than swimming." "My visit to China will always be remembered by me" is improved by, "I will always remember my visit to China." Use *thus* instead of *thusly*, *now* instead of *currently* or *presently*, *met* instead of *held a meeting*, *agreed* instead of *reached an agreement*, *because* instead of *due to the fact that*, *public works* instead of *infrastructure*.

Avoid overused words. Instead of saying a point is *important*, *exciting*, or *obvious*, just make it so. And if you are clear, you seldom have to use *clearly*, *plainly*, *doubtless*, or *most assuredly*. Colorless words make even the freshest ideas and prose seem stale. The joy of writing is getting it right in as lively a way as possible.

Beware of clichés. They can't be completely avoided but they usually sound lame. Examples: *few and far between, busy as a bee, water under the bridge*. Use them sparingly, if you have to, with discrimination and shun them when they substitute for precise thinking.[24]

Also, avoid telling us what you are about to tell us. Just say it. Impeach wordy introductions such as *it is interesting to note that, also important is the fact that, therefore it seems that, I would at this juncture in my paper ..., it is now time for this writer to admit her own ..., the thesis here is that ..., and the point I want to make here is that we ...,be that as it may ..., and in conclusion*. Eliminate *history tells us* and *at this point in time*. Junk the phrase *further research is needed*. It always is.

Curb phrasing that makes repetition necessary to keep the sentence on track; strings of nouns depending on one another; prepositions, conjunctions, and adverbial expressions made up of two or more words: *with reference to, in conjunction with, in terms of, in the event that, in the nature of, as to whether, in lieu of, in relation to.* Often a single, one-syllable word will do: *in, with, for.*

Avoid "doubleheaders": *beck and call, bound and determined, safe and sound, clear and simple, nuts and bolts, full and complete, first and foremost, hope and trust, each and every, fair and just.* See if one word will say it all. "Lawyers love paired words with related meanings, like null and void, part and parcel, aid and abet, sum and substance, irrelevant and immaterial," laments Rene Cappon. But these doubleheaders are "kissing cousins of redundancies."[25] Legal writing rarely wins prizes for readability.

Avoid "Twinkie" Words and Phrases

A "twinkie" word takes its meaning from junk food, which has little or no nutrition. My nominations for twinkie awards are *needless to say, to say the least, interesting, nice, meaningful, exciting, hopefully, key, insightful, great, there are, there is, there were, and so forth, and the like, and so on, crucial, drastic, stimulating, sensitive,* and *parameter.* Omit *with reference to, in the nature of, the fact that.* These have been spoiled by excessive and careless use until they have become hollow.

Avoid jargon. Adding *-wise* and *-ize* to the end of words may be fashionable, but it undermines clarity. The suffix *-wise* has a place in established forms like *clockwise, otherwise,* and *likewise,* but adding it to nouns to indicate *in relation to* is sloppy writing. Made-up words like *politicswise, P.R-wise, leadershipwise, policywise, datawise,* and *mediawise* are unpleasant to both eye and ear.

Although *finalize, prioritize, divisionalize, definitize, analogize,* and *bureaucratize* are formed by the same process that created the acceptable *popularize, concertize,* and *modernize,* skip them. Better words can be employed. For *finalize,* try *complete, conclude,* or *end.* Also avoid trendy words like *scenario, input, interface, impact, effectuate, bottom line, cool, chill,* and *awesome.*

Be Correct

For most of us, English is the primary language we'll use when writing. Learn its rules of grammar and syntax. Master them. Learn to spell. I'm mildly dyslexic, and I prize the saying that only creative people know how to spell a word three different ways. Still, when in doubt, I look it up. Bad spelling and grammar imply a lazy writer who is indifferent to the reader. Worse, by calling attention to themselves, bad spelling and grammar interrupt the flow of ideas. Readers won't stick with a careless writer.

Be careful not to use *feel* when you mean *believe, consider, think.*

The word *but* is commonly misused when *yet* is appropriate. *But* cancels what you have just said. *Yet* is used when you are merely adding to what you have said or want a softer reversal than *but. Yet* can mean *nevertheless*, too. "The candidate said he was going to win, *but* the campaign is now over and he came in second." Fine. "The candidate is not sure she can use Jack Jones as a pollster for this campaign, *yet* she believes Jones is a gifted opinion analyst." Fine.

The thoughtful writer is aware of the distinction between *that* and *which* and uses these pronouns with precision. *That* defines, *which* informs. *Which* adds further information about the noun. For example, "The party, *which* was defeated, pulled itself together and prepared to wait until next time." Here the *which* explains something about the party and helps readers understand the context of why the party needed to pull itself together.

That restricts the meaning of the noun and makes it more specific. "The party that was defeated pulled itself together and prepared to win next time." In this sentence, a *that* clause defines the particular party the writer is talking about; it was the defeated party, not the victorious party, that pulled itself together. It is not just any party, but a specific party.

A good rule is this: if commas can be inserted around the clause, the correct word to use is *which*. Which is a bit more formal than *that*, and most writers prefer thats to whiches for readability and flow. We use *that* far more than *which* when we are talking. Good writers, however, try to avoid both words. Thus, it is better to revise the sentence above to read: "The defeated party pulled itself together and prepared to win next time." *That* can be deleted in about one-third of its appearances. "He said that it was expensive" is crisper when written, "He said it's expensive." If you have a sentence with these pronouns, challenge yourself to rewrite and eliminate them. Hooray for "whichless" and "thatless" sentences. They're shorter and more readable.

Take special care when using *this*. Pronouns refer to previous nouns. Some students use *this* to refer to everything they just said, as in "This explains why John Kerry lost the election." Such usage confuses rather than clarifies. The careful writer avoids sentences beginning with *this*.

Criteria and *data* are the plurals of *criterion* and *datum* and require plural verbs. *Media* is plural.

Use gender-inclusive language. All executives aren't men, nor are all of those who fish or put out fires. Instead of *fireman*, try *firefighter*. Instead of *congressman*, try *representative*. Use plural forms to avoid sexist language. Instead of "A president will use his veto power," try "Presidents use their veto power." *Human being, humankind, person*, and *chair* are all proper substitutes for *man, mankind*, and *chairman*.[26]

Additional Style Suggestions

I like reading forcefully argued papers, yet I dislike overstatement. Effective writers learn the right balance.

Use contractions (e.g., *can't* for *cannot*) when writing conversational prose. People use them when they speak, so they make for natural, readable writing. Write as you speak—unless of course you mumble or your everyday talk is incomprehensible. Contractions, however, are often unacceptable in formal writing. A careful writer knows how to get the right voice and when contractions are appropriate.

Use the exclamation point sparingly; once a paper is enough! Overuse robs it of its force. Avoid underlining, italicizing, and boldfacing for the same reason. A well-constructed sentence creates its own natural emphasis.

Phrases or words in parentheses disrupt the flow, as do dashes and hyphenated words. One critic assails the overuse of hyphens as "hyphenitis." A hyphen, however, can avoid ambiguity and make life easier for your readers. Sometimes hyphens are essential to understanding. Do you mean an *old film buff* or an *old-film buff*? In general avoid hyphens. When in doubt, consult the dictionary or the *Chicago Manual of Style*. (Note: Social scientists, among others, rely on the *Chicago Manual of Style*, yet English professors and many people in the humanities disciplines rely on the Modern Language Association's *MLA Handbook for Writers of Research Papers*.)

Novelists occasionally use dashes to simulate speaking or dialogue. But writing is different from speaking. A dash can help provide a dramatic shift in tone or amplify a point. Yet nonfiction writers limit their use of dashes to avoid choppiness. Language maven William Safire cleverly satirizes the dramatic writer's penchant for the dash and similar punctuation novelties: "Writers of drama must write speech, not writing, because real people do not speak writing. Hence we have pauses, delays—you get my drift?—half-stops, restarts, stammering, and exclamatory grunts (ugh!) and drifting off into pre-dot-com ellipses . . . . To put this speech in written form—that is, to transcribe it—we have seen the powerful punch—pow! right in the kisser—of illustrative punctuation."[27]

Vary the length of sentences and paragraphs, and vary how you begin sentences. If all your sentences have ten words and all your paragraphs ten sentences, you'll bore your reader. Try an occasional one- or two-sentence paragraph. Variety, counterpoint, and change grab the reader's attention. Write directly to your reader. Keep your audience in mind, and awake. Nothing bores a reader more than a string of paragraphs beginning "Harry Truman said . . . ," "Harry Truman declared . . . ," "Harry Truman noted . . . ," "President Truman pointed out . . . ," "As Truman wrote . . . ," or "There was . . . ," "There are . . . " "There is . . . ," "There were . . . ."

Colons (:) are a punctuation mark used chiefly to call attention to a list, explanation, or quotation. Thus, "The legislator brought home the bacon: a bridge, a new post office, and an expansion to the veteran's hospital." Semicolons (;) are used to indicate a pause longer than a comma yet shorter than a complete stop. They should normally be used only between two independent clauses (groups of words that could stand alone as sentences) and never to separate a dependent and an independent clause (as in "Although the candidate had innovative ideas; she had little speaking ability").

Commas help break up a sentence. Yet too many can be confusing. The best way to learn about the proper use of commas is to pay attention to their use by excellent writers. "Reverse engineer" their sentences.

The comma helps a reader understand that one clause or phrase has ended and another begun. "The comma was invented to help readers. Without it, sentence parts can collide with one another unexpectedly, causing misreadings."[28] Avoid using a comma, however, to take the place of a period between sentences.

Tables and Numbers

Use tables only when necessary. Sometimes they are. I like tables and visual displays of data. Yet readers have a tendency to skip past them, viewing them as intrusions or merely as evidence for a point the author makes in the prose. Try summarizing the contents of a table in prose and showing it in an eyecatching visual (as in *USA Today* or CNBC) so it can be grasped at a glance.

As a rule, tables or figures should stand on their own. They should be understandable to the reader who has not yet read the narrative. The meaning of numbers should be clear. Yet tables and graphs shouldn't be relied on to make a point not already made in the text; they should only amplify a point.

A table can help summarize data or highlight particular things to clarify research findings for the reader. "Including a table in a paper does not," however, "relieve you of the obligation to describe specifically what is in that table," writes political scientist Raymond Wolfinger. "You should not solve the problem of data description by instructing readers to look at Table 2 if they want to know what you found."[29]

Write out numbers from one to nine, except when using percentages. Thus it is 44 percent, eight vetoes, 62 legislative measures, 10 court rulings, and 3,000 words. Spell out a number when it begins a sentence. Spell out *percent* except in tables, when the % symbol is proper. Ordinal numbers are spelled out, as in the twenty-first century, the top one-tenth of the population. Legislative sessions and dates use numbers: 110th Congress and January 20, 2007.

Make sure your numbers add up correctly in all tables and charts. Writers often have a difficult time with numbers; errors, especially in percentages, easily creep into books and reports.

Quotations and Citations

Use quotations selectively. Few observations are truly original. The use of too many quotations conceals from the reader what you know and what you think. Quotations interrupt the flow just as readily as too many tables, parentheses, or foreign phrases. Include long quotations only when the exact wording is crucial to your argument.

After you have read widely on a topic, you develop a sense of what is common knowledge. Dictionary definitions, the date of Picasso's death, or Ronald Reagan's career in Hollywood do not need to be cited or quoted from other sources. Paraphrase agreed-on definitions and common knowledge. If you know something, you can say it just as well as someone else did, and adopt the explanation to suit your purposes. You should shorten it as well. You can still give proper credit to the author who inspired your thoughts. Reserve quotations for material that is colorful, opinionated, or distinctive. Also quotations should merely support your argument rather than make the point for you.

If you use a quotation that runs more than seven lines in your typescript, set it off as a block quotation. Indent it several spaces from the left margin of the text, and double-space it. (I prefer the old way of single- spacing quotations but new writing handbooks now mandate double-spacing.) Block quotations don't need quotation marks. Keep in mind, however, that most of us let our eyes dance past block quotations. Shortening them so that they're integrated into the text increases reader attention.

Another device to keep your reader with you is to identify the author in the middle of a quotation rather than in the more traditional beginning or ending tag. Instead of "As E. B. White aptly puts it . . . ," try "I suppose I have written *the fact that* a thousand times in the heat of composition, revised it out maybe five hundred times in the cool aftermath," writes E. B. White. "To be batting only .500 this late in the season, to fail half the time to connect with this fat pitch, saddens me, for it seems a betrayal of [my mentor] who showed me how to swing at it and made the swinging seem worth while."[30]

Keep note cards or a journal of quotations you might later decide to use in your writing. Take down the author's words accurately, and record the source in full. Countless errors occur in quotations and citations, and retracing your steps to correct them is both time consuming and frustrating at later stages in your work.

To shorten a quotation a writer can use the ellipsis notation (. . .). *Ellipsis*, a Greek word, is defined as leaving out. Thus you can leave out an unneeded phrase in a sentence, as in "The President . . . reiterated his support for the constitutional amendment," so long as what remains is grammatical. When omitting a full sentence, use four rather than three spaced periods, as in (. . . .).

Give credit to the appropriate sources for direct quotations and the distinctive ideas you paraphrase from others. The more you write, however, the more you will want to skip the verbose quotes you may have cited when you were less well read. Learn to be selective: "The art of handling quotes comes down to knowing when to quote, when to paraphrase, when to forget the whole thing."[31]

Footnotes are required tools. Footnote information you have learned from a book, article, newspaper, or interview if it is something others would not know without access to that source. Also occasionally footnote passages to encourage your readers to explore ideas or related topics in greater detail elsewhere.

Plagiarism is copying part or all of another's work without citing the source. It also refers to using someone's phrasing and ideas without proper citation or credit. Plagiarism is cheating. "Your research paper is a collaboration between you and your sources," writes Diana Hacker. "To be fair and ethical, you must acknowledge your debt to the writers of those sources."[32]

Plagiarism, both accidental and intended, occurs all too frequently, both in college and in professional life. Whenever you use another writer's exact words, you must enclose the words or sentences in quotation marks. Changing one or two words doesn't make it your sentence.

Leads and Conclusions

Be creative about choosing an apt, and if possible, intriguing title. An effective title telegraphs your theme and arouses interest.

Your essay's first few sentences are especially important. An effective lead signals your thesis and hooks readers with calculated teasers. As they look at your title and leading sentences, readers are asking, What's the big idea? Where is this writer going? What's in this for me?

Reporters devote considerable energy to making what they call "the top of the story" accurate and arresting. Why? Most readers never get beyond the first two paragraphs of most stories in newspapers and magazines. If journalists grab your attention up front, they at least have a chance to hold your interest for the duration.

> The lead must capture the reader immediately and force him to keep reading. It must cajole him with freshness or novelty or paradox, or with humor, or with surprise, or with an unusual idea, or an interesting fact, or a question. Anything will do as long as it nudges his curiosity and tugs at his sleeve.
>
> Next the lead must do some real work. It must provide a few hard details that tell the reader why the piece was written and why he ought to read it. But don't dwell on the reason. Coax the reader a little more; keep him inquisitive.[33]

Although news writing is different from college essays, corporate reports, or public policy papers, introductions in every form of writing are important. Students have the good fortune—although they might quibble at this description—that professors are paid to read student papers from start to finish even if the leads aren't arresting. Yet duty doesn't guarantee interest. Students must make a case for the significance of their essays at the outset.

Often good leads can't be written until the essay is finished. Try writing several leads after you've finished your first draft. Don't be too quick to settle on the first. Let the lead emerge from your work.

For long papers—over 20 pages—subtitles are helpful in indicating transitions to new material or new sections. Subheads can add to a paper's readability and, cleverly used, can save words. Yet, as most college writing assignments are five to 15 pages and focus on a few major points, subheadings and section breaks may be unnecessary. Beware, however, of using them as a crutch to avoid writing necessary, yet difficult, transitions.

Conclusions should flow from the rest of the paper. They don't need signals like *in conclusion* or *in summary*. They should tie ideas together, not simply restate what already has been said. Nor should they introduce new topics or information. The best conclusions explore the significance of the ideas in the essay, sometimes by making recommendations.

ON FORMAT AND PRESENTATION

Take your reader into account. It pays to ask in advance if your intended reader, especially a professor or supervisor, has specific format rules.

Here is a set of suggestions I share with students. They are simple, commonsense guidelines. Most students already know them, yet what students know and what they do are not necessarily the same.

- Use good paper and make sure your machine produces dark enough copy for easy reading.
- Type double-spaced with margins of at least an inch on all sides—perhaps a bit more on the left. (Teachers and editors need space to make comments and corrections.)
- Number your pages, preferably at the top of each page after your first page.
- Staple the paper in the upper left-hand corner. Vertically or slanted is better than horizontal, for easier page turning.
- Skip the plastic wrappers or cellophane binders; they are a nuisance.
- Proofread your paper at least two or three times before submitting it. Even then, however, you'll spot an occasional typo or error. What to do? Minor errors may ordinarily be corrected by pen. Yet you'll find many professor and most professional or business supervisors will insist on error-free products.
- Retain a copy of what you write.
- Short essay papers usually don't need a separate title page. Save paper. Present your title at the start of your paper, leaving proper space before you begin your text. Put your name, date, and other necessary information in the upper right-hand corner of your first page. Here again, however, some instructors will ask that you put your name at the end of the paper, or even on the back of your last page, so they can read the paper without knowing who wrote it. Check on this.
- Strive for a consistent format on quotations, citations, punctuation, and indentation. When in doubt, check a reliable style handbook.

- On occasion you may want to append at the end of your essay a brief *Author's Note*. This is not a place for excuses or apologies, but rather a place to indicate your personal feelings about the topic or controversy, or how your views changed as you did the research and writing. It might be a place, too, to mention some unusual circumstance under which you wrote. Or perhaps you just want to note how joyous or exacting the assignment became. Once again, teachers and supervisors may object to this practice. You'll have to judge whether the context warrants an *Author's Note*.

Oh, and by the way, creative writers often ignore traditional rules and invent their own.

ON TRANSCENDING WRITER'S BLOCK

All writers, regardless of age, are daunted by writing assignments. Writers have to overcome fear and put anxiety on hold.

How does a writer overcome procrastination, get "in the zone," and encourage "flow"? "Like climbing a mountain, writing a book is exciting at the beginning, exhilarating at the end, but tedious, frustrating, and hair-raising in between," writes Ralph Keyes.[34]

Keyes suggests "courage boosters" for writers; one or more of these may help you to transcend writer's block:

- read about successful writers, paying attention to their fears and how they dealt with them.
- take a writing course or two.
- attend an occasional writer's conference.
- join a serious writers' group.
- develop anxiety-easing rituals, no matter how eccentric.
- devise fear-taming work techniques no matter how gimmicky.
- write at times of day when you're most productive and least anxious.
- identify your censor-in-chief and mentally rehearse how to deal with that person.
- get to know yourself well enough not to be terrified by what escapes from within onto the page.
- convert fear into excitement.
- write.[35]

Most "writing problems" are human problems. Courage and honesty are as important and perhaps more important than talent. Fearlessness and discipline are key. Yet nothing is as important, as noted earlier, as the urge to tell the truth, share stories, and say what we believe needs to be said.

Concluding Thoughts

Begin to write early enough so you have plenty of time to revise and proofread. If you can, put your edited draft aside, and reread it after it has receded a bit from memory. And, as noted, have a friend or roommate read your work. A later, detached reading will be as revealing as it is rewarding. Gaps between what you wrote and what you meant become apparent. Awkward transitions or unnecessary apologies jump out at you. Doubleheaders, redundancies, clichés, and "twinkies" pop up. Proofread your writing twice on your own. Remember the virtues of reading your work aloud. Ask a colleague, relative, or friend to read it too. We all learn from feedback, positive as well as critical.

Set high expectations for your research, yet not so high you paralyze your ability to get it done. Perfectionists seldom finish. Plus perfectionism undermines playfulness, creativity, and the liberating process of writing. Some people become so compulsive in the research stage that by the time they are ready to write, their data have become obsolete. "Analysis-paralysis" can undermine an otherwise healthy undertaking.

"Perfectionism is the voice of the oppressor, the enemy of the people. It will keep you cramped and insane your whole life," writes Anne Lamott. "I think," she adds, "perfectionism is based on the obsessive belief that if you run carefully enough, hitting each stepping-stone just right, you won't have to die." The truth is that messiness and improvisation are the writer's friend.[36] The main differences between effective writers and those who never get much written are discipline, focus, concentration, tenacity, and physical stamina.

Pace yourself. Too much time devoted to research often leaves too little for sophisticated writing. An executive friend of mine has a helpful 70 percent rule: Though having all the information would be perfect, having two-thirds or so of the available information usually ensures making the appropriate decision.

Few scholars can obtain all the data, all the interviews, and all the evidence they'd like to have before making judgments. Executives or writers who wait for 100 percent assurances will probably still be waiting long after it has been worth the effort. Beware the "ready, aim-aim-aim" syndrome. Writers must be willing to make decisions, come to judgment, commit, and write. Set smart goals and realistic deadlines; schedule sensible cutoffs. Reward yourself on meeting these. Do your best, yet be prepared to move on to the next stage of your work.

Good writers invent their own rules and occasionally ignore traditional usage and style if these impede their writing. Mark Twain broke rules and told his stories with poetic and lyric descriptions, similes and colloquial turns of speech; Faulkner went on and on and on, and yet he succeeded because he made long sentences sing and paragraphs dance. Walt Whitman was a congenital rule-breaker. Hemingway redefined lean writing. James Joyce cherished breaking the mold.

Yet even the great ones acknowledge at least a few basic guidelines. To be good, you have to read and observe extensively. To write well you have to revise extensively. "I began to write seriously when I had taught myself the discipline necessary to achieve what I wanted," observes novelist Bernard Malamud. "When I touched that time, my words announced themselves to me." Revision, he notes, became not only essential but also one of the exquisite pleasures of writing. He would write everything three times: once to understand it, the second time to improve the prose, "and a third time to say what it still must say."[37]

Writing is a performing art. Yet unlike music, drama, or sports, no conductor, director or coach leads your reader through the performance. Word selection and punctuation are the only aids suggesting how fast or slow or loud the writing should be. Reading is a solitary, detached experience. Careless writing repels and confuses. Dull writing bores the reader. Active, clear writing, on the other hand, informs, persuades, entertains, empowers, liberates.[38]

In the long run, learning to conduct research and to write well correlate highly with extensive reading of skillfully executed research projects and good writing. If you want to become an effective writer, read classics, read great books, as many as possible, as soon as possible. Writers in the Western tradition invariably have read the major Greek classics, the Bible, and Shakespeare. Also read well-written, well-edited magazines, such as *The New Yorker, The Economist, The New Republic,* and *The New York Review of Books.* Keep a journal with your own comments on fine writing and what you like and dislike. Start a collection of words you might use. Heighten your awareness about the power of words.

Adopt gifted writers as your mentors. Read and reread your favorite writers, columnists, and social scientists. If you have no favorites, try Jefferson, Emerson, Lincoln, Twain, Churchill, Hemingway, Fitzgerald, Faulkner, Russell Baker, Saul Bellow, Raymond Carver, Robertson Davies, Nadine Gordimer, Joe Klein, Anthony Lewis, William Manchester, David McCullough, John McPhee, Clinton Rossiter, Arthur Schlesinger, Jr., Lewis Thomas, Calvin Trillin, Barbara Tuchman, John Updike, Eudora Welty, Molly Ivins, Tim O'Brien, John Irving, George Will, and Garry Wills. Also read the Latin writers Carlos Fuentes, Gabriel Garcia Marques, and Manual Puig. Read their earlier works. Discover why they are so good by trying a little of that "reverse engineering" mentioned earlier. Do they follow a clear, logical outline? How do they structure it? How do they capture your attention? How do they marshal evidence? What do they do to simplify, clarify, convince, and persuade?

Hemingway said the way a young writer learns the craft is just to go away and write. Yet Hemingway grew up on a steady diet of Mark Twain and other notable essayists. And after World War I, he went to Paris and enjoyed "tutorial sessions" with Gertrude Stein and Sherwood Anderson. Young writers profit from sharing work with others and going over it, line by line.

Most important, the younger writer must find voice, purpose, and inner drive. "What I have most wanted to do throughout the past ten years is to make political writing into an art," writes George Orwell. "Looking back," he adds, "I see that it is invariably where I lacked a political purpose that I wrote lifeless books and was betrayed into purple passages, sentences without meaning, decorative adjectives and humbug generally."[39] To write honestly, with power, voice and courage, you may first have to make an appointment with yourself and come to terms with your personal values. You have to write from the "inside out" rather than the "outside in."

Here are the questions readers will ask about your writing: Does it have focus, character, unity, and integrity? Does it have a clear beginning, a meaty middle, and a sound conclusion? Is it well researched and well written? Is your opening paragraph catchy enough to make us continue reading the paper? Is your evidence convincing? Does your paper have something new and fresh to say? Does it persuade? Did you learn and display this learning? Did we learn?

If you have important ideas to share, writing badly is better than not writing at all. Most of us are prisoners of compulsive teachers in our past who railed against sloppy sentences and couldn't have cared less about what we were trying to say.[40] This is the tyranny of form over substance. What we have to say is more important than the search for the perfect sentence. What's the use of elegant writing wholly allergic to substance? This problem reminds me of the person who could speak fluently in seven languages, yet had nothing of note to say in any of them.

Writing matters. But what matters even more is the power of ideas. Be brave. Writing is invariably an act of courage. Just as leaders define, defend, and promote important mutually shared values, so also writers help define and clarify critical choices. Writing is a grand opportunity to tell your story, to tell the truth, to advocate beliefs, and to share creative ideas. A writer writes to understand, teach, persuade, celebrate, criticize, caution, inspire, lead, entertain, and share stories.

Great writers help shape their times. Churchill's influence came from his ability to inspire by both spoken and written word. So also with Martin Luther King, Jr. His *Letter from Birmingham Jail* and his "I Have a Dream" speech galvanized the U.S. civil rights movement in the early 1960s. Rachel Carson's *The Silent Spring* and Betty Friedan's *The Feminine Mystique* helped launch impressive political movements. The writings of Karl Marx and Milton Friedman redefined economic debates in their day. Inspirational writers from Thomas Paine and Henry

David Thoreau to Elie Wiesel and Richard Warren have transformed people's lives just as the writings of Peter Drucker recontextualized our understanding of modern management. The power of the pen (or word processor) may be different from the power of the sword yet should never be underestimated.

The first challenge of all writers is to write well; the second is to help us understand ourselves; the third is to take on cliches, myth, sentimentality, and hypocrisy. "One task of literature is to formulate questions and construct counter statements to the reigning pieties," wrote Susan Sontag. "And even when it is not oppositional, the arts gravitate toward contrariness."[41]

Notes

*   Two earlier versions of this essay were published by Prentice Hall in 1990 and 1993. Several people have helped improve this work over the years, especially Carolyn Shultz, Margo Scribner, Serena Hoffman, David Lowland, Holly Carter, and Jon Goldstein.
1. Kurt Vonnegut, "How to Write with Style," *Newsweek on Campus*, April 1987, pp. 54–5.
2. Pico Iyer, "In Praise of the Humble Comma," *Time*, June 13, 1988, p. 80.
3. Ernest Hemingway, excerpts from letters to friends, in Larry W. Phillips, ed., *Ernest Hemingway on Writing* (New York: Scribner's, 1984), p. 77.
4. Alexander Solzhenitsyn, Nobel Prize address, 1970, in John Hersey, *The Writer's Craft* (New York: Knopf, 1974), pp. 148 and 151.
5. Gerald Graff and Cathy Birkenstein, *They Say/I Say* (New York: W. W. Norton, 2006), p. 3.
6. David Pion-Berlin, "Reflections on Writing a Dissertation," *PS: Political Science and Politics* (winter 1986), p. 64.
7. For more on this topic, see Thomas S. Kuhn, *The Structure of Scientific Revolutions*, 2d ed. (Chicago: University of Chicago Press, 1970). Follow the lead of Columbus, Galileo, and Darwin.
8. Somerset Maugham, quoted in James Charlton and Lisbeth Mark, *The Writer's Home Companion* (New York: Franklin Watts, 1987), p. 77. See also George Orwell, "Politics and the English Language," originally written in 1946;

reprinted in George Orwell, *The Orwell Reader* (New York: Harcourt, Brace, 1956), pp. 355–66.

9. Kate L. Turabian, *Student's Guide for Writing College Papers*, 3d ed. (Chicago: University of Chicago Press, 1976), p. 40.

10. Wendy R. Leibowitz, "Technology Transforms Writing and the Teaching of Writing," *Chronicle of Higher Education*, November 26, 1999, p. 67.

11. Sylvan Barnet, *A Short Guide to Writing about Art*, 2d ed. (Boston: Little, Brown, 1985), p. 74.

12. Peter Elbow, *Writing with Power* (New York: Oxford University Press, 1981), p. 299.

13. Ibid., p. 123.

14. Stanley Kunitz, answering a student question in a poetry class at Whitman College, November 5, 1997.

15. Kunitz, "Speaking of Poetry" in his *Passing Through: The Later Poems* (New York: Norton, 1995), p. 11.

16. Jacques Barzun, "Lincoln the Writer," in his *On Writing, Editing and Publishing*, 2d ed. (Chicago: University of Chicago Press, 1986), p. 81.

17. James J. Kilpatrick, *The Writer's Art* (Kansas City: Andrews, McMeel and Parker, 1984), p. 54.

18. William Strunk, Jr., and E. B. White, *The Elements of Style*, 3d ed. (New York: Macmillan, 1979), p. 23.

19. Rene J. Cappon, *The Word: An Associated Press Guide to Good News Writing* (New York: Associated Press, 1982), p. 22.

20. John Kenneth Galbraith, *A Life in Our Times: Memoirs* (Boston: Houghton Mifflin, 1981), pp. 535–6.

21. Theodore M. Bernstein, *The Careful Writer: A Modern Guide to Usage* (New York: Atheneum, 1965), p. 140.

22. William Zinsser, *On Writing Well*, 2d ed. (New York: Harper and Row, 1980), pp. 7–8.

23. These suggestions come from Joseph M. Williams, *Style*, 2d ed. (Glenview, IL: Scott, Foresman and Co., 1985), p. 88.

24. See Diana Hacker, *A Pocket Style Manual*, 4th ed. (Boston: Bedford/St. Martin's, 2004), pp. 19–20, and Theodore M. Bernstein, *The Careful Reader* (New York: Atheneum, 1965), pp. 103–5.

25. Cappon, *The Word*, p. 110.

26. In general, see Casey Miller and Kate Smith, *The Handbook of Nonsexist Writing*, 2nd ed. (New York: Harper and Row, 1988).

27. William Safire, "Dash It All," *New York Times Magazine*, May 28, 2000, p. 19.

28. Hacker, *A Pocket Style Manual*, 4th ed., p. 17.

29. Raymond E. Wolfinger, "Tips for Writing Papers," *PS: Political Science and Politics*, March 1993, p. 88.

30. E. B. White, intro to Strunk and White, *Elements of Style*, 3d ed., p. xiv.

31. Cappon, *The Word*, p. 71.

32. Hacker, *A Pocket Style Manual*, 4th ed., p. 157. See also Richard A Posner, *The Little Book of Plagiarism*, (New York: Pantheon Books, 2007).

33. Zinsser, *On Writing Well*, p. 60. See also Marshall Cook, "How to Write Good Article Leads," *Writer*, June 1987, pp. 16–8.

34. Ralph Keyes, *The Courage to Write* (New York: Henry Holt and Co., 1995), p. 190.

35. Ibid., pp. 200–1.

36. Anne Lamott, *Bird by Bird: Some Instructions on Writing and Life* (New York: Anchor, 1995), p. 28.

37. Bernard Malamud, "Reflections of a Writer," talk at Bennington College, October 30, 1984, in *New York Times Book Review*, March 20, 1988, p. 18.

38. I am indebted to David N. Lowland for ideas in this paragraph as well as for other editorial suggestions.

39. George Orwell, "Why I Write," 1946, quoted in Bernard Crick, *George Orwell* (Boston: Atlantic—Little, Brown, 1980), p. xiii.

40. Bruce Ballenger, "The Importance of Writing Badly," *Christian Science Monitor*, March 28, 1990, p. 16.

41. Susan Sontag, *At the Same Time: Essays and Speeches* (New York: Farrar, Straus Giroux, 2007), p. 204.

RECOMMENDED WORKS ON STYLE AND USAGE

Sheridan Baker. *The Practical Stylist*. New York: Crowell, 1969.

Sylvan Barnet. *A Short Guide to Writing about Art*, 8th ed. Boston: Little, Brown, 2005.

Theodore M. Bernstein. *The Careful Writer: A Modern Guide to Usage*. New York: Atheneum, 1965.

Wayne C. Booth, et al. *The Craft of Research*, Chicago: University of Chicago Press, 1995.

Rene J. Cappon. *The Word: An Associated Press Guide to Good News Writing*. New York: Associated Press, 1982.

The Chicago Manual of Style, 15th ed. Chicago: University of Chicago Press, 2003.

Fredrick Crews. *The Random House Handbook*, 3rd ed. New York: Random House, 1980.

Timothy W. Crusius and Carolyn E. Channell. *The Aims of Argument*, 6th ed. New York: McGraw Hill, 2008.

Peter Elbow. *Writing with Power*. Oxford: Oxford University Press, 1998.

Peter Elbow. *Writing without Teachers*. Oxford: Oxford University Press, 1973.

Rudolf Flesch. *The Art of Readable Writing*. New York: Collier, 1949.

Rudolf Flesch and A. H. Lass. *A New Guide to Better Writing*. New York: Warner Books, 1983.

Joseph Gibaldi. *MLA Handbook for Writers of Research Papers*, 6th ed. New York: Modern Language Association of America, 2003.

Karen Elizabeth Gordon. *The Deluxe Transitive Vampire: The Ultimate Handbook of Grammar for the Innocent, the Eager, and the Doomed.* New York: Pantheon, 1993.

Gerald Graff and Cathy Birkenstein. *They Say/I Say: The Moves that Matter in Academic Writing.* New York: W. W. Norton, 2006.

Diana Hacker. *A Pocket Style Manual*, 4th ed. Boston: Bedford/St. Martin's, 2004.

Donald Hall. *Writing Well.* Boston: Little, Brown, 1985.

John Hersey. *The Writer's Craft.* New York: Knopf, 1974.

Thomas S. Kane. *The New Oxford Guide to Writing.* New York: Oxford University Press, 1994.

Ralph Keyes, *The Courage to Write: How Writers Transcend Fear.* New York: Henry Holt and Co., 1995.

James Kilpatrick. *The Writer's Art.* Kansas City: Andrews, McMeel and Parker, 1984.

Anne Lamott. *Bird by Bird: Some Instructions on Writing and Life.* New York: Anchor, 1995.

Richard A. Lanham. *Revising Prose*, 2nd ed. New York: Macmillan, 1987.

Andrea A. Lunsford. *The Everyday Writer.* Boston: Bedford/St. Martin's, 2001.

Andrea A. Lunsford and John J. Ruszkiewicz. *Everything's an Argument*, 3rd ed. Boston: Bedford/St. Martin's, 2004.

Casey Miller and Kate Smith. *The Handbook of Nonsexist Writing*, 2nd ed. New York: Harper and Row, 1988.

Gabriel L. Rico. *Writing the Natural Way: Using Right-Brain Techniques to Release Your Expressive Powers.* Los Angeles: Tarcher, 1983.

Rainer Maria Rilke. *Letters to a Young Poet*, revised and reissued edition. New York: W. W. Norton, 2004.

William Strunk, Jr., and E. B. White. *The Elements of Style*, 3rd ed. New York: Macmillan, 1979.

John R. Trimble. *Writing with Style: Conversations on the Art of Writing.* 2nd ed. Englewood Cliffs, N.J.: Prentice Hall, 2000.

Kate L. Turabian. *Student's Guide for Writing College Papers*, 3rd ed. Chicago: University of Chicago Press, 1990.

Eudora Welty. *One Writer's Beginnings.* New York: Warner Books, 1984.

Joseph M. Williams. *Style: Toward Clarity and Grace*, rev. ed. Chicago: University of Chicago Press, 2000.

William Zinsser. *On Writing Well*, 7th rev. ed. New York: Harper Collins, 2006.

William Zinsser. *Writing with a Word Processor.* New York: Harper Trade Books, 1983.

Jennifer L. Hochschild, Harvard University

Writing Introductions

5

"The beginning is half the whole."
Pythagoris

"Well begun, half done."
My Grandmother

Every book, article, or journal issue has only one first sentence and paragraph. So it is essential to get them right (which often implies that the first sentence is written many times, most crucially after the rest of the document is finished). Getting them right means several things—writing in a style that will motivate your reader to move to the next sentence and paragraph, making a clear and important point immediately, articulating a distinctive position, and conveying the genre in which you will be writing (fiction? ruminative essay? cut-and-dried social science?). Hard as it is to do all of those things well in the first paragraph, it is possible since they are not separate tasks. One can write engagingly in a particular genre while articulating a distinctive position on an important point.[1]

The rest of the introduction should build on and elaborate the central point of the first paragraph. That is presumably true for any piece of (linear) writing, but an introduction to a social science document has, in my view, a rather distinctive flavor. It is a more personal, direct invitation to the reader to come at least partway behind the veil of ignorance than is available at any other point in the document. This is the section of the article, book, or journal in which the language can be relatively informal, and in which the writer can display aspects of her personality or even reveal relevant bits of information about his private life. It is also the section in which the writer more or less directly tells the reader what motivates the project, that is, what matters enough so that the writer was willing to make all of the effort that we know to be essential for completing a good document. Basically, the goal of the introduction as a whole is the same as the goal of the first sentence and paragraph—to induce readers to keep reading and thereby to teach or persuade them of something that they previously did not know or agree with.

An analogy might be useful here. I think of an introduction as rather like a good cover letter that is part of a package of materials sent by a job applicant to a departmental search committee. The package will contain book chapters or articles, syllabi, and other evidence of the content and quality of scholarship and teaching. It will also contain a curriculum vitae, designed to convey the candidate's academic history as succinctly and objectively as possible. Finally, it will include a cover letter which, in my view, is the candidate's chance to show what really motivates and ties together the items on the vitae or in the writing and teaching materials. As a wise friend once counseled me, "Remember that you are hiring a person, not a set of articles or teaching record." The cover letter can demonstrate how the person thinks and why she cares and you should care about a particular subject, ideally in a way that will convince a search committee that this is someone who would greatly enhance the department.

I find that analogy helpful, but it still does not directly explain *how* to write an introduction that draws readers in, focuses their attention, and articulates a distinctive position on an important subject. There are no cut-and-dried rules, of course; otherwise I would not have been asked to write this essay. Nevertheless, a few precepts emerge from my starting point.

First, the introduction should, in the words of the classic cliché, focus on the forest and not on the trees. That is probably the best way to entice readers and direct their attention the right way. Thus for a book, a detailed outline of each chapter, the methods, or the underlying epistemology are not appropriate. Each of those elements should be edited down to a few sentences; the reader needs a quick architectural tour of the entire project, not a summary of each chapter or an abstract justification of the enterprise. In parallel fashion, for an empirical article eschew a summary of the findings table by table in favor of a few sentences indicating the most crucial or surprising or interesting pattern of results. For a philosophical or analytic article, a summary of the logical or normative stances that led to the conclusion should be edited down to a statement of the conclusion itself, perhaps with notice of a few key landmarks along the way. Finally, for a journal issue or symposium, the introduction should identify (or invent, as the case may be) a few central themes that tie the whole set of articles together and that reveal something important about each.

To put the same point a different way, the introduction should bear a closer resemblance to the conclusion (*not* to a summary) than to any section of the intervening chapters of the book, sections of the article, or elements of the symposium. The point is not to summarize all the steps or all the underpinnings; it is to explicate the central message of the document, with just enough hints of how the author(s) reached that message to assure readers that you are a reliable source of further enlightenment.

In my experience as a journal editor,[2] this advice about "focus on the forest and not on the trees" requires different modifications of the usual style in different subfields of political science. Political theorists typically frame their papers in one way, and scholars of international relations in another. Like all generalizations, this one has important exceptions but even if my claim that these styles are characteristic of certain subfields is exaggerated, the styles themselves should sound familiar—and my suggestions with regard to revision of each will, I hope, be helpful.[3]

To begin with, when I was its editor, papers submitted to *Perspectives on Politics* in the subfield of security studies were almost always structured around several dominant paradigms.[4] The modal manuscript started by outlining three standard theories: realism, liberalism, constructivism (sometimes subdivided into realism and neo-realism, liberalism and neo-liberalism, and so on). The next paragraph then diverged slightly—some authors claimed that they would show how to combine these apparently different theories to prove X; others promised to show that one theory is right and the other two wrong, as evidenced by an explanation of X; a few argued that none of the three quite suffices to explain X, so he or she would provide a new theory (or more frequently, a variant of one of the old ones). Our advice, as editors of *Perspectives*,[5] usually ran along what became a well-worn track: begin the introduction with your own central point, minimize the literature review (or move it to much later in the article if it seems essential), tell us early on why we should care about your concern, and then tell us what kind of evidence you will use. Only after the introduction, if then, should the three dominant paradigms be wheeled into action.

The modal political theory manuscript sent to *Perspectives on Politics* had a very different feel.[6] The first paragraph focused on one or several persons rather than one or several paradigms, and it frequently included dates: "Machiavelli's theory of X, in *The Prince*, 1513, states such-and-such, but Locke's theory of X in *Two Treatises of Government*, 1689, states so-and-so." (Theorists will note the implausibility of this comparison. A contemporary political theorist's last name was the first word in early (and later) paragraphs of an astonishing number of papers ; the paragraph then summarized what that theorist has written about Machiavelli or Locke, or what that theorist has written about another theorist's view of Machiavelli or Locke: "Smith argues that Machiavelli believes XX. Smith disagrees with Jones who argues that Machiavelli believes YY." And so on, through many Smith's and Jones's. Our editorial advice for revision? First, we had something close to a rule that *Perspectives* would not publish any theory article with a name and a date in the title—it is completely unappealing to non-theorists.

Second, we urged authors to rewrite the manuscript so that the whole article as well as each paragraph started with an idea—preferably the author's own—and not with proper nouns. We urged authors to try writing at least the introduction (and preferably the whole paper) from the assumption that readers care about the arguments but are indifferent to which contemporary scholar is making them; names matter only after the central claim, its key supporting arguments, and its most important implications are introduced.

Papers in the sprawling and disparate field of comparative politics (a.k.a. the rest of the world, for we Americanists) varied greatly. I have space here to describe only one modal type: a tightly focused case study with huge capital-T Theory framework that occupied most of the introductory paragraphs. When I earlier served on the editorial board of a distinguished university press, we received a manuscript with a title something like *Birth, Life, and Death: Agricultural Communities in Bulgaria, 1757–1767*. That book became the board's touchstone for determining how well framework and evidence were aligned; it could similarly be the touchstone for many comparativists' papers. That is, scholars often introduced an intriguing and provocative case or small set of cases only after describing a large theory (about, say, the causes of civil war, the corruption of democratic governance, the rise in income inequality). Their goal was presumably to show that the particular case was the grain of sand illuminating a substantial and important part of the political universe; sometimes that claim was justified but too often the big framework merely made the case seem puny. Our advice to comparativists, therefore, was often to first orient readers to the most intriguing elements of the particular case(s), to temper the theoretical claims and exposition at least in the introduction, and finally to promise to show concretely how the theory and the case are linked. The theory might illuminate the case(s); the case(s) might require a modification or development of some aspect of the theory; the introduction might even insist that the case is intrinsically important on its own terms. Only after the reader is really persuaded that framework and evidence will be persuasively linked should the author move into the body of the article.

Papers in American politics submitted to *Perspectives* typically promised in their introductions to "fill a gap in the literature." Perhaps because this subfield is blessed with many data sets or formal analyses that can be mined over and over for worthy insights, it becomes easy to believe that identifying an undeveloped idea or mode of analysis is sufficient to motivate readers. In my view, however, it is not; I have told students in my graduate seminars that they will fail the course if their final papers are predicated on filling a gap in the literature (no one has yet called my bluff on that assertion). Many literatures have many gaps— perhaps for good reason. So our advice to scholars of American politics was to explain in introductions what led you to this topic and this angle of vision. What can *you*—not "the literature" or its holes—teach or show readers? Only after the authorial voice is firmly established should you explicate others' arguments on the subject (preferably by focusing on ideas, not names and dates—see the paragraphs above about political theory manuscripts).

These quick characterizations are, of course, unfair to the many fine authors who write compelling introductions followed by convincing arguments and evidence. But perhaps they are helpful as negative ideal types—common ways of starting a document that, in my opinion at least, ought to be eschewed.

Let me add a few comments about writing introductions to an issue of a journal or edited volume. That is an unusual task which few are ever in a position to take on, but some of my suggestions might be useful for introductions to other types of collected works. The crucial act is to find (or invent) a theme that runs through all (or at least most) of the pieces. Sometimes that is easy, and occasionally impossible—but I discovered in editing *Perspectives on Politics* that it is usually not as hard a task as I had initially imagined. When it works well, finding or inventing a common theme leads readers (as well as the editor and even the authors) to look at each article or chapter in a new light, thus broadening the potential audience and showing that authors are more multi-faceted than even they thought they were. The danger in this exercise is that the editor will distort the central meaning of a piece in the effort to tie disparate works together; there is a fine line between revealing a hidden meaning or message, and imposing one's own point of view on a document written with something else in mind.

A final suggestion: I am constantly on the watch for a clever or illuminating quotation from my favorite authors to serve as an epigraph, final sentence, or jolt of pleasure in the middle of an introduction. Here too there are dangers; I hope never again to read that W. E. B. Du Bois predicted that the problem of the twentieth century would be the problem of the color line or that John Kennedy asked Americans to think not of what their country could do for them. . . . Nevertheless, a few people simply have extraordinary talent as writers or happened onto the perfect combination of words and ideas in a brief compass, and we may as well take advantage of their brilliance or luck. In addition, one can sometimes make a sharp or pointed observation by using a phrase from Shakespeare, the Bible, the Koran, or Jane Austen that would sound too blunt coming directly from the editor of a volume or journal issue.

An introduction should end with an idea, fact, or question that leaves the reader wanting to find out more. Like everything else in this essay, that is much easier said than done. In the spirit of that observation therefore, I close with one of my own favorite quotations. It too is perilously close to being a cliché, but it still comforts me when I despair of my own writing. Red Smith, the elegant sports writer, once explained that "there's nothing to writing. All you do is sit down at a typewriter and open a vein." We no longer use typewriters, but the process has not changed.

NOTES

1.   The final paragraph may be even more important because it is your last chance to imprint on readers the central point that you want them to remember after they have forgotten your name or the document's title. After all, as Daniel Kahneman and colleagues demonstrated in a classic and gruesome experiment involving interviews with people having colonoscopies, the peak and end moments of an extended experience are what people remember and use in evaluating it. D. A. Redelmeier, J. Katz, and D. Kahneman, "Memories of Colonoscopy: A Randomized Trial" *Pain* 104(2003): 187–94.

2. I edited *Perspectives on Politics* from 2003 through 2005, for its first three volumes.

3. An earlier version of the next few paragraphs was published in *Qualitative Methods*, the newsletter of the Organized Section on Qualitative Methods of the American Political Science Association, in fall of 2005 (volume 3, issue 2): 11–3.

4. A colleague once observed that the standard IR article consists of pushing a huge rock of theory up a steep hill, in order to roll it down to smash a few pebbles of fact at the bottom. Articles in the other main segment of international relations—international political economy—often had a similar structure, but in this brief essay I am ignoring them.

5. Unlike most academic journals, I and the five associate editors worked closely with a subset of people who submitted manuscripts in order to develop those manuscripts into a format appropriate for *Perspectives*. Our model was more that of an activist editor at a top-notch university or commercial press than that of a conventional journal. All articles in *Perspectives*, however, went through the standard double-blind peer review.

6. Here I am mostly ignoring interpretivist and post-modern political philosophy. Introductions to papers in this genre tended to be very abstract and to present complex ideas in complicated sentences. Our main advice to writers in this arena was to write the whole paper, and especially the introduction, with less idiosyncrasy and more conventional clarity.

Jeffrey W. Knopf, Naval Postgraduate School
Iain McMenamin, Dublin City University

6

How to Write a Literature Review

"If I have seen further [than certain other people] it is by standing upon the shoulders of giants..."

Isaac Newton

A literature review summarizes and evaluates a body of writings about a specific topic. While there are excellent courses on qualitative and quantitative methods, for their literature reviews, most students have had no option other than learning by doing. In a world where the Internet has broadened the range of potentially relevant sources, however, doing a literature review can pose challenges even to an experienced researcher. This essay seeks to describe the general functions of a literature review in political science and to offer some practical pointers to make learning by doing easier and more productive.

In general, a literature review has two key elements. First, it concisely summarizes the findings or claims that have emerged from prior research efforts on a subject. Second, it reaches a conclusion about how accurate and complete that knowledge is; a literature review presents considered judgments about what's right, what's wrong, what's inconclusive, and what's missing in the existing literature. The literature review is both a process and a text. The final version should not be a text that reports the process of selecting, reading, and thinking about relevant sources; rather, this process makes it possible to produce a text that reaches conclusions about the literature. In contrast to some other ways of surveying a body of literature, such as an annotated bibliography, the literature review is a work of synthesis, meaning it should focus on the body of work as a whole.

CONCEPTUAL MATTERS: THE FUNCTIONS OF A LITERATURE REVIEW

Three Contexts for Literature Reviews

Literature reviews are produced in one of three contexts: as a stand-alone product; as the preliminary stage in a larger research project; or as a component of a finished research report, such as a dissertation, article, or book. In the latter two contexts, it is important to remember that the literature review is a means that should serve the larger research project's ends. In any of these contexts, a literature review can address either theoretical or practical questions. In academic settings, review essays most often focus on the theories scholars have proposed to explain some phenomenon, but a literature review can also be used to determine and assess the current practical know-how or "lessons learned" in regard to which measures are likely to be effective or not in dealing with a certain problem.

To return to the first context, reviewing existing knowledge can itself be the primary goal if one simply wants to ascertain the current "state of the art" on a particular subject or problem. In this context (as well as the other two), it is important not to simply summarize the available research, but also to evaluate it critically. Such critical analysis should not be exclusively negative; it is also important to identify positive results to take away from the existing work.

Second, a review of existing knowledge can be a preliminary step in a larger research project. Such a literature review is often required for a thesis or dissertation proposal; it is also frequently an element in proposals for research grants. The most basic reason to undertake a literature review in this context is to make sure the proposed research question has not already been answered. Assuming no prior study has solved the problem of interest, then the purpose of a proposal's literature review is to situate the proposed project in relation to existing knowledge. This is important because those who review a proposal ask "what is the expected contribution to knowledge?" or "what will be the value added of completing this research?" The goal here is to show that people who read the final research product are likely to learn some new or different information or argument compared to that found in existing studies. In short, a literature review in a research proposal provides an overview of existing scholarship in order to explain how the proposed research will add to or alter the existing body of knowledge.

Third, a literature review can be a component of a finished research report. Its purpose is to show how the final conclusions relate to the prior wisdom about the subject. In this context, the literature review should again function as a means to an end. Its merit can only be judged by the contribution it makes to the article, book, or dissertation of which it is a part. Many students writing a thesis or dissertation commit the cardinal mistake of treating the literature review as an end in itself. They fall into the trap of producing a literature review that merely summarizes a body, or bodies, of literature. In contrast, a good literature review is an argument about the literature that justifies the selection of the question the student wants to answer and the basic approach to answering that question. This is the difference between identifying the giants and hoisting yourself up on their shoulders.

Ways to Frame the Contribution to Knowledge

The literature review in a research proposal is used to frame the proposed research's expected contribution to knowledge. Knowledge, in this context, does not mean "Truth" with a capital T. Rather, knowledge refers to beliefs; in particular, beliefs that some individuals have a degree of confidence in due to study or experience. In the social sciences and policy research, most hypotheses cannot be proven conclusively. When reviewing literature, therefore, it is common to refer to the "claims" or "arguments" advanced by a study or school of thought. Hence, a typical review identifies the claims made in a literature and assesses the strength of the support offered for those claims.

It is helpful to think of knowledge as having two elements: what we believe and how strongly we believe it. Further research can affect either or both of those elements, either positively or negatively, and any of these results would be a contribution to knowledge. This is similar to the logic of Bayesian analysis in statistics. In Bayesian statistics, if one believes a statement has a certain probability of being true and then obtains additional pertinent data, one can revise the estimated probability that the statement is true using a mathematical formula provided by Bayes' theorem. Even where such precise quantification is not feasible, one can attempt an analogous qualitative assessment.[1]

This provides a framework for thinking about the possible consequences of new research. Further research could create a new belief in an area where people have no prior knowledge, it could alter an existing belief, or it could change how much certainty people feel about a current belief. Most obviously, something brand new is a potential contribution to knowledge; this might be new factual information, a new theoretical proposition, or a new policy proposal. In addition, information or reasoned argument that changes our degree of confidence in an existing belief is also a contribution to knowledge. This might be new evidence or analysis that corroborates a particular belief or that challenges a particular point of view. If new information or analysis is powerful enough, it might convince people that their prior belief was wrong and lead them to embrace a different perspective. When using a literature review to indicate where proposed research might make a contribution to knowledge, therefore, it is helpful to think in terms of identifying the existing beliefs people have and the level of confidence with which they hold them. This facilitates the task of showing where additional research could make a difference.

PRACTICAL MATTERS: THE THREE-STAGE PROCESS

The process of reviewing the literature can be divided into selecting, reading, and writing. Before a researcher can write a literature review, that individual must first identify and select relevant sources and read them in a way that advances the goals of the review.

Selecting Sources: Begin Conventionally and Continue Imaginatively

The first problem in a literature review is deciding which literature to review. It is a good idea to select your reading both conventionally and imaginatively. For example, take a student who wants to study the Indonesian military. The conventional selection is to read books and articles on the Indonesian military, politics, and society. Once a student has done a certain amount of conventional reading, however, she should start trying to select readings more imaginatively.

Sticking with the example of the Indonesian military, an imaginative choice might be to read about the principal-agent theory in economics, which was originally developed to analyze the management of firms. A cursory reading of the literature on Indonesian politics and the military shows that there is an issue of political delegation to the military, which is essentially similar to that analyzed by principal-agent theory. One of the great challenges of Indonesia's transition to democracy has been civilian control of the military, and it is likely that the principal-agent approach could illuminate this problem and even suggest concrete institutional solutions.

A combination like this of hitherto separate literatures is a simple and effective strategy for successful research. After having read the conventional accounts of a particular issue, students should try to identify analogous problems in other subjects they have studied. Otherwise, they may end up assuming that the only literature relevant to the Indonesian military is the literature on the Indonesian military. By broadening the review to consider principal-agent analysis as well, the student's choice of literature means she can potentially write a great thesis without generating any new empirical data on the Indonesian military and without developing any theoretical innovations within the principal-agent approach.

Cast Your Net Widely

Just as it helps to be imaginative about other bodies of research that might be relevant to one's topic, it also helps to be imaginative about the types of sources one consults. The traditional literature review focuses on books published by academic presses and articles published in academic journals. However, on many questions, especially those involving a policy dimension, actors besides university-based academics might issue relevant reports. In addition, the development of the Internet has made it easier to disseminate research reports in formats other than academic publications. This growth in alternative research producers and outlets for disseminating research makes it advisable to consider a wider range of sources when conducting a review.

Other entities that might produce relevant research include government agencies, international governmental organizations, nongovernmental organizations, think tanks, and independent, freelance researchers. Some of their reports are still produced in print form and are available through any good library collection. Increasingly, though, many of their reports are released electronically and can be found through careful searching on the Internet. Traditional academics are also using the Internet as a vehicle for disseminating their work. Scholars are increasingly posting conference papers, working papers, and monographs on the Internet,[2] and these postings may be work that has not yet been published in a book or journal article.

At the same time, the Internet must be used with great caution. Most academic publications go through peer review, which in most cases helps ensure that the published work meets certain standards of scholarship. In contrast, anyone with access to the necessary equipment can post anything they want on the Internet. Many postings are based on little or no research, make no attempt to be unbiased, and contain factual claims that are questionable. Before including sources found on the Internet in a literature review, be sure to consider carefully whether the items are credible and meet at least minimal standards of scholarly research. Look to see whether the authors have provided their credentials and consider whether these make them credible sources on the subject. Also examine whether an item contains documentation of its sources and whether these appear to be credible. Despite the risks, valuable sources of research exist beyond traditional academic books and journals, and it is worth using the Internet to seek these out. Be sure not to limit your search for sources to just the Internet, however, as any college or university library will have many items on its shelves that are still not available electronically. To produce a good literature review in today's world will in most cases require doing research using both the Internet and the library.

The Problem of Too Few Sources and the Problem of Too Many Sources

Students sometimes choose a research topic, such as how to address a new policy problem or what can be learned about a recent event, because they think no one has yet studied the issue. In such cases, students expect that there will not be any literature relevant to the question they want to research. It does not pay to be too skeptical on this score; a search for sources often yields more than one expects. Even a search that comes up empty, however, is not a wasted effort. To be able to report that a serious search uncovered no examples of studies that have examined a proposed research question will help demonstrate that the proposed research will fulfill the "contribution to knowledge" criterion for evaluating proposals.

This still leaves the problem of what to discuss in a literature review. The problem of too few sources can usually be solved by thinking in terms of two tiers (or circles) of literature. The first tier (or inner circle) involves studies that directly address the proposed research question. The second tier (or outer circle) broadens the review to consider publications that are relevant to or overlap some part of the proposed research question, even though they do not directly address the same point. In the example of Indonesian civil-military relations discussed above, principal-agent theory would be literature in the second tier. If there is a reasonable body of work in the first tier, in many cases this will be all that a literature review discusses. As the Indonesian example demonstrates, though, even in this case there can be advantages to thinking creatively about literatures outside the inner circle that might supply a specific theory, policy proposal, or research method that could be applied to a proposed research question.

If there is nothing or very little that is directly on the topic a student wishes to research, then the literature review will need to consider some items in the second tier. It can be helpful here to think in terms of analogies to situations or problems that are similar to the one a researcher is proposing to study. For example, if a student were interested in identifying ways to protect crops from agro-terrorism and could find no studies directly on this topic, she could consider looking for research on efforts to protect crops against natural disease outbreaks. If this literature review revealed findings about ways to address the latter problem, the student could then propose research to consider whether these techniques could be adapted for her problem of interest.

Once a researcher begins to consider literature in this second tier or outer circle, she is likely to encounter the problem of too many sources. The number of potentially relevant publications, especially in well-developed areas of theory, could be vast. Hence, researchers need a way to restrict their focus. It is important not to simply select a few books or articles that one finds at random; instead, here are three rules of thumb for selecting sources:

1. Focus on the leading authorities. Certain authors or studies are likely to be cited quite frequently in the literature. These are probably considered key works, so it is a good idea to respond to what they have to say, even if it means ignoring some less influential studies.

2. Focus on recent studies from high-prestige or high-visibility sources. It usually makes sense to emphasize the most recent research. Among recent studies, look especially for those that have been published in a high-prestige outlet: examples include books from a highly ranked university press or articles in the leading journals in the field in question. Sources that garner a lot of attention are also important to evaluate: in some cases, for example, it might be relevant to assess a book on the bestseller list.

3. Focus on the studies that are most relevant and helpful for your question of interest. The more a study is directly on point for the proposed research, or the more a proposal relies on a study for inspiration about how to approach the research, the greater the role it should play in the literature review.

When there is an abundance of literature, it is not necessary for a review to be comprehensive. The literature review should focus mainly on those parts of the literature that relate to and help advance your specific interests; omit the rest.

Reading

In a literature review, you do not read a book for its own sake. If you are interested in how culture influences politics, you might well decide to review Huntington's *Clash of Civilizations*. You would do so not to find out what the great man has to say, but to see what his work can do for your literature review; you are not interested in the *Clash of Civilizations* for its own sake but only in so far as it contributes to the literature you are reviewing. It is important to remember that most works, especially books, contribute to more than one "literature" simultaneously. Thus, your motivation is instrumental and your attitude is ruthless. No matter how prestigious, interesting, or enjoyable a book, if it does not make a contribution to your specific review, put it down and find a book that will.

Inevitably, a lot of research is largely, or even entirely, based on secondary literature. In this situation, there is a grave danger of the literature review engulfing the whole research project. Avoid this outcome by focusing strongly on the different reasons for reading different sources. Readings that have been consulted for different reasons should obviously be treated differently. There are four standard reasons for reading secondary sources, two of which are relevant for a literature review.

The first reason to read a book is to look for interesting questions on which a research project might focus. For example, while reading Huntington (1996) you might notice the statement that the break-up of a state is more likely in a state where there are substantial communities belonging to different civilizations, as opposed to merely different cultures (137). Both the hypothesis and the evidence are stated very briefly and unsystematically, but seem plausible. A systematic investigation of this hypothesis might make an interesting piece of research.

The second reason to read a book is to look for potential answers to a question that you have already chosen. For example, a student trying to solve the puzzle of the rarity of democracy in Arab countries might look for answers in the literatures on Arab political culture, oil and politics, and U.S. foreign policy. A discussion of both questions and answers is found in the literature review. In both cases, the material should be treated instrumentally. For example, it is not what Huntington says about global politics that matters, but only his treatment of "cleft countries," the states through which civilizational borders run. A scholar trying to explain the rarity of democracy in Arab countries looks at U.S. foreign policy not to understand its sources or its variation across the world, but its effect on the political regimes of Arab countries. Although such reading is focused and instrumental, it also should be conducted with an open mind as to possible questions or answers.

The third reason to read the secondary literature is to find useful methods to replicate or adapt your research. A project examining the impact of regional organization membership on democracy in the post-Cold War era will need to decide which countries are democracies. In this respect, a student may want to apply and cite Przeworski et al.'s (2000, 23–8) method for deciding whether countries which have not had an alternation in government should be classed as democracies.

A fourth reason for consulting a secondary source is to look for data. Przeworski et al. (2000, 59–69) categorized almost all states in the world between 1950 and 1990 as democratic or authoritarian, and their dataset would be relevant to numerous dissertations. Neither of these references belongs in the literature review section. The methodological reference noted in the prior paragraph belongs in a methodology section, and the data reference noted in this paragraph belongs in either a methodology section or the empirical core of the dissertation.

A final caveat involves avoiding a tempting shortcut. For many subjects, literature reviews already exist in books and dissertations, as review essays in journals, and in online formats such as Wikipedia. While reading such sources to see how others have characterized a field of research can be helpful, it is essential not to rely on others' summaries of existing studies. There is simply no substitute for your own reading. Read for yourself the sources that are most critical for your own interests and draw your own conclusions.

Writing: *Getting Past a Simple List of Sources*

A literature review, even more than most phases of a political science research project, evolves through multiple drafts. Early versions may actually be a list of summaries of books, with occasional critical comments or queries, but the final version will be a focused argument. Some material may survive from first to final draft, but the material that has been changed or omitted will still inform the review and any larger project it is part of as a whole. Intellectual dead-ends and tangents should not end up in the literature review, but this does not mean that they represent a waste of time. A literature review is also a process of elimination, a distillation of a wide-ranging literature down to a specific argument about the state of knowledge in a well-defined field.

As a result, the review should be selective. It is often not necessary to discuss every item you read. The text should discuss only the studies that have a direct bearing on the central focus of your review or your proposed research. In addition, rather than summarizing the studies in their entirety, the review should focus only on the aspects of those studies that are relevant for your purposes. In other words, the content of the final literature review should be decided on a need-to-know (Dunleavy 2003, 61) not a look-at-what-I've-read basis. As Goethe remarked: "Some books seem to have been written not to impart any information to us, but merely to let us know that their author knew something." If you cloud your argument in an attempt to show how much work you have done, your review will make much less impact.

A literature review is not a succession of book reviews. It should not simply summarize, item by item, each publication you have read. A literature review should *not* have the following structure: paragraph 1 notes that book A says X; paragraph 2 notes that article B says Y; paragraph 3 notes that book C says Z; etc.

The literature review *is* an argument not a list. It must establish the intellectual geography of a research topic and locate the author's project within it. This entails the classification of the literature. To do this, it often helps to group individual studies into larger "camps" or "schools of thought." One can do this in terms of different theories they propose or defend, different methodological approaches they take, or different policies they favor. If you group similar studies together, rather than discuss three like-minded authors separately in three successive paragraphs, you can mention all three together in a single sentence such as "A, B, and C argue that policy X has been ineffective and propose policy Y instead."

This grouping will be easier if you get into the habit of associating individual authors and major camps or points of view with each other. In academic writing, scholars often use the last name of the author of a study as shorthand to refer to the theory or argument advanced by that author. For example, in International Relations, Kenneth Waltz was one of the leading developers of a theory known as "neo-realism." In writing about this approach, other authors will switch back and forth between referring to Waltz, to the Waltzian approach, and to neo-realism.

Another way to classify the intellectual landscape is to look for intersections in partially separate literatures. For example, take a student who has decided to write about the role of the European Union (EU) in the failure of democratization in Belarus. There are large literatures on both the EU and processes of democratization. These overlap to some extent. The EU's existence is argued to be a major democratizing influence on non-EU European countries, especially those that are closest to its borders. The EU also directly and intentionally affects democratization with its policies toward other countries. These actions are part of EU foreign policy and EU policy toward Belarus is part of that foreign policy. This procedure clearly locates the review at the intersection of certain literatures, while also establishing the relationships between the different literatures.

The treatment of individual works should not take the form of a straightforward summary of the work in question. Each work should be subjected to critical analysis, but not criticism for its own sake, nor even criticism for the sake of political science, but criticism focused on the review's research question alone. Critical analysis does not consist of merely, or even always, evaluating a book. In many cases, a piece of literature is not wrong but just not very useful for the project. If you have chosen your research topic well, your argument will not be that many works are wrong, but that they are irrelevant to your topic because you have framed the question or issue in a slightly different way than have previous authors. So, for example, an article on the role of semi-presidentialism in the *transition* to democracy in Poland would undoubtedly mention the work of Linz and Stepan (1996). Your literature review would probably not argue that Linz and Stepan's work was wrong but rather that it is inapplicable to your topic since their work focuses on semi-presidentialism's threats to democratic *consolidation* (276–83).

Scholars should always strive to engage with the most charitable interpretation of the literature. This is not a matter of fairness but of usefulness. If Huntington is dismissed as a befuddled Orientalist, as frequently happens, his ideas are unlikely to move a research project forward. However, if his ideas are presented as plausible given certain conditions, they may suggest a theoretically significant research project; such an approach might also identify tests that could help determine whether his critics' charges are valid. A really successful literature review can move from being a summary of existing work to becoming a fruitful dialogue with the literature.

Getting to an Overall Evaluation

A literature review summarizes and evaluates the overall state of knowledge or practice on a particular subject. To do this, it helps to describe the literature in terms of what the existing works have in common, disagree about, and overlook or ignore. It can be especially valuable in a research proposal to summarize existing studies in terms of these three categories:

1. Areas of consensus or near consensus. On some issues nearly all of the relevant experts may agree. Such conclusions can be either positive or negative; i.e., they can involve beliefs about what is true or what works or what is false or does not work. Areas of consensus represent the "conventional wisdom" about a subject.

2. Areas of disagreement or debate. In many cases, there exists information and analysis about a topic but no consensus about what

is correct. These areas of debate usually give rise to the alternative "camps" or "schools of thought" mentioned above.

3. Gaps. There may be aspects of a topic that have not been examined yet. These gaps in knowledge might involve questions no one has tried to answer, perspectives no one has considered, or bodies of information that no one has attempted to collect or to analyze.

Once you have identified where there is conventional wisdom, where there are debates, and where there are gaps, you can use the literature review to describe what will be the contribution to knowledge of the research you are proposing. Your contribution can address any or all of these. For example, you might believe there are reasons to doubt the conventional wisdom. In general, you should not accept areas of agreement uncritically. Probing for potential flaws in the reasoning or evidence related to an area of consensus is a way to justify proposed research that might challenge the conventional wisdom.

Weighing in on an existing debate is another possibility. Here, one uses the literature review to show the likely value of research that could help judge the relative merits of conflicting points of view or that could help point the way to a useful synthesis.

Finally, proposing to fill a gap in existing knowledge is an obvious way to frame the usefulness of a suggested piece of research. The relevant gaps can be broad or narrow. In some cases, a topic might essentially be virgin territory: no one has studied any aspect of it. More often, however, the gap will be narrower. People will have studied some, but not all, aspects of a problem, or they will have examined a problem using some theories or methodologies, but neglected others. In this situation, if your goal is to fill the gap you identify, your research proposal would state something like "researchers have studied a, b, and c, which are related to the problem of X, but they have not studied d, which is also relevant to understanding and/or solving X."

When identifying areas of debate, it is important to try to ascertain the reasons for disagreement. Scholars might disagree because they start with different assumptions, because they apply different theories or follow different lines of logical argument, because they rely on different empirical evidence, or because they use different methodologies. By identifying and comparing the assumptions, theories, data, and methods of the studies you review, you can pinpoint the underlying disagreements responsible for debates in the literature. You can then target your own research on one of the underlying disagreements, which could help resolve an existing debate. By evaluating each of these elements critically, you can also show where there are problems or flaws in existing studies and then target your own research on fixing one or more of these problems in the literature. Finally, as noted previously, you can also look for important issues that the existing research has overlooked and frame your research as an effort to fill this gap.

CONCLUSIONS

A literature review should concisely summarize from a set of relevant sources the collective conclusions most pertinent to the questions a researcher is interested in answering. It should also evaluate the state of knowledge in terms of what's right, what's wrong, what's an area of uncertainty or debate that cannot be resolved using the existing research, and what's missing because no one has yet considered it carefully.

The work of academic giants is not generally composed of lengthy literature reviews, but it usually displays a mastery of the literature. A mastery of the literature is not a mere ability to hold lengthy and detailed discussions on different writings, but rather an ability to put the literature to work to ask new questions and propose new answers. The golden rule of the literature review, as with all sections of a research report, is that it must be rigorously focused on fulfilling its role in the type of research of which it is a part. In a dissertation or book, the literature review's role is to elucidate and justify the choice of question and possible answers that were considered. Reviewing the literature is not a process that should be reported as it occurred in the final text, but is rather a process that informs a focused setting of the scene for the argument developed in the text.

Whether one is producing a stand-alone review essay, a literature review for a research proposal, or a literature review section in a finished report, when one proceeds systematically and aims to reach a considered judgment about the state of knowledge on a given subject, the resulting literature review can itself make a useful contribution to knowledge. An awareness of the general functions of the literature review and the practical issues in writing one makes it more likely that a scholar might enjoy the view from the giants' shoulders.

References

Dunleavy, Patrick. 2003. *Authoring a PhD: How to Plan, Draft, Write and Finish a Doctoral Thesis or Dissertation*. Basingstoke: Palgrave Macmillan.

Huntington, Samuel P. 1996. *The Clash of Civilizations and the Remaking of the World Order*. London: Touchstone.

Linz, Juan J., and Alfred Stepan. 1996. *Problems of Democratic Transition and Consolidation: Southern Europe, South America and Post-Communist Europe*. London: Johns Hopkins University Press.

McKeown, Timothy J. 1999. "Case Studies and the Statistical Worldview." *International Organization* 53: 161–90.

Przeworski, Adam, Michael E Alvarez, José Antonio Cheibub, and Fernando Limongi. 2000. *Democracy and Development. Political Institutions and Well-Being in the World, 1950–1990*. Cambridge: Cambridge University Press.

Wonnacott, Ronald J., and Thomas H. Wonnacott. 1985. *Introductory Statistics*, 4th ed. New York: John Wiley & Sons.

Notes

1. For an introduction to Bayesian statistics, see Wonnacott and Wonnacott (1985, 75–9 and 515–75). For a discussion of the relevance of Bayesian reasoning in qualitative research, see McKeown (1999, 179–83).

2. For example, many political science materials of this sort are available through Political Research Online (PROL); this includes papers presented at Annual Meetings of the American Political Science Association (APSA). See www.politicalscience.org.

KAREN O'CONNOR, AMERICAN UNIVERSITY

TEXTBOOK WRITING 101

Textbook writing comes in multiple forms, though there are two main forms of textbooks: "small" texts geared toward a subfield class adoption such as Congress, the presidency, or interest groups, and "big books" such as those designed for American politics classes. In this essay, I devote most of my attention to writing "big books." Both kinds of textbooks can be generated by inquiries from publishers, which can come from a variety of sources—from the sales reps who pop into your office at the worst times possible, to the acquisition editors. They also can be the result of self-generated proposals.

Most of the small books are published by an increasingly shrinking number of smaller commercial presses, such as Westview, Routledge, or Rowman & Littlefield. University presses, too, are often on the lookout for "scholarly" books that can also be used as core texts in upper-division courses; these can generate sufficient sales to help underwrite the publication of smaller run, purely scholarly volumes. Many of the larger presses, such as Pearson—which has subsumed Little, Brown, Macmillan, Allyn & Bacon, Prentice Hall, and Longman, as well as Houghton Mifflin, or Wadsworth—are quite different from smaller presses in that they invest huge amounts of money to launch new textbooks, especially American politics texts, which have the largest potential for the publishing house to earn money. And, because so much money is involved, it is rare that successful books are launched by major presses with newcomer authors. Almost all successful books are written by established scholars who are able to turn their scholarship into writing for mass audiences. Thus, unless you are an established scholar, it is far more likely that you will be approached by a representative of a publishing house than it is that you will be able to obtain a contract on your own, especially to write a new text from scratch. It has become common lately for publishing houses to add one or more new writers to established successful textbooks, as initial authors have retired, died, or simply are no longer as interested in investing the significant amounts of time necessary to update and revise existing textbooks on a regular basis.

While a well-written proposal to write a textbook for a smaller audience may generate an offer of a contract, as noted above, big book offers generally are publisher-driven; publishers see a void in the market and seek authors or teams of authors to write a book with a particular perspective, or an author or team who have name recognition within the profession. Thus, while one must generally have created a significant body of scholarly research through refereed journal articles and books, the irony is that once you have written for scholarly audiences, you must be able to change your writing style if you are to write a successful text, as described in greater detail below. Good writing alone, however, is frustratingly not enough to produce a successful text. Sure, a badly written book doesn't key you off to a good start, but publishers, editors, development editors, copywriters, photo researchers, designers, art directors, marketing managers, and sales force size offer key components of textbook success, and those factors are often out of the control of the author(s), as discussed in Section II below.

Below I set out some of what I have come to believe are critical factors in writing a successful textbook. As the co-author of one of the leading American politics texts now in preparation for its 10th edition (O'Connor and Sabato 2008a; 2008b; 2008c; 2008d) as well as a women and politics text in its 4th edition in preparation for its 5th edition (McGlen et al. 2004), I offer the following questions and observations that may help those thinking about undertaking one of these major projects.

DO YOU REALLY WANT TO WRITE A TEXTBOOK?

First, I believe that you need to decide if you really want to write a textbook, especially a big one. Is it the right time in your career? How does your institution view writing textbooks, especially for junior scholars? At one time I was at an institution that considered textbook writing under teaching and the time spent working on a text as time taken away from writing scholarly works. This really often depends on your university, rank, and departmental culture.

Writing a textbook requires you to know why you are writing a textbook. Do you offer a perspective that currently is not addressed by the 70-plus American politics books already in print, for example? Will your textbook have a unique point of view, such as that offered by Greenberg and Page's (2007) struggles inherent in American democracy? Or akin to that presented by Janda, Goldman, and Berry's (2007) concepts of freedom versus equality? Our text presents students with more history than any other book on the market; a design reinforced by a strong emphasis on how history has influenced current political debates. As a frustrated historian, I thought this approach made sense and allowed me to shape a book that paralleled the way I teach all of my courses, which are heavy on timelines, a feature that was incorporated into our textbook.

Whether you have a point of view or theme or not, it is important that you stay true to your vision. While it might be difficult for you to change your writing style to appeal to 11th graders (the level at which most college textbooks are written), it is important that you go to bat for features or information that you believe critical. For example, several editions ago, I included a short paragraph on senatorial holds. At that time, according to our development editor (DE), no textbooks mentioned holds. Since one of my colleagues at Emory (and later at American), Bob Pastor, had had his nomination to be the U.S. ambassador to Panama blocked by a hold from Senator Jessie Helms (R-NC), I thought that this inclusion was important. It is the DE's task to survey other textbooks to make sure that yours is somewhat in the "mainstream" of what is being published. This, however, often produces cookie-cutter books that are way too similar. Today, I avoid looking at other textbooks because I have often seen photos that I have laboriously searched for to include in our book become standard fare in our competitors'. And, I have also found myself in friendly discussions about why I disagree that certain proposed features are silly, too low-level, too hard to keep current, or just too difficult to write within certain timeframes, especially those that must be written right after national elections.

Second, you must understand that writing a textbook is a full-time job. It does (at least in my case) take away from time spent on more scholarly works as well as family life. Elections always come around in November and last-minute rewrites and revisions, especially after major elections, often dramatically intrude on family life as well as grading at the end of the semester. But, on the plus side, textbook writing often makes preparing for classes easier.

Third, depending on the number of co-authors (if any) you have, textbook writing requires a willingness to write and research outside of your comfort zone. No matter how well you were trained in graduate school and how extensive your research agenda is now, it is impossible to keep current with every development in American politics. Thus, you may want to consider one or more co-authors. With but few notable exceptions (Dye 2007; Patterson 2005; O'Connor and Sabato 2008a; 2008b; 2008c; 2008d; 2008e; O'Connor, Sabato, Haig, and Keife 2008; Wilson and Diiulio 2006; Greenberg and Page 2007), the most successful texts are written by teams of three or more co-authors (the original 1952 team of Burns, Peltason, and Burns, then Burns, Peltason, and Cronin, then Burns, Peltason, Cronin, and Magleby, and most recently, Magleby, O'Brien, Light, Peltason, and Cronin 2008; Fiorina, Peterson, Johnson, and Mayer 2006; Lowi, Ginsberg, and Shepsle 2006; Ginsberg, Lowi, and Weir 2007; Edwards, Wattenburg, and Lineberry 2007; Janda, Goldman, and Berry 2007; Bardes, Shelly, and Schmidt 2007; and Welch, Gruhl, Comer, and Rigdon 2007). Just as in the case of Burns, Peltason, and Burns (1952), several books have added authors over the years. (While this list is not meant to be inclusive, it is interesting to note the paucity of women on it.)

Fourth, in deciding whether to write a textbook, it is important to keep in mind that—at the very minimum—it is at least a full-time investment of two years. If an overly anxious editor, publisher, or development editor attempts to tell you that a good book can be produced in less than two years, run, don't walk, away from that company. You do not want to invest a significant proportion of your time writing a book that will die in its first edition. A quickly produced book is likely to look cobbled together and be rife with mistakes. Textbooks that do become successful offer their own additional time challenges. Largely because of the used book market, most major textbooks are now on a two-, rather than a four-year cycle. This means that once your book comes out, you almost immediately must begin the process of revising, writing new features, and updating. Moreover, it is not uncommon to have to produce a special "election update" version in which you must revise items in an existing text to fit the outcomes of a recent election. These editions generally must be updated within a week of the election to make sure that books are out of the warehouse by January 1 for spring adoptions. Such editions generally require a week or two of 14- to 16-hour days to enter the new information. Major sea changes in the electoral sphere— such as the Republican landslide congressional victories in 1994 or the Democratic congressional take back in 2006—require special fine tuning because even if your co-author has a crystal ball, you cannot foresee all of the vagaries of the American body politic and their ephemeral moods.

Fifth, writing an American government textbook requires the ability to make complex ideas simple, and a genuine love of all things American politics. It is not surprising, then, that many successful textbooks are written by individuals who are also very interested in politics as well as political science. I subscribe to three daily newspapers and rip out and place into a chapter file at least one article a day; these give me examples, provide items to base vignettes or boxed features, and overall facilitate the updating of my chapters (as well as my co-author's). In many ways, writing a textbook completely changes the way that you view the news. Everything that I read in a newsmagazine or newspaper is potentially a good "update" for one of my chapters. And, stylistically, journalistic accounts often are closer to the way you need to write for a textbook. Examples, especially current ones that might grab a student's interest, generally come from these sources. My files of news stories are a key source of tables, figures, and graphs that are more current than the data that are often available to scholars. Compiling these articles and data as they are reported provide inspiration for new material and save an enormous amount of research time when it comes to writing or updating.

Writing a textbook requires the ability to look for items that will interest students. All publishers get comments from commissioned reviewers that students don't read their assigned textbooks. Thus, there is increased pressure on authors to write in simpler, more readable, and more interesting ways to attract student interest. Textbooks that simply contain facts and a lot of boxes (which students often do not read) don't sell well. Thus, there is a strong correlation between high teaching evaluations and the ability to write a good textbook. You need only look over the list of the authors of the most successful textbooks. Most of them still teaching have won major teaching awards from their respective institutions. These professors—in all likelihood—already had good current examples in their lectures; those examples and ways of explaining complex concepts allow them to write to student interest while maintaining high standards of inclusiveness and the attention to important theoretical concepts that must be included in a textbook.

Sixth, I cannot sufficiently underscore how important it is to be able to stick to deadlines and budget your time. All of us have written dissertations and many of us scholarly books. But, nothing really prepares you for writing a "big book." You must allot a set amount of time for writing, revising, or updating each chapter; the set amount varies depending on whether this is a solo effort. When Larry and I first signed our contract with what was then Macmillan, which became Allyn and Bacon, which became Longman, which became Pearson (I am not making this up), I got a big desk calendar and put the number "3" in the corner of each day. This was to remind me that I had to finish at least three pages each day before I went to bed. This, in turn, allowed me to turn out about one draft chapter a month. I never once went to bed without finishing three pages, no matter how good or bad they were. It was that constant "I must finish three pages . . . or more"—the more being that if I was going to be unable to write on one or more days in a particular month, the three pages for those days had to be written before the day or days that I was going to miss that month. Why the three pages? This is part of finding your work style. Yes, I can turn out 15 to 20 pages in a day if necessary. But I quickly found that it was a pace I could not keep and that my three-a-day plan worked best for me. I recognize that this is a plan that won't work for everyone . . . but you must very quickly find one that works for you!

Allotting a month to the initial draft of each chapter allowed me to budget my time and preserve my sanity. Writing the 11 chapters for which I am responsible for our text meant that I basically had a year to write and a year to rewrite those chapters. Textbook writing relies on conducting new research and surveying recent literature (convention papers are often very useful for this and are now online, which was not the case when I first began writing); these are very time consuming when coupled with the need to turn out three pages a day. In search of a way to juggle these time-consuming tasks, I found myself for the first time looking back to fourth grade where I was taught the importance of outlines. Deciding how to present so much information in each chapter, which for us usually runs about 100 or so type-written pages, requires a considerable amount of thought about how to arrange the material. In our case, with history as our guide, each chapter begins with an overview of the historical evolution of the office, institution, or topic, which at least gave us a starting point. But, to use our Congress chapter as an example, how and where you choose to cover issues such as running for office—here or in a campaigns and elections chapter; PACs—here or with interest groups; impeachment—here or with the presidency, are all issues that must be resolved. Some items must be covered in more than one place, but it takes a tremendous amount of coordination among authors, usually with the help of a good development editor and/or copyeditor riding herd over the entire process to check and double check for redundancies and, more important, inconsistencies.

Writing a textbook requires that you abandon your penchant for footnotes and referencing. Because I was trained as a lawyer as well as a political scientist, I am happiest when I am given free reign to footnote. I just love footnotes, and when I cannot footnote, I go crazy with in-text references. This is something that you cannot do when writing a textbook. Thus, while you should make every effort to include the latest political science scholarship relevant to whatever issue or concept you are tackling, it must be treated far differently in a textbook than in a piece of scholarship. This can be very frustrating. But you need to remember that though you may find debates over how Supreme Court justices decide cases fascinating, you must be able to synthesize myriad debates in the literature without getting into the kind of detail that you might in a judicial process textbook or, of course, in a book chapter or scholarly article. And, while, of course, you may use an endnote (which, as per publishers' style, is likely to be buried in 8-point font at the end of the book), you may highlight major books in the area by including them in a suggested readings section at the end of the chapter. Those suggested readings, however, to my knowledge, exclusively contain books and not journal articles. This underscores the dilemma faced by anyone writing a textbook: how do you present the basic facts necessary for students to understand how the American political system works in context with far more nuanced political science work that may, at times, have little or no bearing on how the political system actually works? To use the judicial process example again, while I believe that it is critical that students know that a debate exists about the proper role that judges should play in interpreting the Constitution, is it necessary that students know each Supreme Court justice's position on this issue (when most students can't even name all of the justices)?

Interest does, however, often find its way into your textbook—sometimes even with positive results. Because of my interest in the judicial field, for example, I have always included a fairly extensive section on selective incorporation including a detailed table of which amendments have been incorporated in one of my chapters. I was surprised to find, a few years ago, that we were the only text to do so. The Advanced Placement (AP) American Politics exam included an essay question on selective incorporation and the AP instructors conducted a lively online exchange about the unfairness of the question since the subject wasn't covered in the textbooks that they were using. Believe me; most textbooks now include that discussion.[1]

Seventh, when pondering whether to write a textbook, you also need to look inward to see how well you deal with criticism. You will get this from your co-author(s), editor, development editors, copyeditors, as well as adopters, students (your own as well as those eager beavers who contact you on their own), and paid outside reviewers. Our publisher provides us with about 20 to 25 outside reviewers of the whole book or chapters or sets of chapters for each edition. Many of their criticisms are right on the mark; others really can be out in left field. No, I will not add a feature on aliens (space not illegal); yes, it is a good suggestion that we pay more attention to the emerging role of Asian Americans in politics.

You need to be prepared to accept that your book, unlike an article, or book chapter, will never be perfect and that you can never please everyone. First, there are so many people involved that some errors are simply out of your control. No matter what you do, and how many times you review pages, there will be errors in your book, which will immediately be pointed out to you by several people. Some of these are very embarrassing. Photo captions are particularly tricky because, at times, space is left for a last-minute photo that you might not get to see before publication. While co-authors are useful in the blame game, ultimately you are responsible even if you didn't see the photo of Susan Collins (R-ME) that was captioned: "Hillary Clinton addressing the Senate." I try to block out such errors, but do admit that I read and reread *U.S.* v. *Korematsu* as 1944, not 1964 as it ultimately was printed in the text. My favorite from a competitor's book was seeing Associate Justice David Souter captioned with the incorrect first name. These things happen. You cannot beat yourself up about them, although I admit to a sick feeling in my stomach every time I spot one. And, at least for me, it is worse when your students catch it before you do.

Tables and figures can also be a source of considerable dismay. In general, both Larry and I submit charts, figures, or tables that we have found from other sources to our DE who turns them over to artists to render. (I love the *New York Times* figures highlighting division on the Supreme Court where the justices look like bobble heads.) These kinds of "pickups" from other sources present the least opportunity for error. Drawings done by others must be checked carefully for accuracy and readability. It is really embarrassing when your students say they can't understand a table or figure and you can't either. (We can also never adequately thank Harold Stanley and Dick Niemi for their phenomenal annual compilation of statistics and Shelley Goldman and Elliott Slotnick for always giving us access to their judges' statistics before they are in print.)

Eighth, to be able to write the sheer volume that is required for producing an American politics textbook, you need to determine what your best working hours are. I wrote the first edition of my text while a single parent. Thus, I had to juggle carpools, swim meets (actually not a bad place to write), pizza parties (Chuck E. Cheese also not a bad place to write if you can tune out the god-awful background music), and other situations while sticking to my deadlines. You also must factor in the intangibles; when I learned that my DE had two children under four, I told my unmarried and childless editor that we would have to calculate in an additional two months of lost time for strep throats, chicken pox, as well as for your own (un)foreseeable personal emergencies. The main point is that you have to keep writing. You also need to make sure that your co-author(s) are also writing and that your writing styles are complementary. While my students say that they can tell which chapters I write because "they sound like I do in class," for the most part, texts succeed when co-authors' specialties are complementary and writing styles similar. After nearly 20 years working together, Larry and I have yet to try to kill each other, which many of us cannot say about our spouses or significant others.

Ninth, to handle all of this work, you probably need to be willing to consider bringing on new co-authors when necessary. As noted earlier, the oldest book on the market, now Magleby et al. (2008), was first published in 1952 and has had a host of different authors over the years. Author fatigue, especially the pressure to produce new editions so quickly, has led to a plethora of books with several authors; even many that started out with only two authors have expanded quite a bit.

Tenth, to write a successful book, you must stay current without falling into the trap of writing a popular history book. It is always tempting to get swept away by current political developments. Thus, I believe most of us who write textbooks are torn about using recent events to illustrate critical points without overkill. Should the issue of gay marriage, for example, be used to illustrate federalism and Article IV issues, or civil liberties or civil rights issues, or election issues, or domestic policy issues, let alone interest group issues? While gay marriage could be covered in all of these chapters, you really don't want it in every chapter. Similarly, in the aftermath of the terrorist attacks of 9/11 or in the wake of Hurricane Katrina, how much space do you allot to a particular tragedy? And, just as important, it is key to remember the age of your audience. With the growing preference to offer American politics as a high school AP course, your audience may be 16 or 17 year olds. These students don't remember the Vietnam War, or Jimmy Carter, let alone George H. W. Bush, and you have to remember that.

Eleventh, familiarity with technology is becoming increasingly critical in textbook writing. The online components of a textbook are huge and growing. Simulations for every chapter, pretests, test banks, instructor's manuals, PowerPoint presentations, podcasts, and text messaging are now becoming required ancillaries. Since I have had an iPod for a year and have yet to download a song or figured out how to use the text message function on my phone, these new requirements can become real challenges—but they are now considered must-haves of any successful text. More often than not, your publisher is responsible for these features, yet their usability and accuracy is often critical to your book's success. After frustration with the test bank for my text, for example, I actually agreed to write the most recent one for our text. This was one of the dumbest things I ever agreed to do. Multiple-choice question writing is an art in and of itself and it took me about six months to write about 1,500 questions, greatly increasing the number (and hopefully quality) of the test bank. I had received complaints over the years about the quality of questions, and once I took a close look at ours, it was easy to see why. Most publishers contract out the writing of test banks for minimal amounts and it is easy to understand why many test banks are deficient. Moreover, as the author, you know which facts or figures you believe are of greatest importance for students to know. Thus, your perspective on which concepts deserve status as multiple-choice, true/false, identification, short-answer, or essay can be underscored if you write or are very involved with the production of the ancillary materials that accompany your book.

The above comments address textbook writing and what I believe are important factors for potential authors to consider. But, I don't believe that an essay on textbook writing would be complete without a discussion of the role of publishers. You can write the best textbook in the world, but if it isn't supported by your publisher it is unlikely to sell.

WHAT KIND OF SUPPORT SHOULD YOU LOOK FOR FROM YOUR PUBLISHER?

Highly successful textbooks can generate a significant amount of outside income for authors, yet you never know if yours will be one of the books that make it to the top five or ten. So, writing a text is a risk, but a publisher can make or break your success in a variety of ways. What kind of support you can expect is really the $64,000 question. When I first was approached by a publisher, it was to be a fourth author on one of the leading textbooks. It was at a time when publishers actually were looking for prospective female co-authors to respond to criticisms largely raised by the APSA's Commission on the Status of Women and the Women's Caucus for Political Science that material about women or women's issues basically were absent in current texts. I decided that I would rather write my own textbook than "womanize" someone else's. (At that time several publishers were asking women to add items about women throughout their all-male-authored textbooks for minimal sums and no co-authorship credit.) At that point, Larry and I had several offers from publishers. Some offers simply didn't make sense. One offer from a major publishing house actually wanted us to complete the entire book in a year—clearly an undoable task for two people. Moreover, while the advance was substantial, it wasn't as much as Macmillan was offering, and the first company's DE was very inexperienced. Thus, we went with Macmillan—a publishing house that at the time had no other books with which we had to compete and had an enthusiastic young editor who promised us an outstanding freelance DE who was well known within the publishing community. Without that editor and one of the best DE's in the business, our first edition would not have been as strong and could have resulted in a one-edition book—a disaster for any first-time textbook authors as well as the publishing house.

The number of competing books on a company's list is an important factor when you are thinking about writing a textbook. Are you to be one of one or of five or ten? This makes a big difference in how your first as well as subsequent editions are to be marketed. We were lucky to have three years before a second book was added to what by then had become Allyn and Bacon. Had we signed with a company with multiple texts, I simply don't know how our book would have been treated. Acquisitions editors may promise you the moon, but in my experience, you often cannot count on their promises. I have lived through six different editors and DEs and god only knows how many marketing managers. This is a source of constant frustration as each person "new" to the project has their own expectations and goals about your book. We actually had one editor who tried to sink our book by bringing out one edition only in paperback with the ugliest cover in the history of textbooks, but we were able to survive and reenergize our sales with a new publisher, editor, and DE, as well as a commitment to publish several different editions of our textbook, which is key to infiltrating all types of markets.

Building market share is often simply out the hands of the author(s) even if they have impressive professional reputations and the ability to write an interesting and well-written book. Top-notch publishers will push your book through a variety of means. Many of us, for example, received a t-shirt accompanying a new book on the market. Larry and I have had mugs, notebooks, and note cubes used as give-aways for our book. Publishers also expect their authors to make regular trips to large adopters—all of us spend a lot of time in Texas during adoption season—as well as lecture at schools with large adoptions. That is the fun part of the process. Putting your ideas about politics and political science to print not only makes you a better teacher, it provides you with the opportunity to interact with colleagues and students around the country and to stay abreast with politics in a manner unlike many of our colleagues, whether it is out of interest (in my case) or of necessity. So, while I have tried to provide pointers in this essay, they are just that. They don't apply to everyone and should not be intended to discourage anyone. I still love writing my textbook (on most days), and it has made me a better political scientist and teacher.

References

Bardes, Barbara, Mack C. Shelley, and Steffen W. Schmidt. 2007. *American Government and Politics Today*, 13th ed. New York: Wadsworth.

Dye, Thomas. 2007. *Politics in America*. New York: Prentice Hall/Pearson.

Edwards, III, George C., Martin P. Wattenburg, and Robert L. Lineberry. 2007. *Government in America: People, Politics, and Policy*, 13th ed. New York: Longman.

Fiorina, Morris P., Paul E. Peterson, Bertram Johnson, and William G. Mayer. 2006. *The New American Democracy*, 5th ed. New York: Longman.

Ginsberg, Benjamin, Theodore J. Lowi, and Margaret Weir. 2007. *We The People: An Introduction to American Politics*. 6th ed. New York: W. W. Norton & Company.

Greenburg, Edward S., and Benjamin Page. 2007. *The Struggle for Democracy*, 7th ed. New York: Pearson/Longman.

Janda, Kenneth, Jerry Goldman, and Jeffrey Berry. 2007. *Challenge of Democracy*, 9th ed. New York: Houghton Mifflin.

Lowi, Theodore J., Benjamin Ginsberg, and Kenneth Shepsle. 2006. *American Government: Freedom and Power*. New York: W. W. Norton.

Magleby, David B., David M. O'Brien, Paul C. Light, J. W. Peltason, and Thomas E. Cronin. 2008. *Government by the People*, 22nd Edition. Upper Saddle River, NJ: Pearson/Prentice Hall.

McGlen, Nancy, Karen O'Connor, Laura van Assendelft, and Wendy Gunther-Canda. 2004. *Women, Politics, and American Society*, 4th ed. New York: Longman.

O'Connor, Karen, and Larry J. Sabato. 2008a. *American Government: Continuity and Change*. New York: Pearson/Longman.

———. 2008b. *American Government: Continuity and Change. Election Update Edition*. New York: Pearson/Longman.

———. 2008c. *American Government: Continuity and Change. Alternate Edition.* New York: Pearson/Longman.

———. 2008d. *American Government: Continuity and Change. Essentials Edition.* New York: Pearson/Longman.

———. 2008e. *American Government: Continuity and Change. Essentials Edition.* New York: Pearson/Longman.

O'Connor, Karen, Larry J. Sabato, Stephan Haig, and Gary Keife. 2008. *American Government: Continuity and Change.* New York: Pearson/Longman.

Patterson, Thomas. 2005. *We The People*, 6th ed. New York: McGraw Hill.

Welch, Susan, John Gruhl, John Comer, and Susan M. Rigdon. 2007. *Understanding American Government*, 11th ed. New York: Wadsworth.

Wilson, James Q., and John Diiulio. 2006. *American Government: Institutions and Policies*, 8th ed. New York: Houghton Mifflin.

NOTE

I should note that there is an increasing pressure to write textbooks to appeal to large adoption committees, especially in regard to being eligible for placement on the list of texts approved for AP courses. This can sometimes put authors in a dilemma. While all of us are accustomed to discussing "values issues" such as same-sex marriage, abortion, prayer in school, etc. in our classes, some high school teachers do not have similar freedom. The issue of content as well as the impact on college majors are probably issues that should be addressed by the APSA.

Andrea Pedolsky, Doug Goldenberg-Hart, and
Marc Segers, CQ Press

8

There's More to Book Publishing in Political Science than Monographs: The Joy of Writing Reference Books

L et's begin with some definitions: What *is* a reference book?!

Most simply, a reference book is a "look it up" resource, used to find specific, factual information, on an as-needed basis. Classic reference works in political science come in a variety of formats. Most familiar are the encyclopedia, dictionary, almanac, atlas, bibliography, data compilation, thematic guide, and yearbook. Recent innovative formats include the document-based history and hybrid works that combine elements of the various formats. A reference work can take on a narrow topic and cover it in depth, for instance, an encyclopedia about the presidents of the United States, or it can choose a broad-based topic, like a guide to democracy around the world. Unlike textbooks or monographs, reference books are not usually read cover to cover—researchers dip in and out of them, as their needs require. While reference books are often considered "secondary sources," whose content are summaries of information found elsewhere, in actuality many reference books are based on original research—and break new ground in their scholarship. The best reference works bring together information in ways that stimulate new scholarship and interest in a subject. At the time of this writing, only a few colleges and universities recognize authorship of a reference book as part of the tenure process; we certainly hope that will change over time. In the meantime, once you've written that obligatory monograph, the world of reference publishing awaits.

FORMATS AND DELIVERY SYSTEMS

A relatively short time ago, reference was a print-only world. In today's digital world that is no longer the reality. Some reference pundits are positing that in the not-so-distant future, most if not all reference books will be available online only. How quickly—or whether—that happens is, of course, an unknown. And who drives the outcome is also uncertain: Will libraries take the lead and start demanding reference in an online environment so they can satisfy the needs of a multi-campus student body? Will publishers use the economics of the cost of paper and printing as the rationale to migrate away from print? Will authors insist that their reference ideas will exist best in an online environment? It will be interesting to see how this plays out. For now, though, most reference-book publishers are making decisions about print vs. online on a case-by-case basis. Usually their approach is to always have a print edition of any title being offered as an e-book or part of a digital reference collection. And while some libraries are opting for digital reference only, others want to see their bookshelves filled.

There is no typical size or length to a reference work, but suffice to say, a standard reference work could be considered stiff competition to anything James Joyce ever wrote! A reference book may comprise one volume or eight. It can be published in hardcover, paperback, or as an e-book. Most reference books are published in one color, but some—often atlases—require color. Illustration of some kind is found in most reference books, the type and quantity determined by the editorial needs of the volume—as well as the overall cost of acquiring or creating images.

A variety of reference formats have developed over time, each one used to present information in a way that best meets a researcher's particular need. Among the most ubiquitous are the encyclopedia, atlas, data compilation, dictionary, documentary history, and thematic guide. (See Table 1 for brief descriptions of each.) Each of these formats has been applied successfully to topics in political science.

TABLE 1: TYPES OF REFERENCE BOOKS

ATLAS	Every picture tells a story, and a collection of maps can tell a vivid story through the representation of data patterns and trends across geographical boundaries.
DATA COMPILATION/ ALMANAC	Data can also tell a story when historical and/or contemporary statistical information is presented in tables, charts, and graphs.
DICTIONARY	What could be simpler than an A to Z listing of words and their definitions?
DOCUMENTARY HISTORY	An engaging combination of primary-source documents and context-providing narrative.
ENCYCLOPEDIA	A collection of informational articles of varying length, covering a single-topic or range of topics. Usually organized alphabetically, but can be organized thematically or chronologically, and then alphabetically.
THEMATIC GUIDE	Rather than using the traditional, linear A to Z format of an encyclopedia, the thematic guide organizes around topics and ideas.

WHY WRITE A REFERENCE BOOK?

Below are five compelling reasons to write a reference work:

1. *More people use reference works than read monographs:* Think of a reference work as making your scholarship accessible to your peer group and beyond—potentially to an audience of thousands. And that's because a reference book is generally the first stop in anyone's research project, whether the result is a paper, a study, or a speech, because they are known to house authoritative, summary information, data, and documents. Reference book users span the universe of information seekers, from grade school students to college professors, from public servants to senior citizens or community activists. The right reference resource can reassure the user that one is on the right track (and point to other resources for further research), or it can help the novice by providing invaluable basic information for starting the research process.

2. *If you've already written a monograph, a lot of the work has already been done:* The research you've conducted for that must-publish monograph is the research that could very possibly provide the framework for a reference book. In addition, you most likely have myriad surplus material that could not fit in the confines of the monograph's page count, but which a reference book can easily accommodate. Unlike a filmmaker who suffers over what ends up on the cutting-room floor, you will be cheered that so much more of your "couldn't fit" research will make it into your reference book. Any reference librarian can testify to the value of a reference work that deftly dispatches the difficult-to-answer but inevitable-to-be-asked question. If one source performs this miracle often enough, it enters into a special revered status (and librarians are an exceptionally loyal bunch).

3. *Writing a reference book is a creative process:* While a monograph follows one particular format, reference books provide a variety of formats to best present your idea. More than that, by their very nature, reference books are a unique combination of text, data, and documents, historical and contemporary, which you bring together.

4. *Writing a reference book can be a collaborative process:* While some reference works are single-authored, many are contributed works, guided by an editor in chief (this could be you) and an editorial board (formed by you). In addition, most reference-book publishers are very involved in the development of the books they are going to publish, providing editorial guidance and support throughout the process. One reason for this greater level of involvement is because many reference books are conceived by the publisher who then seeks a content expert (you!) to take the idea and mold it into a must-have resource. Another reason is that reference books are used differently than monographs, and reference publishers often more closely develop the format of a book's content to fit the vision of how it will meet end user's information needs.

5. *Writing a reference book results in a work that has staying power:* Monographs come and go, but a successful reference book takes root

and is recommended as the seminal work in its subject category—for years to come. And that's because reference books help bring the relevant facts, concepts, and data to people who need them. The most successful reference titles live on in numerous new or revised editions.

CHOOSING YOUR TOPIC/CHOOSING A PUBLISHER TO WORK WITH

Like any other type of writing, the reference book starts with an idea and a perceived need or information gap. Sometimes that topic is the brainchild of the editor/writer—you, but just as often, a publisher will identify a need and network into the scholarly community in search of an editor. Many an author/publisher relationship develops after a chance— or scheduled—meeting at an APSA conference.

Either way, it's important to know what other titles have already been published on your topic, what formats were chosen, the expertise of the writer/editor, and the market for which it was written. That someone has already published on your topic is not an obstacle to moving forward, as long as you can determine how to distinguish your book from what's already out there.

In fact, one of the most important aspects of planning a new reference book is deciding on the format, which requires you to think about the needs of political science students—the ultimate consumers of the information you will be compiling. The grid below (Table 2) is a visual representation of the types of formats available, and some general political science categories that most college and university syllabi cover. Using the descriptions of each of these reference types from Table 1, you can start imagining how you might best cover a topic in one of these areas.

TABLE 2: MATCH YOUR TOPIC TO THE RIGHT FORMAT

TYPE OF BOOK	American Government	Congress	Presidency	Courts/ Judicial Process	Public Policy and Public Administration
Encyclopedia A to Z Thematic					
Data Book					
Documentary History					
Dictionary					
Yearbook/ Almanac					
Atlas					
Directory					
Biography					
Quotation Book					

Elections & Political Behavior	Political Parties, Interest Groups, and Social Movements	Political History	State and Local Government	World Politics & International Relations	Political Theory and Philosophy

Understanding the Reference Marketplace

While the customers for most reference books are institutions like libraries—primarily because of cost—reference-book users comprise any number of people, including: librarians, students, teachers and professors, scholars, practitioners, and researchers. And so, reference books are developed with particular markets and users in mind: *always envision the ultimate "consumer" of the information in your book, and write/compile to that person's level.* Some formats, like research handbooks, may be aimed at high-level users, while others, like A to Z encyclopedias, may be written to help novice readers get an introduction to concepts, theories, and notable figures.

Of course, while researching the market, you should become aware of which publishers you will want to contact about your reference book idea—start keeping a list. You will soon discover that while there are numerous reference-book publishers, the number whose publishing programs include political science titles is fairly finite. For each that you identify as publishing in political science, record the title, author(s), and a brief summary of each reference on their list that is similar to your idea, as well as their format, page count, trim size (e.g., 8-1/2 x 11, 6 x 9), and price.

Pulling the Pieces Together...to Write a Book Proposal

Topics. Formats. Market. All of the thinking you have expended around these topics is going to help you immensely when you are ready to write a book proposal (see Table 3 for guidelines to writing a book proposal). Think of the book proposal as part editorial plan, part marketing plan—it has sections that focus on the book's editorial content, and others that focus on the type of libraries/users you think will be the book's audience. Writing a book proposal takes time and effort, but it pays off in helping further clarify your rationale behind writing the book, both to yourself and to the editor and reviewers. Bottomline: Without a book proposal, you're unlikely to get a book contract—it's the document most publishers use to make a publishing decision.

TABLE 3: BOOK PROPOSAL GUIDELINES

1. OVERVIEW

Think of the overview as marketing or dust-jacket copy—this should really sell the project and give a sense of the scope of the work. Assume potential reviewers (your potential publisher) know very little about your subject and include a little background information on the topic/issue your work covers.

a. Briefly outline the goals of the work.

b. Describe yourself briefly, focusing on how your experience has preparedyou to write this book.

2. PURPOSE OF WORK AND ITS MAJOR CONTRIBUTIONS/INNOVATIONS

Explain why your proposed work is important, expanding on the goals mentioned in the overview. Describe how your work is unique and how it will make a contribution to the field. Is it providing new information or analysis? Filling a niche? Presenting information in an innovative format?

3. COMPETITION

List what you consider to be the 5–10 competing works. For each, include title, author, publisher, publication date, and a sentence or two describing their strength/weaknesses vis-à-vis your proposed new work. This information will help further explain why your work is unique and an important reference for scholars and libraries. (It may help to consult your reference librarian.)

Include a paragraph or two that explicitly explains why/how your book fills an information gap, or is a better alternative to a similar source.

4. AUDIENCE/MARKET

It is important for your work to be written and organized in a way that makes it accessible to the market for which you are writing—and for your potential publisher to know what you think that market is.

Identify the primary and secondary audiences for your work (undergraduates, high school students, interested citizens, professionals, etc.).

Include some ideas about how students could potentially use this volume. Are there courses that might directly tie into this volume?

5. ORGANIZATION

Explains to the publisher the format you've chosen, and why (e.g., alphabetical encyclopedia format? Thematic? Chronological?).

6. WORKING TABLE OF CONTENTS

Here you will list the organizing structure of your book. For instance, if it is an encyclopedia you will list all of the headwords to be included; if it is a thematic guide, you will list the chapter titles; etc.

7. MAPS/PHOTOS/TABLES

Let the publisher know if you plan on including maps, photos, and/or tables. If a major portion of the work (e.g., maps in an atlas), estimate how many will be required.

8. PERMISSIONS

If materials in your proposed work will require permissions, estimate the number and expected costs here.

9. TIME FRAME

What is your anticipated manuscript completion date? In general, and depending on the size of the work, i.e., a one-volume documentary history or a multi-volume encyclopedia, reference books can take from one to three years to produce.

10. AUTHOR BIO

Your potential publisher wants to know about you! Write a narrative biography that includes such information as academic background, work experience, other authored/edited journal articles and books, speaking engagements, conferences you attend, and any other information relevant to this work that will help position it and you in the marketplace. It's also a good idea to include copies of reviews of your published works. Attach a recent C.V.

11. SUGGESTED REVIEWERS

Most publishers send book proposals to scholars and librarians for feedback on the proposed work's scope, organization, and market. While many have a source of names to refer to, it's helpful to be able to offer the names and contact information for four to five scholars who you think would be able to give the publisher useful feedback. These scholars should be specialists working in your field. Reviews are most helpful when scholars have time to really think about them, so be sure to take availability into account when creating your list.

> ### 12. Sample Chapter or Entry
>
> No matter what type of book you are writing, your potential publisher is going to want to see a sample of your writing. Provide a writing sample from your proposed work consisting of 20–40 double-spaced pages. So, for instance, if you are proposing an encyclopedia, you would write entries for several of the head words; if you are proposing an atlas, you would prepare sample maps and write the narrative that would accompany them; if you are proposing a documentary history, select several representative documents and write accompanying contextual headnotes.

As noted above, few if any publishers will consider a book idea without a book proposal. However, you are unlikely to be left alone to flounder with the book-proposal writing process. If your idea has intrigued an acquisitions editor, he or she will want to make sure the proposal is the best it can be, since it's their job to acquire, develop, and publish the project in the best way possible.

THE BUSINESS SIDE OF PUBLISHING

Although every publisher works a bit differently, there are certain staple aspects to the publishing process, no matter who the publisher. Once you and your editor have decided that the book proposal is ready—and that will include sample writing and feedback from reviewers—your editor will bring the idea before a type of editorial board, usually consisting of the publisher, marketing director, national sales manager, head of finance, and editor-colleagues. The discussion will cover both the editorial and marketing aspects of the project, in addition to the financial projections for sales. Leading up to the meeting, your editor will have distributed information about the project based on the book proposal you submitted, as well as project expenses and sales (the financial component is called a "P & L"—profit and loss statement). If your proposal, the reviews, and your editor all make a strong case for the book, and the finances look good, the editorial board will approve the project and your editor will offer you a publishing contract.

There are many guides to negotiating a book contract, available in print and on the Internet (see, for example, the Author's Guild, which provides free contract advice to members, www.authorsguild.org), and we recommend that you research the language and terms of any agreement you are offered, as much contract language is laden in legal jargon. Most contracts are written from the vantage point of the publisher, and are created to set out author responsibilities, with a certain amount of space given to publisher responsibilities. In terms of author responsibilities, a book contract will likely cover such topics as: author's editorial responsibilities and due date for the manuscript, including the number of words in the manuscript; what is considered an acceptable manuscript and what happens if a publisher determines that the manuscript received is unacceptable—or if it comes in late; who is responsible for getting permissions for use of quoted material or entire documents; who holds copyright to the work; advance and royalty payments; revised editions; what happens when the book goes out of print, is no longer available, etc.

There are many legally-based clauses in a publishing contract that you should read, and read again, until you fully understand them. Here are just a few terms for you to "look up": warrants and indemnities, assignment of rights, copyright, rights of reversion, and subsidiary rights.

In addition to the publishing agreement's main body, there will likely be exhibits that further define the work involved. For instance, while you will have agreed to a due date in the agreement's main body, a schedule of deliverables will spell out a set of dates for "when" you will be sending in "what" to your editor. We've provided a sample Schedule of Deliverables (Table 5) from a multi-volume encyclopedia project where an editor in chief (the person under contract) is working with an editorial advisory board. It is not unusual for the span of due dates to cover at least two years.

TABLE 4: SAMPLE SCHEDULE OF DELIVERABLES

DELIVERABLE	DUE NO LATER THAN	PAYMENT ON ACCEPTANCE
Execution of agreements with Editorial Advisory Board		
Complete A to Z headword list, with scope descriptions, target length of entry, potential contributors, in a spreadsheet format		
Execution of agreements with 1/2 contributing writers		
Execution of agreement with all the contributing writers		
Draft manuscript for 1/3 of the work submitted		
Draft manuscript for 2/3 of the work submitted		
First final-draft manuscript of the work submitted for developmental edit		
Final, complete manuscript including introduction, for acceptance		
Written evidence of all necessary permissions		

DOING THE WORK

With signed contract in hand, you are ready to do the work! Of course, whether you are writing your book alone or working with an editorial board and team of contributing writers will influence how complex the writing process is. Managing a team of one or two writers for a one-volume book is very different from managing a writing team of 20—or 100—for a multi-volume book. You have the perfect guide, with your contract's schedule of "deliverables": It is your roadmap for producing a brilliant, authoritative reference work on time. We suggest you photocopy it and hang it near your desk, and send it to co-authors and editorial board members, to keep them on target as well.

Over the duration of manuscript preparation, you will be in and out of touch with your editor based on your needs and these due dates. However, although no one wants to think about being late—especially at the beginning of a relationship—if at *any* time during the process you hit a log jam and know that you will not be able to meet a date, let your editor know *immediately*. Don't postpone the inevitable—fess up! He or she will help you work through whatever is keeping the project from moving forward. Remember, your editor wants to see your book published, but if they don't know you're facing difficulties, they won't be able to help.

As the Schedule of Deliverables delineates, the hard work of compiling a reference work yields a manuscript, which is often delivered to the acquisitions editor in sections. This occurs so that while you continue writing/compiling, your editor can be reading and reviewing. Considered a draft manuscript, this first submission will be evaluated by your editor to determine whether further development is necessary (i.e., did you fulfill the goals of the book as described in your book proposal), and what that will entail. Depending on the publishing house, the actual development work will be done by your editor or by a development editor. What you will receive in return is a marked-up manuscript indicating where you need to do additional work and a time frame for you to complete that work.

Going into Production

Your manuscript will be deemed "accepted" once your editor reads and approves your final draft manuscript. And it is at this point that the manuscript is handed off to production to become a book. This doesn't end your involvement with your book—you will have tasks throughout the production process. What follows is a brief description of what you can expect while your book is in production.

The first stage of production sees your manuscript copy edited. What copy editing entails is determined by your publisher's standards. At its most basic, an editor will work with your text, styling it in accordance with the publisher's preferences, eliminating inconsistencies—such as in spelling, capitalization, treatment of numbers, hyphenation, and punctuation—and correcting grammatical errors and lapses in usage. More in-depth copy editing would include making edits to improve text flow and transitions. The editing is done using the "track changes" feature in word processing programs so you can see exactly what changes the editor made to your manuscript. A good working relationship with your copy editor is crucial; be flexible and open to critique, but also stay true to your strength—your content knowledge.

While the manuscript is being copy edited, a book designer will be creating the book's interior and a cover designer its exterior. With design and copy editing complete, the manuscript will be set in type, creating "page proofs"—facsimiles of your future book's pages. You will be sent and asked to review a copy of the page proofs for any possible errors that might have crept in during the editing process. This is your last chance to make changes. While you are reviewing the page proofs, your publisher has likely hired a professional to give the book a final, experienced proofread.

Once all corrections are made, an electronic file disk containing your entire typeset book is sent to a printer. It's not a long wait to see your brand new reference book: a normal printing schedule for a hardcover reference book calls for just six to eight weeks. Voila! A book is born. Now you can sit back and watch the royalty checks roll in.

Clive S. Thomas, University of Alaska, Juneau
Ronald J. Hrebenar, University of Utah

Editing Multi-Authored Books in Political Science: Reflections on Twenty Years of Experience

9

Introductory Note

E diting multi-authored volumes is much more than simply taking a set of conference papers, writing an introduction, putting a couple of rubber bands around the stack, and sending this off to a publisher. To explain this and provide would-be editors with many other suggestions, in 1993, we co-authored "Editing Multi-Authored Books in Political Science: Plotting Your Way Through an Academic Minefield," which appeared in *PS: Political Science and Politics*. Much of the advice in that article still rings true. In fact, as editing multi-authored books is even more popular today in political science as in other academic disciplines, the need to understand the challenges and pitfalls of editing such volumes—where the academic mines may be located—is even more important. So here we draw on the essence of that article but have changed the title because we have added several insights gained in our over 15 years of experience since then.[1]

The Multi-Authored Book: No Easy Route to Getting Published

A rough sample taken by wandering around the book exhibits at an APSA meeting reveals that around 20 to 25% of all books published in political science are compiled by an editor, though the percentage varies considerably among publishers. As mentioned above, editing a multi-authored book is an increasingly popular form of publishing within our discipline, and attempting this type of editing has probably crossed most of our minds at some time.

However, editing such books is, and likely always will be, akin to picking your way across an academic minefield: the project can blow up or disintegrate at any time if major precautions are not taken in directing contributors; and the disparate nature of many edited books makes publishers shy away from them. Many political scientists, the two of us included, tell woeful tales about chapters written for edited books that never got published because the editor did not know the ropes of getting published. Such failure on the part of an editor can trigger the wrath of contributors and reduce one's academic credibility; it can also lose you friends and even make you enemies. There are certainly no 100% guarantees of getting a book published and this is even more the case with multi-authored volumes. Following some of the ideas, procedures, and "golden rules" set out below, however, will certainly reduce your risk of failure considerably, even if it cannot totally guarantee publication.

If you are seriously thinking about editing a multi-authored book, you need to answer three questions before making a definite decision. First, what are the pros and cons of editing such a book? Second, is your temperament suited to the task and do you have the mind for detail and organization that editing a multi-authored volume entails? And third, and most important, what are the technical factors and procedures that will substantially increase the chances of completing and publishing your book, and what are the pitfalls that may doom your project to failure?

THE PROS AND CONS OF EDITING MULTI-AUTHORED BOOKS

In terms of enhancing your career, an edited book may not provide what you need. In most political science departments, editing a multi-authored book ranks just above writing an article for a popular magazine, newspaper, or non-refereed journal, and often ranks well below writing a textbook. Some departments don't even count editing a multi-authored book as publication credit. Even if your department looks upon editing multi-authored books favorably, we can't emphasize enough that editing a book is *not* a quick and easy way to get a publication. In our experience, editing and dealing with contributors is far more time-consuming than writing articles or authoring books. If you are an untenured faculty member, editing can sidetrack you from turning out the refereed journal articles, book chapters, and one or two single or co-authored books that will likely assure you tenure. From a career perspective, it is probably best to wait until you are tenured before you edit a multi-authored book.

There is, however, a positive side to multi-author editing. As is the case in preparing and teaching a class, you can learn a great deal about a subject from editing a book. With the vantage point of reviewing all the chapters and, if you are a diligent editor, by doing preliminary background work and checking references and material during the editing phase, you will become intimately familiar with the literature in the subject area of your book. This can be of great value in your own writing, not to mention in your teaching.

A well-planned and integrated edited book can make an important contribution to your subfield and perhaps to the discipline in general. Edited volumes enable a compilation of scholarship that could otherwise not be achieved by one or two individual authors without a large grant and an army of research assistants.

Three other advantages can accrue from editing a multi-authored book. One is that you may well make some good contacts (and maybe some friends too) for future collaboration, convention panels, and a host of other things. But, as we mentioned above and will do again below, also be prepared to lose some friends in the endeavor. A second advantage is that you can get a tremendous sense of satisfaction and achievement from originating, organizing, and shepherding a project to fruition through what, given the myriad problems of editing, is the academic equivalent of a war zone. Finally, if you have thoughts or ambitions of becoming a department chair or other administrator, your experience in organizing a book project and in dealing with contributors will give you an indication of your management and interpersonal skills (or lack thereof) and whether an administrator's life is for you. Such experience may also look good on your vita when applying for such positions.

ARE YOU SUITED TO BE AN EDITOR?

The task of editing a multi-authored volume involves much more than the academic element. In terms of time, it breaks down to about one quarter organization and management; another quarter interpersonal communications in dealing with contributors; which means that only about a half of your time involves the academic element.

In many ways the management and interpersonal aspects of the project are the most crucial, especially at the beginning. Poor skills on the part of the editor in these areas have doomed many a multi-authored volume, with resultant bad feelings on the part of contributors and publisher. The major factor in the success of any multi-authored book is good organization and planning, up-front and throughout the project. With anything from half a dozen to as many as 80 contributors, you need to have a good and up-to-date filing system (on your computer and hard copy), a mind for detail, and the fortitude not to be overwhelmed and exasperated by the tedium of administering to the minutiae of the project. Failure to pay attention to what might appear to be a minor detail can cause much pain and suffering later. It may add time to or even doom the project.

For many editors, dealing with certain contributors is the most difficult and unforeseen aspect of editing. Like the students in your classes, 85–90% of your contributors will be nice and cooperative people; but the remaining 10–15% constitutes the problem cases that will cause you difficulties, a few sleepless nights and often much grief. In extreme circumstances, they can destroy the project. All projects have their problem people. And obviously, the more contributors the more likely the problems, and, as E. E. Schattschneider said, the less certain the outcome.

If unfavorable or lukewarm book reviews bother you, then editing is also not for you. It is most likely that your book will not be reviewed at all; edited books have less appeal to book review editors than do authored and coauthored volumes.

Most of all, when you take on an edited book, you take on a major responsibility. Several people are putting their trust in you to do what you have said you'll do—come through with a published book.

Some contributors may be banking on this publication for tenure or promotion. To contribute, of course, was their decision—they could have declined your offer. Nevertheless, you have a professional and personal responsibility to deliver on your promise. There will be many times when you want to quit the whole thing: times when contributors don't deliver, when a contributor harangues you because the project is behind schedule, when a publisher rejects your project. But you must overcome the downsides and the disappointments and persevere.

If you "hate" rejections of submitted articles and book chapters to the point that you can't revisit and revise them, do not become a multi-authored book editor. The same goes for those who are loners who do not have interpersonal and management skills, thick skins, and minds for detail (or the desire to develop these), and those who don't want to take on the responsibility to the contributors that is part of the territory of editing a book. But if you have or want to acquire these qualities, and editing appeals to you, take account of the 10 points that follow before embarking upon a project.

TEN STEPS TO GETTING YOUR BOOK PUBLISHED

The 10 elements set out below are organizational and procedural steps an editor can take to increase the chances of getting a multi-authored volume published.

1. Understanding the Role of the Editor

We mentioned it above, but it is important to emphasize that editing involves much more than the academic element. An editor is the manager, the ramrod, the wet nurse, the salesperson, the person who hires and fires (and some firing may well be necessary, see below), as well as the chief academic on the project. There should be no doubt as to who is in charge of the project and as to who makes the final decisions. This may be difficult when one is a junior scholar dealing with senior, perhaps even big-name contributors, but you have to remain in charge. As soon as you lose control, your project will get away from you.

One problem we've encountered that can work to undermine your authority is the control-freak contributor. This is often a big name who wants to vet other chapters and tell you what and whom you need to include and exclude from your book. Keep them at arms' lengths if you can. If you can't, then get rid of them as soon as you can. If you don't, you'll regret it later if they decide to pull their chapter or keep harassing you to see other chapters. In most cases, however, being firm and deliberate with them and saying "no" usually deals with these control-freaks.

2. Planning and Organizing the Project

Just like in good teaching and in authoring a good article, chapter, or book, the key to successful book editing is planning and organizing. In fact, these two elements are even more crucial in an edited book because you are trying to integrate the work of many authors with different writing styles and perspectives and probably with varying views about how the book should turn out.

For this reason, you need to give great attention to the focus and themes of the book, and perhaps even run these by a colleague or two to get feedback. Before you approach contributors, you need: a fairly clear idea of the format and contents of the book; some detailed instructions for contributors (see point 5, below); a tentative production schedule for the book; and a good filing system for the project.

This is not to say that all of these things will be set in stone. But being and, most importantly, appearing organized will: (1) make your task easier as you deal with masses of paper, a multitude of computer files, and many, many inquiries from contributors down the road; (2) impress potential contributors who, based on past experience, might otherwise be reluctant to join an edited project (this is especially true if you are relatively unknown in the profession and want to get some big-name people who don't really need another publication); and (3) impress potential publishers. Generally, publishers are very leery of edited books, for the reasons we related above in describing the pitfalls in editing them. Being organized is one way to overcome publishers' aversion and at least get them to look at your prospectus.

3. Choosing the Right Contributors

This is a step that is more difficult than it initially appears and that is fraught with pitfalls. For an editor, the perfect contributor is one who:

(1) submits high-quality work in terms of content and style; (2) displays a willingness to fit their piece to the focus/themes of the book (in other words, a cooperative person); (3) is willing to make revisions and will not be offended by a first-draft critique; and (4) takes deadlines seriously. From an editor's perspective, points 2, 3, and 4 may prove more important than point 1—a quality contribution. This, unfortunately, is one of the political compromises of editing.

Let's face it: like in all aspects of life, there are honest, hard-working, diligent, reliable, and responsible people in political science that will fit the ideal contributor, there are people who are the opposite of the personal and professional qualities you need, and there are many people in-between. Political science has its share of entrepreneurs in both the positive and negative sense of that word. For the editor it may often be more important to have contributors with positive personal qualities than an outstanding professional reputation or expertise. Making this determination is not always easy, however, especially if you don't personally know some of the contributors you would like to have in your book. Not only that, sometimes even the people you thought you knew very well personally you really didn't know at all! Here are some pointers to prepare you for this and trying to secure the best contributors you can in an imperfect world.

An old but very true cliché states that you don't know people until you've worked with them. And the chances are that the problem contributor will turn out to be someone you least expected to cause you grief. You may have known colleagues for years, been good friends, shared rooms at conventions, gone to their weddings, helped them through their divorces. But working with them, and particularly critiquing their writing, telling them that they have to make major changes, or finding that they don't deliver by the deadline, may reveal a side of them you've never seen before. It can even ruin your relationship. The moral: don't go into editing if you don't want conflict, don't have a thick skin, and don't like making hard decisions.

On the other hand, an editor needs patience and understanding. People do have problems in their lives that genuinely impede their progress on your project, and you have to accommodate them within reason. Like dealing with students, however, the difficultly comes in distinguishing between the genuine problem and the lame excuse resulting from laziness or over commitment. You can look at the work of potential contributors before approaching them. You can talk to colleagues to find out how easy certain people are to work with and those you should avoid at all costs even though they might be prominent political scientists.

This brings us to the issue of the advantages and disadvantages of involving big-name political scientists in your project. At one time we were all starry-eyed about the big names in our profession, they were sort of demi-gods—the people we aspired to be. As we advance in the profession we may come down to earth about these stars. While the vast majority of them may be perfectly reliable and will deliver a quality product—perhaps a very high-quality one—right on time, some will not be and may leave you in an awful bind. We have first-hand experience of two big stars whom everyone would know in our business who just flat did not deliver, never called us to let us know that they were not going to deliver, and when we contacted them blew us off by telling us they were too busy! This put us in a very tight spot as we had to find substitute contributors, which added six months to the production of the book and made some of our authors very unhappy with us (two of whom have not spoken to us to this day). What is the use of a contribution by a big-name author if he or she won't work to integrate their piece with your book's focus, deliver a draft, or make revisions? So you need to carefully check out the big names to see if they are reliable, will deliver and work to your specifications, and that they won't feel superior to a young, wet-behind-the-ears faculty member/editor to the point where they are impossible to work with.

So what should be your book's ratio of contributions of prominent political scientists to unknowns? Obviously, big-name people can help you get a publisher, and some publishers will be very much concerned with your contributors' prominence, or lack thereof. And so having on board one or more big-name, but easy to work with contributors can benefit your project immensely from both academic and marketing points of view.

On the other hand, don't dismiss newly minted Ph.D.s who are hungry for publications and, for that reason, are most willing to work within your focus and deadlines. Get a fair assessment of their abilities by asking for a sample of their work or by downloading their papers from a convention web site. But once again, be wary of your friends unless you really know them. Remember you are about to embark on a serious academic project, not a social event.

Now some pointers on including people who are not academics in edited books. That is involving political practitioners or political observers—elected and appointed officials, bureaucrats, journalists, among others. At first sight, involving them may sound like a good idea especially if you are editing a book involving recent events, case-studies of the development of particular policies, or need a historical overview of events from the inside. And certainly having some practitioners can add perspective and maybe quality and marketability to a book.

However, before rushing out to get a present or former politico or big-name journalist to contribute to your book, consider the following three points. First, unless they have a social science—preferably political science—background, most practitioners will give you only a series of anecdotal experiences. They will likely not be able to place these experiences in a theoretical framework or comparative context. This means that you'll have to do it for them, considerably rewriting the chapter, if they'll let you. Second, while at first enthusiastically accepting your offer (you've just stroked their ego), some practitioners, though certainly not all, may gradually come to be a little intimidated working with academics and be reluctant to write something that they think may make them look "stupid" and reduce their credibility. So they may pull out just at the wrong moment—when you need their first draft. Third, their time constraints may be such that, this project not being part of their job as it is for academics, they will give it a low priority and, often combined with the last point, their contribution may end up as a "no show."

In most cases, if you want a practitioner's name in your book—maybe on the front cover—have them write a foreword. Likely you'll end up writing this anyway and getting their stamp of approval; but at least you'll get more or less what you want.

Finally, a very important point is to ask all contributors, big-name, practitioners, young scholars and all others, to submit an extended outline of their chapter or contribution. This serves four purposes: (1) it forces contributors to focus on the subject and topic early on and not at the very last moment when the first draft is due; (2) it enables you as editor to see if the contributor is on target in terms of what you need and is not just rehashing what they've done before (we contend that most academics have only two or three subjects we can write about and that we keep rehashing them in different disguises); (3) following on from the last point, if you request changes to bring the outline on track with what the contributor originally agreed to write, their willingness to do so will reveal a lot about how they will be to work with, it will be particularly revealing about the big names; and (4) if you have any doubts about any contributor based upon their extended outline and your interactions with them, this is the time to skillfully drop them from the project and find a replacement.

4. Ensuring Quality Control

A quick perusal of a few edited books reveals that quality control is a problem with many multi-authored volumes. This includes the quality of the academic contribution, of the writing style, and of the book's integration or cohesion. Quality control is essentially a function of four factors: (1) the contributors you choose; (2) your direction telling each author what you expect and your monitoring of the contributions to ensure that they are on the topic agreed upon; (3) your diligence in editing first drafts and your fortitude in making some difficult decisions at this stage (such as dropping those who do not perform adequately); and (4) your skills as the project coordinator. We have already addressed point 1 and some of point 2. The following sections provide a little more on point 2 and a more in-depth consideration of points 3 and 4.

5. Developing a Detailed Set of Guidelines for Contributors

It is absolutely essential that you develop a set of written instructions or guidelines for the contributors to follow. Furthermore, you should leave nothing to chance; be as inclusive in these guidelines as possible. Such extensive directions may seem overkill to the neophyte editor and somewhat of an insult to the senior, perhaps big-name, contributors that you are hoping to secure. But if you think of this document as a way to maximize work efficiency for all concerned, then it becomes clear why a set of comprehensive guidelines is a must.

First, written, comprehensive guidelines make it easier for each contributor to work exactly to your specifications in terms of both content and format. This saves you time spent answering questions and clarifying vague directions. Most contributors will be very appreciative of specific direction because it saves them from wasting time on content and format that will have to be changed later—changes that may well make them upset with you for not having been specific in the first place. Second, guidelines can help produce cohesion in the finished book. Third, guidelines help ensure a good, fairly complete first draft. This is important because most contributors put their major effort into the first draft. A good, fairly complete first draft is also a valuable asset to have when you start to approach publishers.

Comprehensive guidelines are not only important for the content and production of your book, they also serve a psychological, procedural, and marketing purpose. First, they convey to potential contributors that you take the project very seriously. The faint of heart and the contributor who is looking for a quick and easy publication may think twice before signing on. In fact, you should think twice about signing on anyone who complains about your guidelines; this is often the first sign of a problem contributor. To be sure, some contributors will ignore the guidelines and write their chapter the way they want.. So, the second reason to have these clear guidelines is that they give you an easy way to cut contributors who do not follow them. Third, comprehensive guidelines convey to publishers that your project is well thought out. You can submit these guidelines as an appendix to your book prospectus when approaching publishers.

At a very minimum, your guidelines for contributors should include the following sections: (1) the focus and themes of the book; (2) common elements required in each chapter to aid in integration and cohesion; (3) format, length limitation, note/reference/bibliographic style; (4) project timelines for the submission and return of drafts; and (5) times and places that the contributors can contact you. Depending on the specific project, other sections setting out common definitions or detailing methodology may also be appropriate. A section detailing what elements the editor's introduction will cover (such as definitions, a review of the literature, and so on) is often of great value to contributors; it informs contributors as to what commonalities they can omit from their chapters.

6. Understanding the Psychology of the Contributor

As an editor it is important to be aware of how contributors view a project and to be cognizant of the psychological phases that they go through as the project progresses. If you have been a contributor, these will be fairly easy to gauge; but if you have not, or if you have never given the matter much thought, here are some pointers.

First, while as editor this project is one of the most important things in the world to you, to most contributors it is probably just another publication. After all, yours is the only name that will appear on the cover of the book. Not only will some of your contributors not read the guidelines you send out, some probably won't even read their own chapters once the book is published, let alone the other chapters in the book. We've talked to a few contributors to our books who admit to having only browsed the contents of the book to be sure that their contribution was in it. This means that you must be realistic about the level of commitment and goals of your contributors. Their primary goal is to get their chapters written and published as quickly and as efficiently (and in some cases as easily) as possible, with the minimum of changes beyond the first draft.

In terms of the psychological phases that contributors go through, they develop something like this. Stage 1 is euphoria: you have given them an ego boost by recognizing their talents and asking them to contribute to your project. Stage 2 is slight panic as they work to get the first drafts in on time or scheme to think up excuses for why they will be late. Stage 3 is a combination of exhaustion and relief as they send you their first draft. As indicated earlier, this stage is probably most contributors' peak of interest in a project. After this their interest will start to wane, and they will be in Stage 4, the "this project is getting tedious" phase. This is why it is essential to get the best first draft that you can and to request only minor changes after that (though things do not always work out this way) or, if feasible, make most of the change yourself as editor

If things do not move along rapidly after this—if you have a problem getting a publisher, if some contributors hold up the project by not doing revisions, and so on—many of your contributors may progress to Stage 5, exasperation. Further problems may lead them into Stage 6, alienation, when they simply give up. If your contributors get to Stages 5 and 6, you have serious problems and your project may be doomed. Obviously, one of your major goals as project manager is to prevent your contributors from reaching these stages.

7. A Crucial Juncture: The First-Draft Stage of the Project

So far, we have mentioned several reasons why the first-draft stage of the project is so crucial. There are four additional important reasons.

One is the need to deal with chapters that are poor or do not reflect your guidelines for chapter content. The poor chapter is one that is superficially researched, badly written, and generally the sort of thing you wouldn't accept from a sophomore. A second reason, and a variation on the first, is that often a contributor will try to palm off a chapter that is in the area but nowhere near your specifications. This is probably an article or chapter that they could not place somewhere else; or a dusted-off conference paper that they are sending because they misjudged how much work was involved in their chapter and they wanted to get something to you before the deadline. Third, and yet another variation on the poor or off-the-mark chapter, is the contributor who says something like: "I've been really busy and so I'll have to send you a rather rough and incomplete first draft, but I guarantee that I'll do a good second draft." No they won't! Busy means they are either not giving the project a high priority; or, and more likely, that they can't do what you need and didn't realize it until they got to seriously working on the chapter. Fourth, as indicated above, is that often people do not read your guidelines and just turn in the chapter that they wanted to write. Perhaps the most common complaint and cause of exasperation among editors is this seeming lack of regard by contributors for what the editor is trying to do. It has been a very common experience in all of our editing projects.

This is where some tough decisions have to be made by the editor—decisions that can make or break your project. You need to tackle each of these four situations head-on, unpleasant as the prospect may be.

As to poor or incomplete chapters, one of the major lessons that we have learned as editors over 20 years, a lesson often corroborated by other editors, is that if someone submits a really bad or incomplete first draft despite the direction, support and clear timetable you have provided, he or she will not write a good second draft. You should probably find another contributor for this chapter or eliminate it from the book if possible.

One experience we had with a poor, off-the-wall first draft illustrates what odd, unexpected things can sometimes happen. A contributor turned in a first draft with a section haranguing and lambasting his Ph.D. supervisor and the works the supervisor had published. Not only was this tirade a personal attack, it was only tangentially on the subject of his chapter. When we asked the contributor why he'd done this and informed him that it had to be cut, he replied: "I needed to get this dislike for him [his supervisor] off of my chest, he never recognized my talents: I'll prove my abilities to you in my second draft!" Needless to say, we lost no time in edging this person out of the project.

As to the palmed off chapter and the one ignoring your guidelines, these may be salvageable; but you need some concrete guarantees. If in doubt, find another contributor. This sounds drastic. It will certainly add time to the project and probably upset, maybe outrage, these contributors. But the alternatives are even less pleasant: adding much more time to the project as these contributors dally and then perhaps don't deliver; compounding your problems in finding a publisher; and, in the end, if your project has to be abandoned, running the risk of alienating all your diligent contributors and likely some of your friends.

Another important aspect of the first-draft stage is to do a thorough job of editing. This seems obvious, but many editors don't take the trouble to do so because it is hard work, tedious, and runs the risk of bruising some contributors' egos. Remember, however, that this is your major and perhaps last chance, until you can secure a publisher, to get changes made that will improve the quality, cohesiveness, and format of the manuscript.

8. Dealing with Contributors and the Problem Contributor

As an editor you must keep your contributors informed about what's going on: status of the project, changes in timelines, and so on. This includes informing them of the bad news as well as the good. The worst thing that can happen to you is for one of your contributors to find out some bad news—rejection of a manuscript by a publisher, a delay in publication, etc.—from someone other than you. It leads to bad feelings, and if it happens frequently it can even precipitate Stage 6 of contributor psychology—alienation. Set aside a time slot or two each week when your contributors can call you. Communicate with them regularly; and even if there is no real progress to report, you should tell them that. Also be prepared to write lots of letters of recommendation for them for promotion and tenure and letters verifying their participation in the project. This is part of the responsibilities that come with the territory of being an editor.

There are several ways to deal with problem contributors. One, as we suggested above, is to get rid of them when you find that they don't deliver. This is not easy; but it will likely turn out to be the best thing you did for the project and for yourself. If you can't stomach this, if they'll let you, you'll probably end up rewriting their chapter yourself as this may be the only way to salvage it. Then there are contributors who do satisfactory or good work but have fragile egos and get upset at your suggested changes. These you can deal with by smoothing their egos and giving them lots of praise for their work. Then there are those who constantly call you—sometimes to harangue you—because the book wasn't published yesterday! Often these are people who have never edited or published a book themselves, and so are not familiar with the intricacies and pitfalls of the process. The best way to handle these people is to keep them well informed of the progress—or lack thereof—of the project and be up-front about any problems you are encountering. Honesty and forthrightness often disarms people.

If you are co-editing a book it may provide the opportunity for the editors to take on different roles in relation to the contributors; this can often be useful in dealing with the problem contributor. One editor can play the "nice person" role, the other the "task-person role." The different personalities that the editors might have plus their different relationships with the contributors (positive or negative) can also be an asset in dealing with contributors and publishers alike. If you are co-editing, it is worth sitting down together as editors and talking about your strengths and weaknesses, with each editor taking on roles that emphasize the former.

9. Approaching a Publisher and Securing a Contract

Unless you are a star or an ascending star in the profession, have a project that is studded with stars, or an edited book that has a large potential market, the chances are that you won't get a contract until you can send the entire manuscript to a publisher. This means that in organizing an edited book you ask the contributors to embark upon a project with a far from certain outcome. So as editor, from the very beginning of the project you incur a major obligation, a portfolio of debts, and put yourself under great pressure to come through with a contract and ultimately a published book.

There are three key factors in getting a publisher interested in your edited book project and in ultimately securing a contract. First, you have to approach the right publishers. Not all publishers will be interested in your particular subject and some—especially some of the larger commercial houses—will not be interested in edited books. You can find out which publishers might be interested by perusing the booths at a convention, examining the literature, talking to colleagues, or calling an editor. Second, you have to overcome most publishers' natural aversion to edited books. This you can do by showing that you really have a well-thought out and well-organized project. This can be supported by a well-written prospectus, a comprehensive set of contributor guidelines, other supporting materials such as the vita of contributors, research on the potential market, and a good first draft of the manuscript.

Once you've gotten the attention of a publisher who is seriously considering your project, the third key factor comes into play: you and your contributors must be willing to make most of the changes that the publisher wants based on reviews of the manuscript. Because publishers are rarely experts in your field, they rely heavily on their reviewers, who frequently suggest many revisions. Such changes can cause trauma for you and your contributors. However, securing a contract will probably hinge on your willingness to go along with most of these changes whether you like them or not or whether they are justified or not. It is often an annoying but true and practical reality that taking the publisher and the reviewers head-on and arguing against or refusing to make the major changes they want will probably result in rejection of your manuscript. Despite the problems and tedium of dealing with these changes, you can find some comfort in the fact that once you are close to a contract it is easier to reinvigorate your contributors to make the needed revisions.

One final point which should be fairly obvious from the preceding paragraph: when you send the first draft of your manuscript to the publisher you'll heave a great sigh of relief. "Wow, that was a lot of work," you'll say. "Thank goodness it is nearly over." The problem is that only about 60 and at most 70% of your work is over. And, in many ways, the real key parts of the project in terms of producing a good manuscript and making revisions lay ahead.

10. *Moving the Project through the Publication and Marketing Process*

It is obvious that you need to build a good relationship with your publisher's assigned editor and other production staff to ensure that your manuscript gets produced in the best way possible. There is much more to these final stages of the process, however. As indicated above, in many ways this is the phase when attention to fine detail is most crucial as you and your contributors review the edited copy and the page proofs of the manuscript. Unfortunately, however, by now, almost everyone is tired of the project (some sick and tired!), has moved on to other things, and, consequently may be much less diligent than is necessary to avoid glaring errors that will turn up in the printed book. For this reason it may be wise to find someone—a graduate student, a colleague, or a professional proofreader—to help you proof the manuscript. But however diligent you are, whoever proofs it for you, the chances are that when, at long last, you get the book in your hands and open it, the first thing that will be staring out at you will be an obvious typo!

Finally, a few words about marketing your manuscript. If marketing is important to you, you should be aware that some publishers are much better at this process than others; and that some are less concerned about it even though they will never admit it. The big commercial publishers are obviously in it for the money and do a first-rate job of marketing. But most of these do few edited books. Some of the smaller commercial houses and even some of the big ones rely mostly on library sales and will mount only a token general marketing effort. University presses are more likely to be interested in an edited book; but their marketing efforts vary from very good to not so good to pathetic. The upshot of all this is that you may want to get actively involved in the marketing effort for your book. To do this, work closely with the marketing staff at the press; get the word out to journals and other publications; maybe send a letter to interested colleagues; or even develop your own dedicated mailing list. For example, we developed and gave to each of our publishers a mailing list of 1,600 names of those who might be interested in purchasing books from our four-book series on interest groups in the 50 states.

CONCLUSION: EDITING A MULTI-AUTHORED BOOK— THE ART OF THE POSSIBLE

These, then, are what we see as the 10 key factors, the major steps in successfully organizing and completing an edited book project, the pros and cons of editing, and some criteria that you can use to determine whether you should take on editing a multi-authored book. To be sure, many edited books that followed a far less stringent organizational scheme and had a less controlling editor than we are recommending have been published.

Furthermore, experienced editors will disagree on the importance of all of these points and recommendations. But the vast majority of seasoned editors and many of those whose projects didn't make it to press will tell you that the factors set out here, particularly resilience, fortitude, perseverance, and tenacity as well as academic knowledge on the part of the editor, are certainly key elements to success in editing a multi-authored book. Plus, like politics as an activity, editing multi-authored volumes boils down to the art of the possible, not the ideal (even though we might believe that the ideal should prevail in academia). Getting 70% of the book you would have ideally liked published is 100% better than lamenting the ideal book that never saw the printer's press.

In the end, however, the advice in this article is just that—advice. Every project is different and the way to really understand editing is to do it yourself. Nevertheless, our experience has taught us that ignoring this art of the possible in editing books and the other factors we set out in this article, adds extra, potentially very destructive mines to an already well sown academic minefield.

NOTE

1. In regards to the original article (1993), the authors were appreciative of Susan A. Burke for her comments and editing suggestions on drafts of the manuscript. While the central themes of the present article and the original one are based on the extensive experience of the authors in editing multi-authored books over a 20-year period, attendance at the 1992 APSA roundtable discussion on "Managing a Multi-Author Research Project in Comparative Politics" was useful in refining several of the points in the original article. We wish to acknowledge the contributions of that roundtable's members: Kent Weaver (chair), Brookings Institution; Joel D. Aberbach, UCLA; Keith Banting, Queen's University; Nancy Davidson, Brookings Institution; T. J. Pempel, University of California, Berkeley; and Sidney Verba, Harvard University.

REFERENCE

Thomas, Clive S., and Ronald J. Hrebenar. 1993. "Editing Multiauthor Books in Political Science: Plotting Your Way Through an Academic Minefield." *PS: Political Science and Politics* 26 (December): 778–83.

MARK C. MILLER, CLARK UNIVERSITY

MULTIDISCIPLINARY PUBLISHING: REACHING THOSE IN OTHER DISCIPLINES

10

More and more scholars are realizing that their work can and should reach a broader audience beyond just those who read political science journals. Multidisciplinary and/or interdisciplinary publishing presents a somewhat different set of problems and rewards than does publishing solely within one's discipline. Interdisciplinary scholarship draws on concepts and approaches from a variety of disciplines, even when it is published in a single disciplinary venue. For example, those who study political economy are usually working at the intersections of political science and economics, some who study international relations cross the boundaries of history and political science, while political psychology often merges political science and psychology (for a more thorough explication of the various venues in which political scientists can and do publish, see Beth Luey's chapter in this book). Some journals seek out truly interdisciplinary articles. On the other hand, multidisciplinary scholarship as I am using the term is intended to reach an audience beyond political scientists. Most multidisciplinary work is inherently interdisciplinary, but not all interdisciplinary scholarship is necessarily intended to be read by students and scholars in other disciplines. Scholars whose work crosses disciplinary boundaries must figure out how to reach their intended audiences while at the same time keeping in mind how their employers (and outside letter writers for tenure and promotion) will evaluate truly interdisciplinary or multidisciplinary efforts. The point for all authors interested in multidisciplinary publishing is that they must learn the rules and norms of publishing in a variety of disciplines or in truly interdisciplinary or multidisciplinary venues.

This chapter will examine several aspects of publishing across disciplines. There are great benefits of having one's work read by students and scholars in a variety of fields, but there are also some clear risks in publishing beyond political science outlets. Scholars must carefully weigh those costs and rewards before deciding the best avenues for publishing their work. This chapter will explore some of the questions of publishing articles in both interdisciplinary and multidisciplinary journals, as well as publishing articles in journals that are generally read by non-political scientists. The chapter will also discuss the publishing of books versus articles. Perhaps the most important issue to keep in mind as scholars choose outlets for their work is the consideration of how current and future employers (and outside letter writers) will evaluate their products. Although many of my examples in this chapter will draw on those of us who cross the boundaries between law and political science, I think these examples raise important questions for scholars in others areas of political science to consider as well.

Some scholars find themselves teaching and doing research in an environment that encourages interdisciplinary and/or multidisciplinary endeavors. For example, although I am tenured in the Department of Government at Clark University, I am also director of our multidisciplinary Law and Society Program. My university is quite happy to have its faculty publishing in a variety of interdisciplinary and multidisciplinary outlets. My own work is often interdisciplinary because it draws on diverse fields such as political science, sociology, and law. I would like to think that both scholars and practioners in those areas might find something useful in my writings. Therefore, I often seek multidisciplinary outlets for my work. Others find themselves working solely in multidisciplinary programs such as Women's Studies, Peace Studies, International Development, Urban Studies, Racial and Ethnic Studies, or some very broad field such as International Studies. Their publishing and tenure expectations may not be entirely clear to them, including the value of publishing within a specific discipline, in several disciplines, or of publishing in a multidisciplinary venue. It may thus be important for some scholars to learn the rules and norms of publishing in a variety of disciplines. Although most of my experience comes from publishing in the fields of political science and law, I think the concepts apply to publishing efforts for anyone who finds their work of interest to students and scholars in several disciplines.

Publishing in political science journals is a relatively straightforward process. Because of the norms of our discipline, the author or authors can send their proposed article to only one political science journal at a time. Since there is a clear hierarchy of journals within the discipline, most authors start with the most prestigious journal where they think the piece has a chance of being accepted for publication. The editor of the journal may make a determination that the submitted article deserves further attention, or he or she might reject the submittal immediately because the editor feels that the proposed article is not appropriate for that journal. If the editor feels that the submittal deserves further attention, the piece is then set out to reviewers in the discipline as part of the peer-review process. Once the reviewers provide their feedback, the editor might decide to then reject the piece, publish the work as is or with some minor revisions, or give the article the infamous "Revise and Resubmit" status, meaning that the journal will reconsider the piece but only after the author makes substantial revisions. If the author reworks the piece according to the suggestions of the reviewers, then the revised article is sent back to reviewers (sometimes the same reviewers, sometimes new reviewers) for further scrutiny. If the article is rejected or the reviewers want changes that the authors are unwilling to make, only then may the authors decide to submit the article to another political science journal. This entire process can be quite time consuming and frustrating for potential authors (for a more through look at the journal publishing process in political science, see Andrew Polsky's chapter in this book).

While publishing in most social science disciplines follows the same basic pattern of publishing in political science journals, publishing in the world of legal scholarship follows a radically different path. Scholars should be aware of the rules and norms of any discipline in which they want to publish. Because legal scholarship and political science are among the most different in the social sciences in their approaches to publishing, these fields raise some extreme issues for interdisciplinary work but I feel that the questions are universal for anyone who wants to publish outside of political science. Of course, political scientists who want to publish in natural science journals will find that the differences may be even greater, but law and political science are different enough to compare for our purposes.

While most political science journals are associated with a specific membership organization such as the American Political Science Association, the Midwest Political Science Association, or the legislative studies section of the APSA, law reviews and law journals are attached to specific law schools. Each law school in the United States tends to have a general law review, such as the *Yale Law Journal* or the *Harvard Law Review*, plus a number of specialty reviews such as the *Berkeley Women's Law Journal; New York University Journal of Legislation and Public Policy; Stanford Journal of Law, Business, and Finance;* and *UCLA Journal of International Law and Foreign Affairs.* Most of these law journals are edited by law students, and the students themselves often decide which articles will be published. Thus most law reviews in the United States are not peer reviewed.

One of the most important differences between publishing in social science journals and publishing in law reviews is the fact that it is quite common for authors to submit their articles to more than one law review simultaneously. Most social science journals will not accept multiple submissions. If one law review accepts the piece, then the author may use that acceptance to gain an expedited review by other law journals at more prestigious law schools to which it has already been submitted. This notion of multiple submissions and leveraging an acceptance from one law journal to "trade up" to other law reviews would be considered highly unethical in the world of political science journals. Some law reviews strongly prefer that they are the only ones to receive and then review a submitted article, but most understand that authors will be sending their work to multiple law journals simultaneously. Law reviews in other countries such as Canada tend to function more like social science journals in the U.S. For example, the *University of British Columbia Law Review* is a peer-reviewed journal that does not accept multiple submissions. It is important to look at the specific journal's guidelines for authors or guidelines for article submissions to determine whether they accept multiple submissions. When in doubt, it is always a good idea to contact the journal before sending it an article that has also been sent to other journals. When a piece is being submitted to multiple law reviews simultaneously, it is important to mention that fact in the cover letter that accompanies the submitted article.

Potential authors should always get a sense of the length requirements, referencing systems, and other stylistic norms of any journal to which they intend to submit an article. For example, the style of law review articles is also quite different than that of articles published in political science journals. Political science journals generally limit submissions to no more than 35 pages, including charts and graphs. On the other hand, some law review articles can be 150–200 pages in length, although recently most law reviews have been publishing somewhat shorter pieces. History journals tend to accept longer pieces than political science journals, while journals in other disciplines may require their pieces to be even shorter than those in political science. Law reviews tend to want a lot of formal footnotes, both those citing the source of information plus also those that are more explanatory in nature. Often a page in a law review will appear to be one-third text and two-thirds footnotes. On the other hand, most political science journals prefer that internal citations appear in parentheses, with very few notes at the end of the piece. Journals in other disciplines may require the exclusive use of endnotes. Journals published in other countries may prefer the use of British over American spellings. Thus, before writing an article, it is usually best if the author decides at the outset whether to write in the style of political science journals or in the style of law reviews or in the style of the journals of some other discipline. Again, the point for all authors interested in multidisciplinary publishing is that they must learn the rules and norms of publishing in a variety of disciplines or in truly interdisciplinary journals.

When the author has a choice of whether to send his or her work to political science journals, to journals in another discipline, or to multidisciplinary venues, the author should consider how current and potential employers will receive those publications. Some political science departments award a certain amount of points for publishing in the *American Political Science Review*, considered the top journal in our discipline, and fewer points for articles in less prestigious political science journals. These departments often have a hard time giving any points to a law review article because the piece has not been peer reviewed. They may or may not award points to a piece published in a peer-reviewed economics journal, for example, or in an interdisciplinary outlet. Even schools that do not use a formal point system may have a hard time evaluating law review articles since they are not peer reviewed. Law schools often base their tenure decisions on the number and placement of law review articles, but many political science departments are less comfortable with the world of legal scholarship. If a current or future employer will place little value on publishing in a specific journal or type of journal, then the author must think twice before pursuing publication in these outlets.

On the other hand, it is important to publish in venues that will be read by those in the intended audience for the piece. I have had several occasions where judges and even law school professors have told me that they do not read political science journals. At one panel presentation sponsored by the Supreme Court Judicial Fellows Alumni Association, several federal judges noted that they do not read any scholarship that is not included in Westlaw or Lexis-Nexis, two legal scholarship search engines. Political science journals are not included in these programs. From the point of view of very busy judges, they will not waste their time searching to find political science scholarship on law or courts, no matter how useful that scholarship might be to them. If they cannot find the scholarship quickly on Westlaw or Lexis-Nexis, then the scholarship has no relevance to them. Unfortunately, it seems that many law professors also limit their reading to articles readily available in these law-related search engines. Of course, it may not make much difference because a recent article in the *New York Times* noted that judges are citing law review articles in their opinions far less often today than they did in the fairly recent past (see Liptak 2007). Perhaps judges are just not as interested in any kind of scholarship as they were in the past, or perhaps the current academic fads in legal publishing are just not as useful to practioners and judges as they once were.

Scholars should always revise a piece with the specific intended journal in mind before they send that article to the editors for consideration. Some journals are purposefully interdisciplinary or multidisciplinary in nature. Pieces sent to those journals should be revised accordingly. For example, the Law and Society Association draws its membership from law professors, political scientists, sociologists, anthropologists, criminologists, psychologists, and others interested in questions of law and society. This organization's journal, *Law & Society Review*, is intentionally both interdisciplinary and multidisciplinary in nature. Contributors must keep the multidisciplinary audience of the journal in mind. A recent editor was a political scientist, Herb Kritzer of the University of Wisconsin-Madison. In a piece in the APSA's Law and Courts Section newsletter, Kritzer talked about the need to be aware of the readership expectations in an interdisciplinary journal:

> Given that *LSR* is explicitly an interdisciplinary journal, a surprising proportion of articles start with a phrase such as "According to the political science literature . . ." or "As political scientists have shown . . ." While a significant proportion of the readers of *Law & Society Review* are political scientists, an interdisciplinary journal looks for articles that speak to an interdisciplinary audience, not just to members of the author's discipline (Kritzer 2007, 9).

Although the *Law & Society Review* has the word "law" in its title, it functions more like a social science journal than it does a law review in part because it is peer reviewed. The *Law & Society Review* does not accept multiple submissions, for example, but its articles can be found on Lexis-Nexis. The *American Journal of International Law, Law and Contemporary Problems*, and *Law & Social Inquiry* are examples of other peer-reviewed social science type journals that have "law" in their titles, but they do not function like law reviews even though they do appear in Westlaw and Lexis-Nexis.

Thus it is critical that the author consider the expectations of the readership of a journal, and tailor the piece accordingly. *Judicature* is another peer-reviewed interdisciplinary and multidisciplinary journal concerned with legal issues. It is published by the American Judicature Association. Because its readership includes many judges and legal practitioners, *Judicature* prefers readability in its articles. It also prefers that the footnotes be kept to a minimum, which is the exact opposite of practice in the law reviews. Thus many authors who submit their pieces to *Judicature* find that if the piece is accepted for publication, the editor prefers that most of the footnotes be eliminated. This can be a painful occurrence for some scholars. Again, the point is that the author must conform to the readership expectations and thus the editorial norms of whatever journal in which they want to publish.

By its very nature, book publishing tends to be more interdisciplinary and multidisciplinary than publishing in political science journals. However, some books are clearly intended for a readership within a specific discipline, while other books are written for a broader and multidisciplinary audience. While good writing requires that authors carefully define their terms and key concepts, books written for a multidisciplinary audience must be especially attentive to avoiding unnecessary jargon that is familiar only to those in a specific discipline. Also, if a book starts off by saying something to the effect that "political scientists have spent a lot of time on this research question," then the book may not be of interest to a broader readership. Another aspect of publishing a book for a multidisciplinary audience is looking to see whether the author cites sources from several disciplines or whether the bibliography entries would only be familiar to someone within a specific discipline. Although this may be a fairly obvious statement, truly interdisciplinary work draws on the products of scholars in a variety of disciplines. The bibliography of an interdisciplinary book aimed at a multidisciplinary audience should reflect that truism.

One of the key questions for book authors who want to reach a multidisciplinary audience might be finding the right university press or other publisher for the piece. Is the publisher most concerned with textbook sales or is the publisher willing to take a risk on a fine piece of scholarship that might not find a broad readership? Does the publisher market their books to scholars in a variety of disciplines or are their marketing efforts more specialized? It is also important for the authors to think about other books that the press has already published or will publish in the near future. Having complementary books on the press's list makes it easier for people to find your book when they are looking for something in that area. Does the planned book fit nicely into the press's current list or would it be an outlier? Does the press have a series that the book would complement? Is the publisher willing to list the book among several of their series? Does the press have strengths in the several disciplines in which the author is most interested?

Of course, the largest question for most authors of journal articles and books is how their employer or the outside letter writers for tenure and promotion will react to their publications. Although many places claim they want to encourage interdisciplinary or multidisciplinary scholarship, when it comes time to evaluate faculty members or job candidates some departments and universities still do not reward multidisciplinary work. Most potential or current employers still want to see some grounding in a specific discipline. Some departments are more interested in seeing their faculty publish in peer-reviewed journals, some are more interested in having them publish books, and some want to their faculty to publish a mix of both. Junior scholars should clearly ask their senior colleagues, the department chair, or perhaps the chair of the search committee about the expectations of their current or potential employers. It is especially difficult for job applicants to guess what potential future employers may or may not value when deciding whether to publish in multidisciplinary outlets or in venues that are mostly read by non-political scientists.

The reward of publishing in multidisciplinary venues is that the author's work can reach a much broader audience. The downside may be that departments and outside letter writers for tenure and promotion may not know how to evaluate such work. In my department, we use outside letter writers to evaluate the faculty member's scholarship for third-year reviews, for tenure, and for promotion to full professor. We also have a somewhat unique approach to personnel decisions because all members of the department, regardless of their tenure status, vote on all personnel matters for all of our colleagues. Thus I have read a fair number of letters from outside reviewers over the years. My university does encourage interdisciplinary and multidisciplinary publishing among our faculty. However, some of the outside letter writers for various personnel cases were frankly quite hostile to publishing in multidisciplinary venues. They would complain that a faculty member was not focused enough if they were publishing in journals from a variety of disciplines or which were clearly multidisciplinary. Other letter writers would praise the breadth of scholarship present in interdisciplinary or multidisciplinary publishing. Often these conflicting approaches would show up in the same personnel case. One hopes that outside letter writers are chosen carefully, but scholars who publish in a variety of disciplines do face the problem of reviewers wanting something different than what they have already published. For new faculty members, it is always important to get a strong sense of what a department values in publications, and also what criteria are used to select outside letter writers.

The challenges of writing for interdisciplinary or multidisciplinary audiences are many. It does take some time to learn the rules and norms of publishing in a specific discipline or even in a specific journal. One must also take more care to define key terms and jargon that might not be familiar to readers from other disciplines. And authors must learn how their work will be evaluated by their current employers and any potential future employers. On the other hand, many of us feel that interdisciplinary work is one clear path to the creation of new knowledge. We also want our work to be read by a variety of audiences. If one wants to reach out to economists, historians, psychologists, or philosophers, then one must publish in venues that will be read by those people. In some ways, the firm boundaries between disciplines and even between subfields within our discipline seem to be eroding in the academy at large. For example, one can see this trend in the interdisciplinary theme of the 2007 meeting of the American Political Science Association. On the other hand, as long as hiring, tenure, and promotion decisions are made within a specific department or program, then multidisciplinary publishing should be approached with a degree of educated caution. Each scholar must make these choices carefully. On the whole, however, I am one who feels that interdisciplinary and multidisciplinary scholarship is worth the risk.

REFERENCES

Liptak, Adam. 2007. "When Rendering Decisions, Judges are Finding Law Reviews Irrelevant," *New York Times*, March 19.

Luey, Beth. 2008. "Sharing What You Know." In *Publishing Political Science: The APSA Guide to Writing and Publishing*, ed. Stephen Yoder. Washington, D.C.: American Political Science Association, 11–20.

Kritzer, Herbert M. 2007. "From the Middle Out Rather than Top Down or Bottom Up: Looking Beyond Judicial Behavior in Appellate Courts and Public Opinion about the Courts". *Law & Courts* (winter): 17: 9–11.

Polsky, Andrew. 2008. "Seeing Your Name in Print: Unpacking the Mysteries of the Review Process at Political Science Scholarly Journals." In *Publishing Political Science: The APSA Guide to Writing and Publishing*, ed. Stephen Yoder. Washington, D.C.: American Political Science Association, 197–211.

11

DANIEL W. DREZNER, TUFTS UNIVERSITY

SO YOU WANT TO BLOG ...

There are two parts to publishing anything successfully: the act of publication itself and the critical reaction to the published work. Both parts matter. Peer reviewers, editors, and other gatekeepers can erect formidable barriers between the author and the printing press. Surmounting those barriers is an accomplishment in and of itself. How the intended audience reacts to the publication, however, is equally important. Is a journal article or university press book widely cited in the ensuing literature? Does a textbook become widely assigned? Does an op-ed move the policy agenda?

This distinction matters when thinking about how to write a "successful" political science weblog. Compared to all of the other publication venues discussed in this volume, blogs are unique. There are no editorial gatekeepers in blogging. Technical or economic barriers to entry are essentially zero; anyone with access to the Internet can create a blog, for free, in under 10 minutes.[1] The moment a political scientist sets up a blog, he or she has achieved the first component of success. The second component of success—positive audience reaction—is altogether trickier.

An academic political scientist who decides to blog must consider three audiences: colleagues, students, and everyone else. The key to success is to earn positive feedback from as many readers as possible while not triggering a negative reaction from the first two groups. If successful, a political scientist's blog can serve as a valuable complement to research, teaching, and service. An unsuccessful blog carries the risks of alienating other political scientists and confusing students.

This chapter will proceed in four sections. The next section briefly reviews the weblog phenomenon, and how it has penetrated the political science discipline in comparison to other academic fields. The second section reviews the different ways in which a blog can enhance one's professional career, focusing on research and service. The third section discusses the professional perils that come with maintaining an active weblog. The final section offers some practical advice on how to maximize the promise of blogs while minimizing the pitfalls.

BLOGGING 101

For the uninitiated, a blog or weblog is defined as a web page that is subject to minimal to no external editing, provides online commentary, is periodically updated, and is presented in reverse chronological order with hyperlinks to other online sources (Farrell and Drezner 2008). Blogs can function as personal diaries, technical advice columns, sports chats, celebrity or business gossip,[2] political commentary, or all of the above. A blogger is an individual who maintains a weblog. A post is an individual entry in a weblog. The "blogosphere" refers to the universe of blogs, which forms a social network.

Blogs have penetrated the academy—though their prevalence and acceptance varies widely from discipline to discipline. They are most prominent in law, and have become a key resource for legal scholars, judges, and law clerks (Solum 2006; Berman 2006; Balkin 2006). Blog posts have been cited in court opinions and legal briefs, and there is evidence to suggest that law clerks read prominent legal blogs on a regular basis (Solum 2006; Balkin 2006). Legal bloggers know this, and may craft their posts to influence decisions in prominent cases. Blogs have also penetrated other social science disciplines, such as history, philosophy, and economics.

By one quantitative measure, political science falls into the middle of the pack in terms of social science blogging. One web site keeps an updated list of academic blogs.[3] As of March 2007, both history and economics have roughly 33% more blogs than political science. At the same time, political science blogs outnumber those in anthropology, psychology, and sociology.[4] While weblogs have spread into political science, however, they have not necessarily spread far within elite institutions. As of March 2007, very few political scientists at top-20 departments maintained an active blog.[5] In contrast, numerous lawyers and economists at top-20 institutions run weblogs.

Despite the penetration of blogs into the academy, considerable controversy remains about whether blogging should be thought of as a scholarly activity (Boynton 2005). Some academic bloggers take great pains to divorce their professional activities from their blogging output (Althouse 2006).[6] This chapter, however, focuses on blogging about phenomena relevant to political science.

THE PROMISE OF BLOGS

Traditionally, academics divide their work output into teaching, research, and service. A similar triptych works when measuring blog success. Blogs have been used as an online component to facilitate teaching. They can allow professors to link to course-relevant articles, or allow their students to articulate their thoughts on salient topics. For example, Gary King has sponsored the Social Science Statistics blog, facilitating interaction among graduate students on ways to improve statistical techniques and presentation.[7] The real potential for blogs, however, is in the areas of research and service.

Blogging can facilitate conventional research programs in several ways. The simplest and most direct is when a blog acts as an online notebook for nascent ideas and research notes. A blog allows the writer to link and critique news stories, research monographs, and other online publications. Because blogs are archived, it is easy for authors to retrace their thoughts online. Most of these posts will not develop into anything substantive—as is the case with most ideas formulated by scholars.[8] Nevertheless, the format permits one to play with ideas in a way that is ill-suited for other publishing formats. A blog functions like an intellectual fishing net, catching and preserving the embryonic ideas that merit further time and effort.[9]

The research benefits of a blog grow when connections are made with other social science blogs. This allows an exchange of views about politics, policy, and political science with individuals that you might not have otherwise met—an "invisible college," as Brad DeLong (2006) puts it: "People whose views and opinions I can react to, and who will react to my reasoned and well-thought-out opinions, and to my unreasoned and off-the-cuff ones as well." Henry Farrell (2005) compares blogs to the eighteenth-century Republic of Letters, noting that the blogosphere "builds a space for serious conversation around and between the more considered articles and monographs that we write."[10]

In political science, academic blogs have facilitated better scholarship by encouraging online interactions about research ideas. For example, political science bloggers have debated whether international relations theory is slighting the study of al-Qaeda;[11] the sources of the liberal democratic peace;[12] the role of the political scientist as a political actor;[13] and arranged online discussions of noteworthy books in political science.[14] Blogs can act as a substitute for the traditional practice of exchanges of letters in journals, and provide additional venues for book reviews.

Of course, these kinds of exchanges happen offline as well. The blog format, however, enhances and expands these interactions in two ways. First, the networked structure of the blogosphere facilitates the inclusion of more political scientists, more academic disciplines, and more informed citizens than other venues. Second, these interactions also happen much more quickly than in other formats. When presenting an idea on the blogosphere, there is instantaneous critical feedback. Even with the advent of online journal submissions, this quasi-peer review system is *much* quicker than would be the case with a journal or university press.[15]

Weblogs can also be viewed as a form of service. A blog allows a professor to interact with interested citizens beyond the ivory tower. Provided one can write in a reasonably jargon-free manner, a blog can attract readers from all walks of life. Indeed, citizens will tend to view an academic blogger they encounter online as more accessible than would be the case in a face-to-face interaction. This increases the likelihood of fruitful interaction. A blog is an accessible outlet for putting on one's public intellectual hat. As Farrell (2005) observes, "Blogging democratizes the function of public intellectual. It's no longer necessary for an academic to lobby the editors of the *Washington Post*'s op-ed page or the *New York Review of Books* in order to make his or her voice heard. Instead, he or she can start a blog and (with interesting arguments and a bit of luck and self-promotion) begin to have an impact on the public conversation." Survey evidence also suggests that political scientists use blogs as a form of political activism (McKenna 2007).

A successful weblog can also expand publication opportunities. Book publishers, magazine editors, and op-ed assistants all read weblogs. If a political scientist can demonstrate a deft writing style and a clear expertise about an issue on a blog, it sends a signal to these gatekeepers that they can display these qualities in other publishing venues. Blogging is not a substitute to other publications: done correctly, it is a powerful complement.

THE PERIL OF BLOGS

Almost all of the benefits that come from maintaining a weblog require an audience willing to read it. In choosing to blog, political scientists face two problems: people will read their blog, or they will ignore their blog. Let us take the second problem first. It can be dispiriting to put effort into a blog and then find that it fails to garner any traffic. The distribution of links and traffic in the blogosphere is remarkable skewed, with a few blogs commanding the overwhelming share of links and hits (Farrell and Drezner 2008; Shirky 2003). Over time the "elite" blogs have become more and more entrenched, creating a barrier to embryonic political science blogs in building a significant reader base. Latecomers may therefore find it difficult to attract significant numbers of readers.

Even with these barriers, however, political scientists who adapt to the medium should—eventually—be able to attract readers in the hundreds or even thousands per day. This leads to the second potential problem—having your blog read and misinterpreted by colleagues and students. The simple fact is that most political scientists either do not or cannot write for a public audience (Borer 2006). Academics who publish only in peer-reviewed outlets will develop misperceptions about political scientists who do publish in non-scholarly outlets. Because they take words seriously, they will assume that it takes the same length of time to craft a paragraph of blog text as it does to create a paragraph of scholarly text. This is simply not true. This misperception contributes to a massive overestimation of the effort devoted to blogging, and the opportunity costs in the form of lost scholarship.

In some ways, this problem is merely the latest manifestation of what happens when professors try to become public intellectuals. Political scientists currently look at blogs the way a previous generation of academics looked at television—as a guilty, tawdry pleasure that should not be talked about in respectable circles.[16] The problem is more acute now, however, because blogging creates new pathways to public recognition beyond the control of traditional academic gatekeepers. Any usurpation of scholarly authority is bound to upset those who benefit the most from the status quo.[17]

For example, in July 2005 a senior humanities professor wrote a pseudonymous essay (Tribble 2005a) in the *Chronicle of Higher Education* on the academic job market, entitled "Bloggers Need Not Apply." The title aptly summarized the argument. Three months later, this professor responded to the volumes of online criticism with another *Chronicle* essay (Tribble 2005b), observing, "As my original column made clear (and many amid the outcry reiterated) when it comes to blogging, 'I just don't get it.' That's right, I don't. *Many in the tenured generation don't, and they'll be sitting on hiring committees for years to come.* (emphasis added)" Political scientists sympathetic to blogs have fretted about how a blog would impact a junior candidate's chances for tenure. Michigan historian Juan Cole was allegedly rejected for an interdisciplinary chair at Yale because of hostility to some of the content on his blog (Liebowitz 2006).

Another potential problem is how students view a professor's blog. If an academic blogger achieves any kind of public success, then that academic's students are likely to peruse his or her blog. This is not automatically a bad thing, but academic bloggers often display more personal idiosyncrasies on their web page than they would ordinarily reveal in a classroom setting. This can be problematic because students often overinterpret their interactions with professors. They might believe they have a more informal relationship with the professor—or view a blog post as signaling a message when none is intended.[18]

The seriousness of these pitfalls is a function of one's standing in the profession. Tenured professors have little to fear from the downside of blogging—unless they aspire to employment at an elite institution. For faculty comfortably ensconced at non-elite institutions, blogging can provide a new way to engage the scholarly and policy discourse of the day. For junior faculty and graduate students, the perils are greater and harder to avoid. The demographics of blogging suggest that, like Internet use more generally, it is skewed toward the young (Rainie 2005). Even if incoming graduate students are comfortable with the medium, however, they must be wary of their elders—who are clearly less comfortable.

HOW TO SUCCEED AT BLOGGING

The way to publish a successful blog is to attract well-informed readers, while at the same time minimizing the misperceptions of colleagues who might read it. How can this be done? Ten pieces of advice to you, the novice blogger, from a five-year veteran:

1. *Imagine your audience.* Besides yourself, who do you want to read your blog? This is strictly a matter of personal choice, but it is a choice you need to make. Some blogs are intended to reach only their own specialty. Others are intended for a general political science audience. And yet others are intended for an even wider audience. While there are common keys to success for all weblogs, it helps to anticipate the target audience's expected background knowledge.

2. *Think small at first.* Do not expect that you will immediately adapt to the format. When you start your blog, it will not look pretty.[19] The good news is that there is a learning-by-doing curve in blogging, and you can adapt to the format over time. The point is, give your new blog a month or two of shakedown before trumpeting it to other political scientists.

3. *Write clearly and concisely.* We have been trained within an inch of our lives to write for other academics. To the lay person, academics come off as too long-winded, too afraid of emotive language, and too in love with their own jargon to be easily accessible (Borer 2006). Write as clearly and directly as possible.

Even if your intended audience is strictly other academics, there are ways in which crafting a blog post differs from writing for an offline format. One simple rule of thumb: readers will give up on long blocks of unindented prose online long before they get discouraged when reading a similar amount of text on paper. Paragraphs should be no longer than 100 words.[20]

4. *Link, link, link.* Many political scientists who try their hand at blogging mistakenly believe that blogs function as a place to dump rejected op-ed submissions. This overlooks a crucial component of the blogosphere—its networked, hyperlinked structure. As a general rule, try to link to at least one other web page when composing an individual blog post.

It also helps to link to other bloggers' perspectives on the topic of your post. Search out weblogs that focus on similar topics and read them on a regular basis. This serves several useful purposes. First, think of linking as the blog equivalent of a literature review—what are other's takes on a *New York Times* op-ed, for example? Second, reading other's opinions on a similar topic will often provide useful fodder for your own musings. Third, most bloggers want to know if others are talking about them. Various search engines and trackback features within blog software make it easy for other bloggers to find your blog.[21] This allows the possibility of an iterated online exchange of views. If you are really interested in attracting traffic, be sure to email popular bloggers when you have a post that targets their interests.[22]

5. *Remember—you are the editor.* The blogosphere's comparative advantages are speed in publishing and no external editors—but that does not mean that once you have posted something it is sacrosanct. In the hour after I initially post something, I will often

revise it to clean up typos, correct grammar, add relevant links, and bulk up my arguments with more detailed points or supporting facts. I also will update posts over the next day or so in response to feedback or new information. The best bloggers have well-honed internal editing systems—and they use them on a regular basis.

6. *Develop a thick skin.* As someone accustomed to having colleagues rip apart my academic work in workshops and conferences, I have always found the criticism of blog commenters far less damaging to my psyche. That said, the blogosphere is not for the faint of heart.[23] Many bloggers thrive on critiquing any and every post. Commenters can be even more abusive in their language. One category of commenters—referred to in blogging argot as "trolls"—will submit comments that have little to do with the original post. The more popular a blog becomes, the more this becomes a problem. The more you can filter out online rudeness in your own mind, the more productive you will be.

7. *Respect the boundaries.* Senior colleagues take discretion seriously, and episodes of professional misconduct involving weblogs have occurred.[24] One great fear of non-bloggers is that their interactions with you and with others will become fodder for your weblog. You need to reassure others that you blog in a prudent manner. Do not post about what is said at faculty meetings or after job talks. Do not regurgitate campus gossip or hearsay. If a colleague says something that you believe to be blog-worthy, ask him or her for permission to put it online. Do not post about your interactions with students, even if the interactions seem harmless to you. In general, do not post about individual students until and unless they are no longer your students. Be respectful of others. Your colleagues will respond to the tone of your blog—the more worried you are about their reaction, the more careful you should be.

8. *Expect and correct misinterpretations.* In conversation, people assess body language, voice intonation, and numerous other non-verbal cues to interpret the message. In print, editors can pick up phrases that might be misinterpreted. These cues and

checks are absent in weblogs. Because blogs are self-edited and instantaneously published, they tend to resemble email more than any other publishing format. One fact that has become clear from electronic mail is the ease with which misinterpretations arise and mushroom beyond control (Shapiro and Anderson 1985). When misinterpretations arise, be sure to respond quickly and clearly.

9. *Dilute the risk if necessary.* If you want the benefits of blogging but are concerned about how it could affect your academic standing, there are ways to reduce the risks. One possibility is to blog under an alias or pseudonym. Another is to form or join a group blog.[25] The downside to these approaches, of course, is that they also reduce some of the rewards that come with blogging.

10. *If it's not fun, then don't do it!* Done properly, a blog can be a great asset to a political scientist—but it is hardly a prerequisite for a successful career. If you try it out and feel it is not working for you, then stop blogging.

References

Althouse, Ann. 2006. "Why a Narrowly Defined Legal Scholarship Blog Is Not What I Want." University of Wisconsin Legal Research Paper Series no. 1021, Madison, WI.

Balkin, Jack. 2006. "Online Legal Scholarship: The Medium and the Message." *Yale Law Journal Pocket Part 20* 116 (September). Accessed at www.thepocketpart.org/2006/09/06/balkin.html.

Borer, Douglas. 2006. "Rejected by the *New York Times*? Why Academics Struggle to Get Published in National Newspapers." *International Studies Perspectives* 7 (August): vii–x.

Boynton, Robert. 2005. "Attack of the Career-Killing Blogs," *Slate*, November 16. Accessed at www.slate.com/id/2130466/.

Capriccioso, Rob. 2005. "Online Quicksand," *Inside Higher Ed*, November 10. Accessed at www.insidehighered.com/news/2005/11/10/bloggers.

DeLong, J. Bradford. 2006. "The Invisible College," *Chronicle of Higher Education*, July 28.

Drezner, Daniel. 2004. "The Outsourcing Bogeyman." *Foreign Affairs* 83 (May/June): 22–34.

———. 2005. "Why Aren't IR Scholars Paying More Attention to Al Qaeda?" November 13. Accessed at http://abuaardvark.typepad.com/abuaardvark/2005/11/understanding_a.html.

———. 2006. "The Trouble with Blogs," *Chronicle of Higher Education*, July 28.

———. 2007a. *All Politics Is Global*. Princeton: Princeton University Press.

———. 2007b. "Lost in Translation: The Transatlantic Divide Over Diplomacy," in *Growing Apart: America and Europe in the 21st Century*, eds. Jeffrey Kopstein and Sven Steinmo. Cambridge: Cambridge University Press.

———. 2008. "The Realist Tradition in American Public Opinion." *Perspectives on Politics* 6 (March): 51–70.

Farrell, Henry, and Daniel Drezner. 2008. "Blogs, Politics, and Power: A Special Issue of Public Choice." *Public Choice* 134 (January): 1-13.

Farrell, Henry. 2005. "The Blogosphere as a Carnival of Ideas," *Chronicle of Higher Education*, October 7.

———. 2007. "Scholarly Activism," March 27. Accessed at http://crookedtimber.org/2007/03/27/scholarly-activism/.

Gartzke, Erik. 2005. "Reply to Rummel," September 15. Accessed at www.danieldrezner.com/archives/002315.html.

Jackson, Patrick. 2007a. "Weberian Activism," March 22. Accessed at http://duckofminerva.blogspot.com/2007/03/piece-that-i-wrote-with-stuart-j.html.

———. 2007b. "Scholars and Politics," March 31. Accessed at http://duckofminerva.blogspot.com/2007/03/scholars-and-politics.html.

Jackson, Patrick, and Stuart Kaufman. 2007. "Security Scholars for a Sensible Foreign Policy: A Study in Weberian Activism." *Perspectives on Politics* 5 (March): 95–103.

Liebowitz, Liel. 2006. "Middle East Wars Flare Up at Yale," *Jewish Week*, June 2.

Lynch, Marc. 2005. "Understanding Al Qaeda: The Irrelevance of IR Theory," November 11.

McKenna, Laura. 2007. "'Getting the Word Out': Policy Bloggers Use Their Soap Box To Make Change." *Review of Policy Research* 24 (May): 209–29.

Munger, Michael. 2005. "It's True: I am a just another blogging fatality," March 13. Accessed at http://mungowitzend.blogspot.com/2005/03/its-true-i-am-just-another-blogging.html.

"The Primacy of Politics? A Crooked Timber Seminar on Sheri Berman's New Book." 2006. November. Accessed at www.henryfarrell.net/berman.pdf.

Rainie, Lee. 2005. "The State of Blogging." Pew Internet & American Life Project. Washington, D.C. Accessed at www.pewinternet.org/pdfs/PIP_blogging_data.pdf.

Rauch, Jonathan. 1993. *Kindly Inquisitors*. Chicago: University of Chicago Press.

Rummel, R. J. 2005. "The Cato Institute gets it All Wrong," September 11. Accessed at http://freedomspeace.blogspot.com/2005/09/cato-institute-gets-it-all-wrong.html.

Shapiro, Norman, and Robert Anderson. 1985. *Towards an Ethics and Etiquette for Electronic Mail.* Santa Monica: RAND.

Shirky, Clay. 2003. "Power Laws, Weblogs and Inequality," February. Accessed at www.shirky.com/writings/powerlaw_weblog.html.

Solum, Lawrence. 2006. "Blogging and the Transformation of Legal Scholarship." *Illinois Public Law Research Paper No. 65*, Urbana-Champaign, IL, September.

Tribble, Ivan 2005a. "Bloggers Need Not Apply," *Chronicle of Higher Education*, July 8.

———. 2005b. "They Shoot Messengers, Don't They?" *Chronicle of Higher Education*, September 2.

Wolfe, Alan. 2004. "The New Pamphleteers," *New York Times Book Review*, July 11.

NOTES

*   Portions of this chapter were presented previously at the 2005 Public Choice Society meetings in New Orleans, LA. I am grateful to Donald Douglas, Henry Farrell, Andrew Gelman, Leslie Johns, James Joyner, Chris Lawrence, Jacob T. Levy, Laura McKenna, Michael Munger, Daniel Nexon, Fabio Rojas, and Matthew Shugart for their feedback.

1   Popular web sites include Blogger, Wordpress, and LiveJournal.

2   This chapter will not discuss political science blogs devoted to the job market, such as IR Rumor Mill, which consist of information about interview and hirings, as well as anonymous reactions to same. On the pluses and minuses of these sites, see Robert Axelrod's message to department chairs, reprinted at http://irrumormill.blogspot.com/2007/04/robert-axelrod-on-academic-rumor-mills.html, April 3, 2007.

3   www.academicblogs.org/wiki/index.php/Main_Page.

4   These raw numbers should be taken with a grain of salt, however, as they might simply reflect the relative sizes of different social science departments.

5   Curiously, most of those who do are methodologists: Stanford's Simon Jackman (http://jackman.stanford.edu/blog/), Columbia's Andrew Gelman (www.stat.columbia.edu/~gelman/blog/), and Harvard's Gary King (www.iq.harvard.edu/blog/sss/). Other political science bloggers based at elite institutions, such as Princeton's John Ikenberry (http://americaabroad.tpmcafe.com/), Stanford's Joshua Cohen (http://left2right.typepad.com/), and Berkeley's Steve Weber (http://steveweber.typepad.com/) discontinued their blogs.

6   For a political science example, *Perspectives on Politics* editor James Johnson maintains a photography blog at http://politicstheoryphotography.blogspot.com/.

7   www.iq.harvard.edu/blog/sss/.

8   As Jonathan Rauch (1993, 64) points out, "We can all have three new ideas every day before breakfast: the trouble is, they will almost always be bad ideas. The hard part is figuring out who has a good idea."

9   Speaking from personal experience, I can think of at least three projects that had their origins in blog posts. See Drezner (2004; 2007b; 2008).

10   For a dissent, see Wolfe (2004).

11   Lynch (2005); Drezner (2005). Accessed at http://abuaardvark.typepad.com/abuaardvark/2005/11/understanding_a.html.

12   Rummel (2005); Gartzke (2005).

13   Jackson and Kaufman (2007); Jackson (2007).

14   *"The Primacy of Politics?* A Crooked Timber Seminar on Sheri Berman's New Book," November 2006. Accessed at www.henryfarrell.net/berman.pdf.

15   Speaking from personal experience, two weeks after I uploaded a draft version of *All Politics Is Global* (Drezner 2007a) to the blog, I received detailed margin comments from a top-tier economist.

16   After I started blogging, some colleagues averred that they *never* read blogs—and yet, without fail, these same people came into my office on a regular basis to discuss a post of mine. See Drezner (2006).

17   For one semi-serious acknowledgement of this fact, see Munger (2005).

18   This last point extends to any authority relationship. One department chair told me about writing what he believed to be an innocuous post about working hard in order to get tenure. Afterwards, he discovered to his shock and horror that several of his junior faculty members individually believed that the post was directed at them specifically.

19   This is one reason why the leading lights of our profession face a greater cognitive barrier to blogging. Someone who is already a prominent name in the field will attract immediate attention once they start blogging—not all of which will be positive. This is a daunting prospect for academics accustomed to offline respect and/or genuflection.

20   For more online writing tips, go to www.useit.com/papers/webwriting/.

21   Two examples are Technorati and Google Blogsearch.

22   Do *not* simply send an email announcing your new blog to popular bloggers—they get many emails like this a day, almost all of which are ignored.

23   In 2004, one prominent blogger explicitly compared me to "the business elite who dealt with Hitler." See www.danieldrezner.com/archives/001363.html.

24   For one example of such misconduct, see Capriccioso (2005).

25   For three examples of group blogs that transcend disciplinary boundaries, see Crooked Timber (www.crookedtimber.org), The Volokh Conspiracy (http://volokh.com), and Open University (www.tnr.com/blog/openuniversity).

TOPICS IN PUBLISHING

Andrew J. Polsky, Hunter College and the
Graduate Center, CUNY

12

Seeing Your Name in Print: Unpacking the Mysteries of the Review Process at Political Science Scholarly Journals

Introductory Note

This article was originally published in its entirety in the July 2007 issue of PS: Political Science and Politics. We thank the author for allowing us to re-publish his work here.

"Publish or perish." Every graduate student has heard the phrase. Many junior scholars understand that it reflects the cold reality of professional survival in any political science department that bases tenure and promotion decisions, in whole or in part, on a record of demonstrated scholarly achievement. Despite occasional pronouncements by college presidents or faculty committees that teaching should be given greater weight in personnel decisions, the pressure to publish will not soon subside. If anything, it may be becoming more acute, as graduate students entering the job market struggle to publish some portion of their dissertation in a respected scholarly journal so as to distinguish themselves from the pack of applicants presenting otherwise similar credentials.

For all the anxiety that surrounds publication, the process by which journals review manuscripts and the basis upon which they reach decisions remains obscure. I propose here to peel back the lid. I do so with a constructive purpose—to offer some guidance to prospective authors, especially graduate students who hope to see their byline in print by the time they seek an academic appointment. Many manuscripts fail because authors commit serious but avoidable (indeed, sometimes obvious) errors. Although the standard review process of "double-blind" refereeing contains unpredictable elements, authors can take steps to improve their prospects. I also believe an understanding of the process can help ease the minds of those scholars who fear submitting their work to anonymous scrutiny, even as the tenure clock ticks away.

My comments reflect my experience as author, editorial board member, and editor. As with most of my peer editors, I was an author of journal articles before I assumed my present position in July 2005 as editor of *Polity*. My experience as author spanned the full range of decision possibilities: rejection at one journal, acceptance at another; revise-and-resubmit ("R&R") resulting in both acceptance and rejection; R&R multiple times at the same journal; and acceptance pending minor revisions. I have heard of the mythic academic superstar who has never received anything other than a clear accept decision for an initial manuscript submission. Alas, most of us mere mortals have suffered our share of rebuffs. Editors such as myself, then, understand what it means to be on the receiving end of bad news. Since becoming editor, moreover, I have gained a better appreciation of what referees expect of manuscripts and learned to identify pitfalls that can doom potentially interesting and significant submissions.

WHEN IS A PIECE READY TO SUBMIT?

A manuscript should be vetted by other scholars working in the same field before you submit it to a journal. Beware the enthusiastic professor in a graduate course who pronounces your seminar paper ready for publication. It isn't. Typically, a piece will be presented first at one or more scholarly conferences before submission. This gives you an opportunity to receive critical feedback that may identify obvious flaws and/or alert you to important literature you have overlooked. Your argument will be stronger for it. Note, however, that the process of presenting and revising is not the equivalent of receiving anonymous reviews: often graduate school peers, faculty colleagues, and discussants on panels will soften their criticisms so as not to wound or offend.

At the opposite extreme from those who rush prematurely to submit their papers for publication are the junior scholars who delay, delay, delay. They fine tune and polish in the elusive quest for perfection. Even as a tenure decision looms, they hesitate, intending just one more revision. If this describes you, bear one thing in mind: perfectionists don't publish.

My advice to the perfectionist is straightforward. Do not hold yourself to a higher standard than you expect of others. We all read work in graduate school that is flawed, yet still makes a significant, even seminal contribution to the discipline. Similarly, when we teach we include on course syllabi scholarship that is open to criticism—indeed, that is one means by which we teach our students to think critically. And in our own research, we cite literature that we have found useful even when we take issue with it. If imperfect scholarship is good enough for you to use routinely in your teaching and your research, your own imperfect work is good enough to submit for publication.

WHERE SHOULD YOU SUBMIT?

With a multitude of scholarly journals publishing work by political scientists, you will likely face a number of possibilities as you consider where to submit a manuscript. You must make a choice. Scholarly journals insist upon exclusive consideration, so you may submit your piece to only one journal at a time. If a target journal is not familiar to you or is not one of the general political science journals accepting material across the discipline, do your homework to confirm that it publishes scholarship similar to yours. Most journals have an online home page linking you to the table of contents of recent issues; a journal may make some articles available free for a limited period to boost interest. (The home page is also the place to find submission guidelines and policies, such as page limits.) University libraries have paper copies and may also subscribe to services such as JSTOR, which give their patrons electronic access to journal articles a few years after publication.

Opinions vary about the importance of a journal's reputational status for aspiring scholars and junior faculty. My own experience suggests that search committees are more interested in the fact that a job candidate has published than in the prestige of the journal. But the standards are sure to vary across institutions. Much the same applies to junior faculty facing periodic reviews and tenure decisions. In that case, at least, you should be able to learn from senior colleagues the relative value of publishing in particular journals. As a general rule of thumb, publishing in the most highly rated scholarly journals will do more for your career, but their acceptance rates will be quite low. Some top journals in the discipline accept fewer than 5% of submissions.

Of equal concern to job candidates and junior scholars is the review turnaround time. When journals relied on paper submissions and mailed hard copies to referees (a system common until the last few years), it often took five or six months to complete the review process. If a manuscript was rejected at the end of that period, the author had to begin again, faced with the same extended wait. New electronic review procedures at many journals have shortened the review cycle dramatically. Manuscripts can be sent to referees as email attachments; if a referee declines to review a piece, it can be sent to someone else a few days later. Reviews come back just as quickly. (On occasion we have received referee reports within 24 hours of the initial request.) At *Polity*, we guarantee authors a decision within two months of submission, and it rarely takes that long. Some journals that still rely on paper submissions have also found ways to shorten the review cycle, such as by adding a third referee at the outset. Before the *American Political Science Review* made its recent move to electronic submissions, it still completed reviews of hard copy manuscripts within two months. Where time matters, then, you should certainly look first to journals that commit to prompt turnaround.

THE MANUSCRIPT REVIEW PROCESS

When you submit your manuscript, you should receive an acknowledgment from the journal. It may contain a tracking number, an explanation of the review procedure, and a timetable for the review process. If you do not get confirmation within two or three weeks that your submission has been received, follow up to make certain that it has not gone astray. Never assume that silence means everything is going as it should. Editors differ over whether you should bother with a cover letter explaining why the piece is important or appropriate for the journal. In many cases the editor will never see the note (graduate students on the editorial staff may log new entries into the system or the process may be fully automated). I disregard a cover note because I believe the article either stands or falls on its own merits. Some editors, by contrast, find a note useful to help them situate a manuscript on a subject with which they are not familiar.

Journal editors undertake an initial assessment of manuscript submissions, a practice that varies widely across journals and by editors. This step is used as a filter to eliminate manuscripts that editors deem unsuitable for full review. A manuscript may be rejected up front for several reasons: it exceeds the journal's page maximum; it is essentially political and/or ideological rather than scholarly; the journal has a backlog of accepted manuscripts on the same subject or in the same field (an unpredictable factor that means looking at recent issues may actually mislead a prospective author); the piece is poorly written; or the editor believes the piece is deficient in some obvious way that would lead referees to reject it (see the discussion below of common manuscript flaws). Some editors send out most manuscripts for full review while others exercise a significant check during the initial evaluation. The process may also change when a new editor takes over at a journal—I exercise significantly greater discretion in screening out manuscripts upon arrival than did my predecessor.

Rejection prior to external review is one way in which editors function as gatekeepers for professional scholarship, and it raises a question about the openness of the review process. I justify the practice on several grounds. First and most important, no journal exercises a monopoly over publication, even within a subfield. This matters because, however much experience we may have, our judgment is fallible; we may err and miss the substantial merits of a piece where some obvious flaw has caught our attention. Were there no alternative, it would be hard to defend the screening practice. But authors always have other journals to which they can submit a piece when one editor has declined to consider it. Second, we need to be mindful of the burden we place on referees. They volunteer their time out of a sense of professional commitment. To send them a manuscript of poor quality or, depending on the journal's objectives, manifestly unsuitable content would represent an abuse of their dedication. Moreover, although the pool of potential reviewers may be sizable, it is still finite. We risk depleting the available supply if we draw upon it recklessly.

Manuscripts that pass the initial screening will typically be subjected to "double-blind" peer review—that is, at least in theory, neither the referee nor the author knows the identity of the other. I say "in theory" because in the present web-connected world it has become very difficult to conceal the identity of authors. If you have presented a paper at a conference and then used the title (or a close cousin) for your manuscript, a reviewer can do a simple Internet search to find out who you are. Similarly, working papers and graduate student colloquia schedules are often posted online. I believe, then, that we are fast approaching a situation in which journals can hope at best to achieve single-blind reviewing in which the referee's identity is confidential.

External referees will typically be chosen from two pools of scholars. Most journals have an editorial board whose members are expected to participate in the review process in some capacity. Sometimes manuscripts will be read exclusively by the editorial board, although that places a very heavy burden upon its members. At *Polity*, most manuscripts will be read by one editorial board member; because of the general scope of the journal, I ask the board referee to consider especially the appeal of a manuscript for a wider political science audience.

The second pool consists of scholars with expertise in the subject addressed by the manuscript. Journals have several methods for finding such specialists. Some journals cultivate a stable of proven referees, scholars who are reliable and conscientious, and maintain a data bank organized by subject competence. A manuscript itself may be a useful guide—the citations point to potential referees. Online search engines such as Google Scholar help editors identify academics who have recently published or presented work on related subjects. Lastly, authors are welcome to suggest potential reviewers (at *Polity* we usually invite them to do so), recognizing, of course, that the journal is not obligated to use those names. It does no harm to identify potential reviewers with your initial submission.

When potential referees are asked to review a manuscript, they are under no obligation to agree. They receive no compensation and often no public recognition for their services. Nevertheless, many agree to take on the task. Indeed, some do so without ever informing the journal, so the first indication that they have agreed comes when they return the review several weeks after they received the manuscript. (This is why at *Polity* we sometimes have received as many as five referee reports for a single manuscript.) Referee reports are often long and detailed, especially when critical of a manuscript. Having read hundreds of reports over the past two years, I have been impressed with the constructive thrust of the vast majority of reviews: most scholars seek to improve the work they evaluate. Referees are also conscientious about identifying ethical issues, such as when they believe they know who the author of a piece is or when they have previously reviewed the same manuscript for another journal.

Journals prefer two or more reviews for each manuscript placed under full review. Two reviews suffice when they are in clear agreement, but often referees differ. At *Polity* we always seek commitments from three referees (including the editorial board member) to evaluate a manuscript. Three referee reports offer a better chance for a majority recommendation. Authors benefit in another way, too: a third report may provide valuable additional feedback on the manuscript. Standard practice within political science (though, interestingly, not in some of the humanities) calls for journals to share referee reports with authors.

WHAT REVIEWERS WANT AND COMMON MANUSCRIPT WEAKNESSES

Certain attributes make it much more likely that a manuscript will be accepted. First, though the point may be obvious, the piece should have something to say. Presentation also counts. Referees are partial to a manuscript that is "reader friendly." They like a clear structure: the author presents the central claims and establishes their potential significance in the opening section, identifies where the argument fits in the current scholarly conversation or debate, explains and justifies the methodology and choice of evidence, presents the evidence in a logical manner, and concludes by connecting the pieces of the argument and restating the significance of the findings. I do not mean to suggest that only manuscripts following this format will be accepted. However, if you deviate from convention, you should do so for good reason and make that reason explicit.

When I undertake the initial assessment of a manuscript submitted to *Polity*, I first look for a clear statement of the "value added" of the piece. That is, I want to know what the manuscript will contribute of significance to our understanding of political phenomena and to scholarly discourse within a field or across the discipline. Assuming the author can demonstrate through the use of appropriate evidence his/her central claims, how does the result advance some ongoing scholarly conversation? This is, of course, a basic question we pose about all scholarship—the "so what?" challenge. Graduate students are told they will face this question at any job interview. It should not surprise you, then, to learn that journal editors and referees ask the same question. If on first reading I cannot find some clear indication of the value-added of a manuscript, I usually decline to send it out for full review.

Establishing the significance of the research involves in part a judicious review of the relevant and recent literature. Scholarly conversations may be advanced through a variety of contributions. You may intervene in a discourse to clarify a theoretical point that is underdeveloped, to resolve a conflict or tension between two competing theoretical positions by bringing to bear compelling new evidence, to suggest that productive insights may be derived from combining two approaches that heretofore have not been made to speak to each other, or for some other purpose. It is essential that your point of entry into scholarly debate be made clear. Your discussion of the literature also needs to be current. Referees typically do not condemn a manuscript that is missing some recent literature, but they have little patience when the discussion of scholarship is generally outdated.

Referees also appreciate a manuscript that is well written. This point bears some emphasis because as a discipline political science is not known for lucid, graceful prose. Yet many referees comment on the quality of writing. They prefer clear, succinct expression (as do editors struggling with page limits) and dislike repetitive phrasing and excessive use of jargon.

Much as certain qualities increase the likelihood of acceptance, common weaknesses doom many submissions, even though they may have some merit. There is no excuse for ignoring a journal's stated rules about maximum length or formatting conventions. (Editors may not care whether a submission follows the journal's citation style, so long as authors realize that their manuscript will have to conform should it be accepted. If your manuscript does not use the journal's style, check before you submit to determine whether your piece will be considered.) Similarly, a manuscript stands little chance of acceptance if it has been poorly copy-edited or it suffers from many careless writing mistakes. Proofread before submission. Better yet, get a second set of eyes to do so, too.

Many manuscripts fail the value-added or significance test. Sometimes the failure occurs because the project has not been effectively situated. An author may "talk around" a scholarly conversation without making plain the manuscript's unique contribution to that discourse. Vaguely associating your work with some body of literature does not suffice. And be explicit about how you want your work to be perceived: do not expect referees to make a connection for you. Some manuscripts appear to engage a scholarly debate but on closer inspection prove to have waged a heroic battle against a straw-person caricature.

Authors also err in assuming that an analysis of an unstudied or understudied phenomenon is inherently important. At a recent panel of journal editors, John Geer, editor of the *Journal of Politics*, noted that when he comes across the word "gap," it sets off alarm bells. To fill a gap does nothing by itself to establish the importance of what is being studied. This applies to work in political theory as much as to empirical research—a manuscript on an obscure political thinker is not important merely because no one has paid attention to his/her writings before.

Problems of case selection and case-theory relations also undermine many manuscripts. Some research projects are "case-driven," that is, motivated by an interest in a particular empirical phenomenon or text, rather than by a theoretical question. One result is the "case-heavy" manuscript, rich with description and anecdotal explanations but devoid of theoretical context. It is highly unlikely that such work will be accepted by any major general political science or highly-regarded specialized journal. Prospects are not much better for "theory as an afterthought," case-driven manuscripts. Here the author recognizes that the project needs to be joined to some theoretical conversation. Unfortunately, however, because the case has not been selected to test some theoretical claim, the empirical evidence and the theoretical context are poorly integrated. The author often fails to justify the case selection, to explain how it is appropriate to adjudicate between contending theoretical perspectives or how it lets us eliminate competing explanations. In the case of political theory manuscripts, the author offers a new reading of familiar texts without explaining why we should prefer it to other interpretations.

A different kind of problem may arise with manuscripts that rest entirely upon a review of existing literature rather than upon original research. I believe such pieces may have value in suggesting new ways to view familiar phenomena, drawing upon published work in a way that generates fresh insights and that is likely to be productive in sparking future research. (Review essays fall in the same category.) In a discipline given over to highly specialized scholarship, we need work that can knit together the many scattered insights that emerge from our particular inquiries. That said, however, there is no place in major journals for the literature review that merely summarizes and restates what has been published elsewhere.

Editorial Decisions

Referees return their reports to the editor, typically accompanied by a recommendation to accept, reject, or revise-and-resubmit. (Delays may result if a referee fails to return a review by the prescribed deadline and the journal is forced to seek another evaluation.) Journal decision rules vary, from a unanimity requirement for a piece to be accepted to the more common majority principle. But the application of a decision rule may call for significant editorial discretion and represents a key point at which an editor may exercise decisive judgment. Many scholars are loathe to reject a piece outright, preferring instead to call for a drastic recasting of a weak or seriously flawed manuscript. I am guided more by the substance of the referee report. If the report effectively says the author might have the kernel of an interesting idea but essentially needs to start over from scratch, I interpret that as a rejection. Moreover, three-way split decisions are not uncommon: one reviewer recommends acceptance, one calls for rejection, and the third wants to invite resubmission after revision. Here the editor has to decide whether the positives outweigh the negatives sufficiently to justify revise-and-resubmit. Finally, not all referees are created equal. Journals may attach added weight to a report from a member of the editorial board (*Polity*'s practice) or from a reviewer with a proven track record.

As the recommendation hierarchy implies, three types of decisions are possible. First, a manuscript may be accepted or accepted pending minor revisions. Where minor revisions are needed, the piece will not be sent back to the referees for their approval. The editor decides whether the changes are satisfactory. In all but a tiny fraction of cases, a manuscript accepted pending minor revisions will be published.

Second, a manuscript may be rejected. For most journals, the editor's decision is final—there is no group to whom you can appeal a rejection. Editorial boards do not function to oversee editors; nor do the governing associations of regional journals such as *Polity* operate as a kind of appellate court for individual manuscripts. It is unlikely that you will be able to persuade an editor to reverse a rejection decision, though you might attempt to do so if you believe a referee report to be unsound or grossly unfair and you can give compelling reasons why the editor should discard it and seek another review. On the rare occasion when I made the case to an editor that a referee misconstrued something I had written or seemed to be pursuing his/her own agenda, I found the editor to be open-minded. That said, asking an editor to reconsider should be done only under exceptional circumstances. Unless the other referee reports are significantly more positive, it is a waste of time. Pursue some other publication option instead.

Third, and most problematic, a manuscript may be given a revise-and-resubmit verdict. R&R can be troubling for editors and authors alike because it sends ambiguous signals. For some journals, straightforward acceptance upon initial submission is rare and R&R signifies a positive response and a high probability of acceptance. An editor would be reluctant to invite resubmission, then, for anything other than strong manuscripts. At other journals, the invitation to submit a new version of a piece connotes nothing more than a willingness to send the revision through the full review process again. Authors may be puzzled about whether they are being encouraged to try again and what the likelihood of success is. To add to the confusion, referees may call for quite different and possibly incompatible changes.

I try to bring as much clarity to the R& R decision as possible. First, I suggest the most important criticisms to address and to identify common critical themes running through two or more referee reports. In my experience as an author, I have found this type of editorial guidance to be common, and very helpful. Second, I state clearly the review process I intend to use for a resubmission. Most journals send revised manuscripts back to the original referees. I will indicate to an author the referees (identified only by letters) to whom I plan to send the revision and how many must give an affirmative recommendation to publish in order for me to accept the piece. In the case of a "low" R&R, the manuscript may go back to all of the original referees. Some journal editors routinely explain how they will treat a resubmission, but the practice is not universal. It cannot hurt to ask how a revised manuscript would be reviewed as that may help you decide whether to pursue publication elsewhere.

A revise-and-resubmit decision places the author under no obligation. You may take your manuscript to another journal or, if major changes are required or your research focus shifts, choose to abandon it. Journals may set a deadline after which they will not consider a revision or simply treat it as a new submission. Few journals will follow up to inquire about your intention to resubmit.

DEALING WITH REJECTION

Sooner or later a manuscript you submit will be rejected. Indeed, it may well be the first piece you submit precisely because you lack experience and are thus prone to the mistakes beginners make. And since you also may not have the self-confidence that prior success helps engender, rejection may hit you very hard. Draw comfort from the fact that we have all gone through it. You do need to develop a thick skin because many manuscripts have to be submitted to more than one journal before being accepted.

If you treat rejection as a means by which to secure useful critical feedback, moreover, it can have a constructive value. The day you receive the bad news and read the referee reports for the first time, you may feel a certain defensiveness. I speak from experience here. I have read anonymous readers' reports that (I was certain!) misconstrued or misunderstood my arguments, chastised me for not having read something I should have read (sometimes written, I churlishly suspected, by none other than the referee), or suggested I revise my submission to produce the entirely different article the referee thought I should have been writing. But when you look again at the reports after a few days, you may well have a different reaction. You will see that several scholars have taken a good deal of time to offer detailed and thoughtful comments that point out inconsistencies in your analysis, note that your evidence falls well short of confirming your initial claims, suggest different ways of looking at your subject that may yield fruitful insights, call your attention to vital scholarship you overlooked or to work in related subfields that may shed new light on the case(s) you have examined, and encourage you to be bolder (or perhaps more responsible) in your conclusions. In my two years as editor of *Polity*, I have been impressed with the consistent professionalism of the scholars who offer their time to help improve manuscripts even when recommending rejection.

Recognizing that the referee reports you received represent the opinions only of those scholars, you may want to send the piece out immediately to another journal. I advise you to take some time first to incorporate some of the suggestions and address some of the criticisms the referees have raised. There is one very practical reason for doing so. The manuscript may end up in the hands of the same referee(s), solicited now by Journal Two. Although editors may prefer to have a manuscript seen by fresh eyes, we also like to know whether an author responds to feedback constructively. Few referees will be positively inclined toward a piece the second time if the author has simply ignored their suggestions from the first review. Further, almost any piece will be improved through a revision based on thoughtful critical comments. Why send a flawed manuscript to another journal when the opportunity to improve it has been handed to you?

Conclusion

The reviewing process at scholarly journals is designed to put manuscripts through a rigorous process of peer evaluation. Although it is less than perfect, it yields scholarship of high quality and helps improve that scholarship through the review process itself. It is not hard to see where error can occur. Human judgment plays an important part in the evaluation of a piece from the initial submission through the blind review by outside evaluators to the final decision by the editor. An editor may be too quick to dismiss a manuscript up front; referees may harbor an animus to a certain type of scholarship that they choose not to disclose to an editor; or an editor may give undue weight to one negative report that is detailed to the point of nitpicking at the expense of briefer but more positive assessments. For all that, most scholars want to encourage good work, even where they disagree with an author's claims. I have read favorable reports by scholars whose own views were under attack in a manuscript. On the other side, I can count the number of reviews that struck a demeaning and unprofessional tone on the fingers of one hand.

As with many human activities, one can only learn so much about getting published from reading about it or listening to those who have done it. You need to try it yourself—to put your scholarship out there to be judged by others and steel yourself for the early lumps you may take along the way. Expect some frustration. But understand, too, that when your manuscript is accepted, you will have accomplished something quite remarkable—you will have made an original contribution to what the community of scholars knows about politics.

NOTE

*   I wish to thank Jack Jacobs, Lenny Markovitz, Michael Hiscox, and the graduate students at the CUNY Graduate Center and Harvard University for many useful suggestions and comments on the presentations that served as the basis for this article. I have incorporated ideas offered by Jim Jackson, Marianne Stewart, and John Geer at an editors' roundtable in which we participated at the 2006 Midwest Political Science Association meeting. Bob Lineberry and two anonymous referees helped me to clarify certain points in the manuscript. I am responsible for any errors that remain.

ALEX HOLZMAN, TEMPLE UNIVERSITY PRESS

THE QUERY LETTER AND PROPOSAL AS SALES TOOLS

13

It is a truth universally acknowledged, that a new scholar in possession of a revised dissertation must be in want of a publisher.

Did I get your attention with that sentence? It is, as you likely recognize, a riff on one of the most famous first lines in fiction, to be found in its vastly superior original form in Jane Austen's *Pride and Prejudice*. And it illustrates, at the risk of sending Ms. Austen into a spin in her grave, a first principle for anyone approaching a publisher with a book proposal. You need a hook.

Why do you need a hook? Because securing the attention of editors beset by multiple tasks—high volumes of (e)mail, travel to campuses and conferences, and mediating between authors and multiple elements of a press—requires some selling. Think of it this way: the average university press publishes far, far fewer than 10% of the projects it considers. Indeed, the real number is probably around 2% or 3%. So why should it publish yours? You've got just a couple of moments to impress—start selling.

Elsewhere in this volume, Leanne Anderson has written on the etiquette of publishing relationships and Jennifer Knerr includes a thorough section on developing a quality book proposal in her chapter on negotiating a book contract. This chapter focuses primarily on the query letter, where you introduce yourself and your project, before touching briefly on the proposal. There are lots of do's and don'ts, but let's start by looking at some larger issues that get condensed into the query letter.

First, though, a little background that may help explain my perspective. I began my publishing career as a textbook sales rep—then euphemistically referred to as a "college traveler"—and continued selling at a couple of presses for a total of nine years, gradually adding additional responsibilities. When I switched over to acquisitions editing, I was immediately struck by the similarities to textbook sales. With the latter, you have an explicit product, the book, to sell to a specific audience, teachers of the courses for which the book is meant (not the students, the teachers—but that's another discussion). In acquisitions, you sell the attractiveness of your list to new authors by stressing its qualities, like the existing authors whose company a new author would join, the press and its services, and your own qualities as an editor.

It is not much of a stretch from that perspective to conclude that it's your job as author to sell your project and yourself to the publisher. You are selling the quality, clarity, relevance, and originality of your scholarship, your ability to write, and your reliability as author. You have, via the query letter and proposal, only a very brief time to get your positive message across. If the importance that I place on having a good query letter and proposal only adds to the already tense situation created by the tenure clock's loud ticking, take solace in this: editors must find good projects if their careers and publishing houses are to survive. As a general principle, editors want to buy; but they want to buy very selectively. Only the best products will do for their institutions and their personal (all editors take their lists personally) lists.

So, how to proceed? What should a good query letter achieve? What should a good proposal achieve? Simply put, the letter should make me want to see the proposal and the proposal should make me want to see the manuscript for possible publication. Note that for possible publication is not the same as for possible reading. I read books all the time that I wouldn't dream of publishing. And, as Leanne Anderson indicates, one of the little secrets of academic publishing is that editors often publish books they haven't read *in toto*.

As simple as it sounds, the single most important requirement for stimulating a publishers' enthusiasm for your project is to believe in it yourself. If you aren't convinced that yours is an important book worth publishing, then there is no way you're going to convince an editor. So get rid of all the "I thinks" and "perhaps" and "it is possibles" in your academic arsenal. It is time for assertive, straightforward (read, active voice) writing. Show some enthusiasm!

What goes into the letter? As you know by now, I believe in strong starts. It won't kill your project to start by saying "I'm writing to ask if Great Press would be interested in my manuscript," but it's pretty obvious that's why you're writing, isn't it? So jump in with that hook. "My new manuscript uses focus groups and survey research to show that voters choose candidates based on their home state. This directly challenges earlier research, including that by Political Genius in her prizewinning *Why Home States Don't Matter.*" In two sentences you've made a good start on telling me your manuscript's content, importance, research methodology, and relationship to the existing literature. There's a pretty darned good chance I'm going to move on to the third. (Don't laugh—I don't know any acquisitions editor who hasn't rejected proposals upon reading the first sentence of the query letter.)

Once you've gotten my attention, it's okay to fill out the description and address some other issues. If this is a revised dissertation, tell me it's based on work that started that way and tell me just enough about how it's evolved to convince me that this isn't still in too raw a form to be published. Tell me why the book is suited to my press. Is it because my press has a strong list in that field? Have I worked on a strong list in the field elsewhere and recently moved to this press? Does my press have a particular series where you think the book would fit? Why?

Though you may—in both the sense of it is permitted and you might—repeat the information in the proposal itself, it's a good idea to indicate how long the manuscript runs and how much is in a state you're prepared to have others read. You might be getting letters out a little early to gauge interest, but already have a couple of chapters available for the editor now. If so, fine—but do indicate when you think a full manuscript might be ready for inspection. And for heaven's sake, be honest about the word count. This includes footnotes, appendices, bibliographies, prefaces, anything that includes words! You will not win any friends if you say it's a 90,000-word manuscript but neglect to mention that you're not counting the 50,000 words of notes. Sooner or later that little fact will reveal itself and earn you some bad will.

If the project includes a significant amount of tabular material, line art, or halftones, do mention it briefly. If such content is minimal (I realize that's a subjective word, but use common sense), I've always felt it's fine to omit it from the query letter, but mention it in the more detailed proposal. But this is a good place to say that different editors have different preferences. Do peruse the web site of any publisher you're thinking of approaching and follow any specific instructions on what to submit. The principles we've been discussing here will still apply. And clear, concise letters always impress.

Your query letter should also recognize, at least implicitly, that you and the editor have different sets of expertise. Unless you had a publishing career before returning to academe (it happens), your expertise is the subject matter of your book and, more widely, your field. The publisher's expertise includes all things publishing. By all means, suggest that the book might fit in a particular series, and do suggest the audience you think would be most interested in it. But do recognize that on these matters you are not the expert. If you're going to venture into the editor's expertise, then, to borrow a phrase from creative writing programs, show, don't tell. If you're suggesting your work fits a particular series, mention how it relates to another title or two in the series. If you think the audience includes multiple fields and subfields, provide a little evidence. And frame both of the above as impressions you've formed, not as absolute truth. This does not mean reverting back to endlessly qualified academic-writing; it does mean using a little subtlety to demonstrate that you're making suggestions the editor—who in this case really does have more expertise in the matter—may wish to consider.

I offer a slightly extreme example to make a point. More query letters than I care to remember assert that a book will appeal to political scientists, sociologists, area studies specialists, anthropologists, professors, grad students, undergraduate students, and the "interested

general reader." That's pretty unlikely. Mention just the core audience—
let's say specialists in voting behavior and comparative politics—and
leave it to the editor to decide if there are other possible markets. And
if you've made a conscious effort to write to an undergraduate level, by
all means say so; but let the editor decide if you've been successful and
whether the subject matter will actually sell to that audience. A little
humility in recognizing each other's areas of greater expertise can go a
long way toward a good author-editor relationship.

OK, let's say you've decided upon which editors and presses you want
to contact and you have the basis of a good generic query letter. How
do you personalize each one? Should you? In my opinion, you should—
showing that you know a particular list or have reasons for contacting a
particular publisher indicates that you know the field in which you hope
to publish and that you respect the editor's time enough to have done your
research; this is an important first step in establishing a good rapport. And
by personalizing, you'll probably keep from contacting too many presses
at once. While there are no rules governing the number of initial queries,
the exercise of starting with a handful—say up to five—will force you to
think about where your manuscript really will fit best. If you've researched
publishers well, odds are at least one or two will respond positively; if it
turns out that none decide to pursue the project further, then first take a
good, honest look at your query and proposal to be sure it actively represents
your work. If it does, then move on to a new set of potential homes for your
work; if it doesn't, then revise it before sending out another round.

The first rule of personalizing a query letter is to send it to a
specific editor. Press web sites will usually supply this information,
though where there are overlapping editorial responsibilities the answer
may not be entirely clear. Colleagues, Google searches, and glances at
the acknowledgements pages of the press's books that relate most closely
to your work should resolve the mystery.

Once you identify the editor, start with your hook, then launch into
the specifics of why this editor and this press. If the editor has published
an author who recommended the press, say so. (Indeed, if you have a
common contact who knows the editor, it's a good idea to have that

person send a separate note recommending your project.) Don't overdue things—provide just enough detail to make it clear that you've gone to the trouble of researching the press. Some editors will value this more than others, but no editor will hold it against you for doing this homework.

There is one huge caveat about the mechanics of personalizing query letters: Be sure you send the right version to the right press! This sounds elementary, but you'd be surprised. All editors have received query letters addressed to someone at another press. We get a chuckle out of it and personally I won't let that keep me from reading on, but it's pretty darned embarrassing and not the indication you want to send regarding your care and thoroughness as a scholar.

The prevalence of email has increased the opportunity for error. If your query letter is by and large cut and paste, but personalized just a bit, there's always a danger that you changed a word or phrase in the "standard" part of the letter that personalizes it as well. Be sure you've thoroughly scrubbed and fixed the document as you send it to each editor. I've received correctly addressed queries citing something about another press's list or a "colleague" who actually works elsewhere.

Finally, proofread both query letter and proposal again and again. Share them with colleagues, family, or friends and have them proofread. In the same way you don't send a cover letter and vita off with typos when applying for a job, you don't send a typo-riddled or grammatically incorrect query letter and proposal to a publisher. As always, individual editors will vary in the degree to which they're bothered by this, but typos are pure negatives. Though they won't stop an editor in her tracks, typos and grammatical errors will create worries, however mild, that the entire project may be marked by carelessness. Repeated typos cause editors to ratchet up the line for copyediting in the mental project budgets they start to form as they read your materials. This can prove fatal for a project that seems intellectually fine but that straddles the economic borderline of feasibility.

To sum up, query letters should be short, well-written, enthusiastic documents that start to convince an editor that he wants to publish your work as much as you want him to.

THE PROPOSAL

All of the general rules I've described for query letters—direct, clear, typo-free writing—apply to a proposal as well and needn't be rehashed. Proposals differ from query letters in that they do not need to be tailored for each press beyond any specific requirements in that press's manuscript submission guidelines. A first-sentence hook may not be as important here, but an overall hook certainly is. Continue to build the editor's enthusiasm for the core elements of your work.

There are several ways to organize a proposal and sometimes the nature of the project will also dictate form; so long as you convey the necessary information clearly, exact form is not critical. You might write a straight narrative divided into sections for areas like market, competition, timetable for completion, and table of contents. Or you might present a brief description of the project's overall themes followed by an annotated table of contents (my own personal favorite). Editors' preferences on form vary in that they may or may not want particular content. For example, I am not much interested in suggestions for potential outside readers until I actually decide I want to start the peer-review process, but Jennifer Knerr includes reviewers in her excellent list of items to include in a good proposal (see chapter 14). Again, specific details are often available at the press's web site. What's important is that you provide enough information to give a full and realistic portrait of the project.

The proposal should always include information about the nature and the state of the manuscript (completed, partial), the schedule for completion, your *modest* (see above) assessment of market, and any special information, such as the need to clear an unusually large number of permissions or to include art. In addition, indicate whether any part of the manuscript has already been published in article form. Editors will differ on their assessment of how much of a manuscript can be previously published (I generally think that while one or two articles generally whet the appetite for a book, more tend to satiate it and hinder sales), and it is to some extent project-specific, but it is critical that you be upfront about previously published material from the start. You will garner much ill-will if you inform an editor that half the book has appeared in article form after the review process has begun.

A good proposal needn't be terribly long. Though I hesitate to be prescriptive, something around 10–12 pages, with a margin of grace on either side, should suffice. If not, ask yourself what you're including that isn't essential or what you're omitting that is. The real rule is this: include everything you need for the editor to form a good sense of what the project is about, but no more than that.

My parting suggestion—and everything here is suggestion, not rule—is to approach the entire exercise of finding a publisher with a positive frame of mind. You've got a terrific project and you're about to encounter people whose goal is to publish first-class projects. There is nothing adversarial about the process. Even negative responses—at any point in the publishing process—are offered in the spirit of allowing you to publish your work in a form that will reach the largest audience that can benefit from your scholarship. And that should in the end be nothing less than a joy. Good luck!

REFERENCES

Anderson, Leanne. 2008. "The Etiquette of Publishing." In *Publishing Political Science: The APSA Guide to Writing and Publishing*, ed. Stephen Yoder. Washington, D.C.: American Political Science Association, 241–53.

Knerr, Jennifer. 2008. "Negotiating a Book Contract with Grace, Finesse, and Success." In *Publishing Political Science: The APSA Guide to Writing and Publishing*, ed. Stephen Yoder. Washington, D.C.: American Political Science Association, 221–40.

14

NEGOTIATING A BOOK CONTRACT WITH GRACE, FINESSE, AND SUCCESS

Signing a contract is an important event in the life of a book, its author, and its publisher. It is an end in itself, but it is usually only the beginning of a process that can lead to a long, productive publishing relationship—or not. With the long view in mind, I'd like to introduce a process I characterize as "win-win" contract negotiations designed to launch the book publishing process on the right foot and keep it moving forward as a publishing partnership from beginning to new beginning.

DEVELOP A QUALITY BOOK PROPOSAL

First impressions are important and the best way to ensure that you will get a contract offer in a timely fashion is to submit a proposal that leaps out of the daily pile of mail or email that engulfs acquisitions editors. Proposals come in many sizes and shapes, but the best do the following:

a) Have a title that is descriptive of a topic of interest. Titles can be cute or too cute, but the best are straightforward and striking.

b) Begin with a short, succinct statement summarizing the book and why it matters.

c) Include an outline or table of contents of what the book will cover.

d) Position the work in the field, discussing both related scholarship and market competitors or complements. How will your book make a contribution to what is out there? How is it different and how is it at least as good as what has been published? Don't include a full literature review, but name some books with which the editor is familiar. That said, it is not particularly useful to claim that your book will be the next Freakonomics—as much as everyone wishes it would be.

e) Have a clear view of the book's audience—peers, students, researchers, journalists, policymakers, or that most ephemeral quantity, the "educated lay public." If aiming for this last audience, be prepared for greater skepticism and careful scrutiny of your publishing record and media contacts.

f) Present your credentials in a succinct and persuasive statement. By all means, include your CV, but highlight related publications, media spotlights, teaching and research activities, and other relevant features in the body of the proposal itself.

g) Include or offer a sample chapter. When submitting a sample, make sure it is written for the audience you have identified as your main target—i.e., don't submit a journal article written for your peers if the book is intended for student or general audiences.

h) Suggest qualified reviewers for your project; most editors will welcome such suggestions and use them to formulate an appropriate review panel even if they don't or can't recruit those specific reviewers.

i) Make sure the proposal is nicely formatted, edited, and proofread before sending it off. Remember, more is not necessarily better, but enough is essential.

CHOOSE PUBLISHER CANDIDATES CAREFULLY

No matter what your tenure committee has told you, not every book is right for Oxford or Cambridge university presses. Even if it is, not every topic or author can wait for the lengthy review and publication process often required by the most distinguished presses. And while everyone would like to write the next Random House bestseller, very few will.

Just as it is no use submitting a proposal for a work of social science nonfiction to a press devoted to novels and poetry, it is equally futile sending U.S. public policy treatises to a publisher focused on international relations or a proposal on Latin America to a publisher who publishes only works on Asia and the Middle East. Find books in your field that you admire and research where they are published. Carefully match the kind of book you are writing to the kind of publisher who has done such books well. Start with content: Which publishers appear most frequently in your own book's bibliography? If writing a textbook, go to a textbook publisher; but if writing a research monograph, start with a university press. If there is a regional connection to your subject, regional presses (whether academic or trade) might be especially receptive to your work. And if you are writing a hybrid book, be open to hybrid presses that publish multidisciplinary, cross-market books in your subject area.

Once you have selected a set of appropriate publishers, learn about their staff and procedures before submitting your proposal. Does the press consider complete manuscripts or only proposals? If your submission is a dissertation, revise it first before submitting it for consideration, or at least have a clear revision plan to offer. Your dissertation committee is not always best equipped to judge how ready a dissertation is to submit to a book publisher; seek fresh advice.

Find out who the appropriate editor is for your subject. Can you get a referral from an author already published by the press? An editor will respond much more quickly to a name he or she knows than to an unknown inquirer. Always address your proposal to an editor by name, asking that person to pass the proposal along to the appropriate editor if necessary.

PROCESS AND PRIORITY

Once you have gotten in the door, be up front about process and priority. If you have made multiple submissions of the proposal, say so. Some presses require exclusive submission to protect their time and review resources; ascertain this before sending out multiple submissions. Decide whether it is worth it to spend the time those presses require in an exclusive process that may not result in a contract. Ask for a general decision timeline; presses, subject to the same reviewer whims as journals, cannot guarantee a specific decision date, but their best estimate can help you better manage your time.

Commercial presses are usually more open to multiple submissions than are university presses, but not always. In either case, keep publishers apprised of where you are in your own decision process—e.g., letting editors know when you've received reviews or contract offers from other presses, especially if you are still open to further offers.

At this stage of the contract process, it is helpful to know your own priorities and to communicate them in a way that is clear but undemanding. Some to consider include:

a) Turnaround time—for contract, but then later, for publication.
b) Prestige.
c) Editorial attention.
d) Marketing.
e) Advance.
f) Royalties.
g) Format (hardcover, paperback, trade) and price of publication.

Be prepared to state what is most important to you and how you will evaluate any contract offer you may receive. Subjective values are more difficult to quantify but will likely play a role and should be acknowledged.

FLEXIBILITY

If a publisher has questions, suggestions, review input, alternate production or publication strategies, or other kinds of feedback to share, be open to new ways of thinking about the book you have proposed. Flexibility is a two-way street and you can gauge your publisher's openness to new ideas in your response. It is a rare proposal that is accepted for contract immediately and without refinement. Changes in the proposal may be called for before a contract is offered, or a contract may be offered based on an understanding of changes in the project as it develops. Either way, flexibility at both the pre-contract and contract stages is the best indicator of how the publishing partnership will go—hand in hand or hand-to-hand combat.

HOW TO CONSIDER A CONTRACT OFFER

If the process has gone well, you will have a fair contract to consider. Compare it to your stated objectives and priorities—does it meet them? Then look at the contract in light of the unstated process—does it feel right?

- If you have questions, ask them. If there is any room for ambiguity (e.g., about expected changes after signing a contract, about marketing commitments, etc.), get clarification in writing.

- If you have strong needs, register them, preferably right from the beginning but certainly at the contract stage. Do you have an important story to tell but need editorial help to tell it well? Do you require an advance to cover expenses incurred in completing the project? Don't leave discussion or acknowledgement of these needs until the end or (heaven forbid) after the contract process.

- Don't rewrite the contract—e.g., if all pronouns are male, leave them that way, even if it feels uncomfortable. Realize that most publishing contracts are "boilerplate" and that only a few variables exist and matter. Nothing derails a contract process faster than an author who wants to reinvent the contract wheel that has served the publisher well for so many books and years.

- Pick your battles and don't sweat the small stuff.

- But get in writing any major terms or concerns that are exceptions to the boilerplate rule. Be clear on who has responsibility for what, remembering that it is a publishing *partnership*.

COMMON CONTRACT NEGOTIATION POINTS

When it comes to negotiations, George W. Bush is fond of saying that everything is on the table, but when it comes to book contracts, only a few items really count. Here are some of the most important contract variables that authors and publishers focus on and various ways to approach them:

Author

Are you the sole author, a co-author among equals, an editor with contributors, or an agent of a separate institution that is truly responsible for fulfilling the terms of the contract? If you have a co-author, what are your respective responsibilities and what happens if a co-author does not fulfill them? If an outside entity is involved, do you have the rights to or want the responsibility of signing the contract on behalf of the institution? Be sure to understand fully who is encompassed by the "Author" designation and what rights and responsibilities are associated with it.

Working Title

Usually this is based on the proposal or manuscript title the author has submitted, but it may be refined in the review and acceptance process and is subject to further refinement after contract signing. Be aware that publishers often want to modify titles in connection with their marketing-staff recommendations, often in response to reviews or other market indicators later in the manuscript development process. Authors should welcome this input but may want to reserve the right to approve the final title.

Negotiating Points:

- If a particular title is important to you, be sure to negotiate its acceptance before signing the contract and modify the contract accordingly (i.e., final title instead of working title).
- Retain the right to approve a final title change.

Due Date

Just as authors may schedule a sabbatical or teaching relief in order to work on book manuscripts, publishers make publishing plans, production schedules, and sales projections based on contract due dates. When committing to a due date, be sure to understand whether it is a first draft due date or a final manuscript due date—if the latter, allow time for the review and revision process. It is best to be realistic when estimating and committing to a manuscript due date.

If a publisher is pushing an author for a particular manuscript due date, it is for a reason—usually to ensure a timely publication date related to the book's topic or to a targeted publishing season (e.g., textbook exam copy timelines). Authors should determine whether such timelines are feasible and beneficial to the author's own interests. In a true publishing partnership, author interests and publisher interests are aligned, but sometimes a publisher may push an author to deliver a manuscript for reasons unrelated to the interests of the author or the book—e.g., to make a publishing quota.

To reiterate, it's important to be clear about what you are committing to, and then to be sure that you can realistically achieve it. What will happen if a due date is missed? Authors and publishers frequently agree to revised manuscript due dates in the course of a project's development, but it's important to communicate these changes and get agreement in writing (even if only by email) for changes that shift a project from one season to another or—especially—from year to year.

Negotiating Points:

- If the publisher is pressing for a particular final manuscript due date to make a particular publishing season, tie it to an advance payment for on-time performance.
- If it isn't written into the contract, add a clause stating that author and publisher can mutually agree to extend the due date.

Length

Manuscript length is often stated in terms of word count, and word counts are easy to get with word processing software. But does the word count include every element of your manuscript—e.g., table of contents, notes, bibliography, appendices, and, especially, art? Art is best counted not by words but by space allotment (e.g., numbers of pieces or pages allotted to art). Many contracts stipulate art counts separately from the word count; if yours does not, and if your manuscript will have numerous figures and tables, get an art limit or allotment built into the manuscript length.

Negotiating Point:

- Length and book price are intertwined, so if you agree to a shorter book than proposed, tie it to an agreed upon target retail price, realizing that other production or market factors may affect final pricing.

Art

In addition to the impact on length, art poses many publishing challenges for both author and publisher. Figures and tables must be prepared in a certain way to be acceptable. Photos must be provided at a certain level of resolution in order to print well in a finished book. Original art requires special planning and handling. Maps may be simple or complex, may draw on public domain base maps or be specially contracted projections or overlays. Color is very expensive. If your project includes art, be sure art specifications and responsibilities are clearly explained before contract signing. Do not assume that anything on the Internet is reproducible and permissible.

Negotiating Points:

- Who will prepare the final art and according to what specifications?
- Who will pay for art preparation?
- If the author agrees to prepare or secure camera-ready art, will it lower the price of the book?

Permissions

Both art elements and manuscript elements may be subject to reprint permission. Be sure the contract explains who is responsible for both securing and paying permissions. Also ascertain the timing of the permissions relative to the final manuscript due date; usually they are due simultaneously. The permissions baseline holds authors responsible for all permissions responsibilities. In big textbook projects, anthologies of previously published works, or art projects (among others) permissions may be negotiable. A typical textbook scenario may propose splitting permissions fees between author and publisher, with the author's portion charged against future royalties as an advance. Some publishers have permissions divisions that will handle the securing of permissions for a big project, but others require authors to do the legwork. If a project requires securing permission to reprint the author's own work, the author will be able to get such permission more readily and inexpensively (usually without a fee at all) than will the publisher.

Negotiating Points:

- Who will seek permissions?
- Who will pay for permissions?
- Can author payment for permissions be charged against royalties?

Acceptability

Most book contracts are written contingent upon acceptance by the publisher. Acceptability includes both form and content elements. Most contracts spell out what is meant by an acceptable or satisfactory manuscript, and most allow the author the chance to rectify unsatisfactory elements. If there is any question about revisions to an existing manuscript at the time of contract signing, it is important to understand what must occur in order to satisfy the acceptability clause. Most contracts (if not all) reserve the publisher's right to judge final acceptability, and this is not negotiable; the upfront understanding of what constitutes acceptability and how to achieve it is. These are important conversations to have (and record in writing) before signing a contract and throughout manuscript development.

Some contracts are written as "advance" contracts, explicitly signaling the fact that a publishing commitment is contingent upon the development and acceptance of a manuscript that has yet to be written or revised to satisfaction. This is not much different from other contracts in effect, since all are predicated on this contingency. But advance contracts may "feel" more tentative than others.

Negotiating Points:

- If not written into the contract, request a clause that requires the publisher to allow the author the chance to revise the manuscript according to written parameters of acceptability. Such a clause should outline the process and timeframe for acceptance, rejection, and revision.
- Make sure there is a contract clause stating that substantive changes will not be made in the work without author approval.

Copyright

Contracts typically stipulate that the publisher will copyright the work in the publisher's name and that it will publish and register the work with the U.S. Copyright Office and with copyright offices abroad, if relevant. Authors often will negotiate retention of copyright in the author's name. Publishers are usually flexible in ceding this right, because within the same contract the author is granting the publisher the exclusive right to publish, sell, distribute, and otherwise disseminate the work in the U.S. and abroad. Copyright and publication rights are two different things, and an author's retention of copyright does not entitle the author to publish or otherwise disseminate the work in question elsewhere.

Negotiating Points:

- If the author retains copyright, who will file the copyright registration and Library of Congress data?
- If the publisher holds copyright, request the reversion of those rights to the author when the work is put out of print.

Publication Rights

Publishers want to retain exclusive rights to publish, sell, and distribute the work in all countries and all media, now known or yet to be developed. The open-endedness of this last point is a direct result of the Internet and electronic media like DVDs, iPods, e-books, and the like. Over the past 20 years or so, publishers have spent a lot of time and money revising and renegotiating existing contracts to gain electronic rights to work they otherwise control. This is an experience publishers don't want to repeat; hence the blanket claim to rights in media "known and unknown" or "yet to be developed."

Most contracts spell out the royalty distribution to the author from the sale of the work in various countries and media. The author can negotiate any or all of these points, but if the author retains electronic rights to a work, for instance, it may inhibit a publisher from advertising the work on a web site, sending out electronic promotions, or licensing the work to an electronic library service—all actions that are beneficial to the author and the work. When negotiating the retention of foreign rights, be aware that if the contract is too restrictive the publisher may choose not to pursue any foreign rights at all, leaving them all to the author to pursue.

Authors are obliged to seek from the publisher what is typically considered a courtesy permission to reprint from the contracted work in journal articles and other scholarly outlets. Fair use of one's own work doesn't require written permission. But publishers may deny authors (by contract or in declining written permission) use of the work in competing works, or they may charge for such use.

Negotiating Points:

- Authors who have special contacts with foreign publishers may want to retain foreign rights in particular languages, but if you have no such contacts, it may pay off to allow the publisher to retain foreign rights and list your book in its foreign rights catalogue.

- Authors may want to negotiate nonexclusive rights so that both author and publisher can be active in exploiting rights in alternate media.

- Publishers are usually happy to allow scholarly authors movie rights to their work.

Style and Manner of Publication

Publishers want to retain the right to publish if, how, when, and at what price they determine appropriate. Authors can negotiate consultation or even approval on some matters—e.g., cover design—but publishers grant such approvals reluctantly. Authors should clearly understand whether the work will be published in hardcover, paperback, electronically, or otherwise. The timing of paperback releases and other such questions may be negotiated or left open.

Negotiating Points:

- Authors may request consultation or even approval on cover design, but publishers may resist.

- Price of book is determined by many factors, but authors can leverage length, art, and other cost factors in influencing the price of the finished book.

- If a hardcover library edition will be published first, authors should negotiate a commitment to a later paperback edition under certain circumstances—e.g., the achievement of a stated sales threshold.

Editorial and Production Services

Different books are treated in different ways by different publishers. Questions to ask if the answers are not enumerated in the contract include: Will the manuscript be copyedited? Proofread? Professionally typeset? Will the publisher commission an indexer if you do not wish to compile the index yourself? If so, how will the indexer be paid?

Narrow scholarly monographs and technical scientific books are often placed under contract with the expectation that the author will do the production work and provide camera-ready copy or press-ready files. Many authors have access to production units through their universities and publishing software is better and cheaper than ever. Nonetheless, an author inexperienced in book production will find it a challenge.

Editorial and production services may sometimes be traded off for royalties, and sometimes the publisher is able to provide such services for a fee. Freelance production services are also available, although they may be expensive for a new client who is likely a one-time patron. Editorial and production services are expensive and valuable commodities no matter who is providing them, so it is important not to take them for granted.

Negotiating Points:

- If the publisher requires camera-ready copy, request proofreading before final production.
- Offer to forgo royalties if the publisher will agree to copyediting and/or typesetting.

Warranty and Indemnification

Contracts require the author to warrant that the work is original, that the author is the sole owner of the work, that it does not violate another's copyright (except as provided for by written reprint permission), and that it is not libelous, obscene, or unlawful. Contracts almost always explicitly state that a publisher has the right to cancel a contract if the publisher determines any legal difficulty, and short of canceling a contract, authors are required to make changes in manuscripts demanded by the publisher's legal counsel or based on legal assessments.

Contracts also require the author to indemnify the publisher against any legal claim based on author warranties. Indemnification clauses may sound pretty intimidating and demanding—and they are. Authors may feel uncomfortable signing a blanket indemnification but publishers rarely will negotiate this point. Authors can add stipulations to this part of the contract—such as being able to represent themselves (at their own expense) in any legal proceeding—but they cannot strike warranty and indemnification from the contract. The last thing a publisher wants is a lawsuit because of an author's actions or negligence, and it is frequently the case that if a suit is brought, it is brought against the publisher rather than the author (i.e., the unwritten "deeper pockets" rule). Deep pockets or not, many publishers can ill afford a court case—regardless of who wins or loses.

A final note: No warranty or indemnification can ward against crackpot lawsuits, but authors can and must be the strongest bulwark against legal claims by ensuring that their manuscripts conform to the letter of all copyright and libel laws.

Negotiating Point:

- Authors can request the addition of a clause allowing the author to represent him/herself in any legal proceeding, but this will be granted only at the author's expense.

Royalties

Royalties are usually expressed as a percentage of net sales, meaning the total revenue after all discounts are taken by the various wholesalers and bookstores. Some royalty offers are for a flat percentage whereas others start lower and escalate as sales increase over time. Different royalty rates may apply to the hardcover book compared to the paperback edition, or to trade editions, mass-market paperbacks, and other forms of publication. When many authors think about contract negotiations, they think first about royalties. But royalties are connected to many other publishing factors and cannot be negotiated in the abstract.

The primary factors in determining royalty rates are the cost of publication compared to the book's market and sales potential. In scholarly publishing, royalties may not be offered for the first 500 copies sold to allow publishers to recoup publication costs before paying royalties, and even thereafter, royalty rates may be low (i.e., 5–7%). In textbook publishing, rates are higher but likely escalate over time as the textbook catches on and covers what are usually steep costs of production. In trade-book publishing, it is often the question of mandatory deep discounts that governs what royalty rate is offered, especially if the royalty is based on the usually low retail price of the book instead of on net sales.

When negotiating royalties, it is usually easier to negotiate an escalation at the high end than it is to raise the royalty start point. For scholarly publishing, it is important to weigh what the publisher is providing in terms of services (editing, typesetting, marketing, and sales) against higher royalties. Given the many stories about price gouging by textbook publishers, there may be a trade-off between beginning royalty rates and the price of the book; a lower royalty rate may allow a lower retail price of the text, providing a competitive advantage and helping the text catch on. At the same time, it is reasonable to ask whether authors must bear the brunt of the commitment to keeping textbook prices low.

Negotiating Points:

- If royalties start at a low point (or if there are no initial royalties), negotiate a lower price on the initial release of the book.
- Request that low starting royalties escalate quickly—e.g., after 1,000 copies are sold.
- If the upper limit of royalties offered tops out at 10% or less, request an additional escalation (e.g., to 12%) after 5,000 copies are sold.

Advances

Advance payments against future royalties are offered for books that are expected to sell well beyond the costs of publication, usually textbooks and trade books. Advances may come in several forms, some of which are more apparent than others. For instance, if a contract stipulates that an author is responsible for providing an index to the work, and if the publisher agrees to contract out the index with its cost charged against royalties—that's an advance (and not an insignificant one). As mentioned earlier, permission fees may be charged against royalties as an advance. Or an advance may be paid outright, sometimes in response to expressed needs on the part of the author (for office supplies, research assistance, release time, etc.).

Some authors measure the commitment of the publisher to the project or the estimation of the author's reputation by the publisher according to the advance amount offered. Sometimes such a relationship exists, but other times a trade-off may come into play. Publishers must choose where to invest their finite resources. A large advance may in fact take monies from those which could be invested in production or promotion of the finished work.

Advances can be calculated in several ways at several different levels, but a common metric is the royalty payment that would accrue to the author in the book's first year of sales. Remember that an advance is not a grant and must be "earned out." If a contract is cancelled before a book is published, the author is often required by contract to return any advance monies.

Negotiating Points:

- If even a small advance is important but not offered, request an advance payable only upon manuscript delivery or acceptance.
- If an advance is traded off for marketing and promotional promises, get it in writing.
- If no advance is offered, can the index fees be charged against royalties?
- Can permissions be charged against royalties as an advance?

Author Copies

This is a common point of negotiation between author and publisher. If a publisher offers to send out free copies for promotional purposes, the need for additional author copies may decrease, but authors are frequently able to procure additional author copies in the initial agreement. Many contracts offer the author a discount for purchasing copies of the work after the initial distribution. If an author anticipates purchasing a significant number of copies and registers this intent with the publisher prior to the book's going to press, the author can often negotiate an even better discount.

Negotiating Points:

- Request additional author copies for personal distribution.
- Request that the publisher send out a specified number of promotional copies to names and institutions on a list supplied by the author.

Revision Clauses

Most relevant to textbooks, revision clauses cause authors anguish oftentimes needlessly. If your book is a research monograph or other one-time, single-purpose book, you can often successfully request that the revision clause be entirely struck from the contract since all will agree the work's reviseability is limited.

If, however, you are consciously writing a textbook, the revision clause is very important from both the author's and the publisher's points of view. For the author, the amount of notice time for completing a revision is of the essence, especially the first time around. Once a textbook is determined a success, a revision cycle will likely be established at regular intervals to accord with market conditions and the competition. Publishers consider textbook revisions very important to their business and will insist on the right to revise a successful textbook with or without the original author's participation. Thus, it is extremely important that the contract explicitly detail the circumstances under which a revision may be completed without the participation of the original author or with the addition of co-authors. Factors to consider include at what time a co-author may be added, with what agreement by the original author, royalty distributions between and among authors, sequence of author name listings, and so on.

It is important to realize that major textbooks—even successful ones—often do not sell enough copies in their first editions to recoup the considerable investments publishers must make in their production, promotion, and sales. New editions bring rewards to authors and publishers alike over the life of a successful textbook; the revision clause in the initial contract is designed to allow for that eventuality.

Negotiating Points:

- If the work is not a textbook, can the revision clause be stricken?
- Do the terms of the original contract (e.g., advance, permissions arrangements, etc.) extend to the revised editions?
- If the author is unable to revise the work upon request by the publisher, is it possible to negotiate approval over the co-author

recruited? Do you want to be involved in approving the revision even if you can't write it yourself? Do you want your name to be used and if so, under what conditions? Will you continue to receive royalties and at what rate?

Breach of Contract

Book contracts are typically breached by non-performance and what could be called "poor performance" issues. Scholarly publishing is still relatively civilized, so it is unlikely that a publisher will press a case against an author who can't or won't deliver a manuscript promised by contract. Authors and publishers typically agree to part ways (i.e., cancel contracts) when manuscript delivery becomes a problem. If a publisher graciously releases an author from contract obligations, however, the publisher does not expect to see the same project published elsewhere a year later.

Publishers sometimes take a long time to process and publish manuscripts, but rarely do they fail to publish an acceptable manuscript at all unless the publisher has become strapped for cash. Delinquent royalty and advance payments are another signal of a publisher in financial difficulty. Remedies include putting publishers on notice in writing and then initiating legal action if no satisfactory response is forthcoming. Publishers experiencing such difficulties, however, may be unresponsive until they sort out their own legal situations, which often end up with a sale or reorganization of the company.

One of the most disruptive examples of poor performance is plagiarism or libel on the part of an author. If a publisher is prosecuted for violating copyright or committing libel, author indemnification comes into play and the gloves come off if the issue is not resolved.

Negotiating Points:

- Make sure the contract specifies a finite period of time in which the publisher has to publish a final, complete, acceptable manuscript.
- Give publishers a deadline for responding to demands for outstanding royalty or advance payments, after which the contract may be declared null and void.

DEAL MAKERS AND BREAKERS

In many ways, this goes back to the "process and priority" points outlined earlier. Knowing your publishing preferences and priorities will help you establish your own deal makers and breakers, and will allow you to recognize what and when to negotiate to achieve your key contract objectives whether they be financial parameters (do you absolutely require an advance or a certain royalty rate?), production values (do you require a jacketed hardcover trade book commitment, or the inclusion of color art?), or marketing and promotional commitments (do you require the distribution of a certain number of free copies of your book for adoption consideration, or the production of advance bound galleys to reach trade media in advance of publication?).

Interestingly, authors report that deal makers and breakers often hinge on subjective values rather than hard negotiating points. A smart, enthusiastic editor is worth many royalty points from some points of view, and nothing will kill an author's interest faster than a slow or surly editor.

From the publisher's perspective, there are various deal breakers, some of which are financial (e.g., limits on advance monies or royalty rates based on the project's sales potential) and others of which are procedural (e.g., an author who refuses to indemnify the publisher or who wants to rewrite the contract). Given the concept of a publishing partnership as the ideal, it is best to identify deal makers and breakers early in the process and not allow contract negotiations to stall or falter at the end of a long process on the part of either the author or the publisher.

COMPETITIVE CONTRACT SITUATIONS

If you are lucky enough (or your project is attractive enough), you may find yourself with more than one contract offer. Sometimes these have very closely matched contract terms; at other times they vary, which puts negotiation in play. For instance, if one contract offer includes an advance and that is an important factor in your contract decision, you can either accept that offer, or go back to the press that did not offer an advance and see if it is open to negotiation on this point. Alternatively, perhaps one press offers an advance but another offers an inspiring marketing plan. Marketing plans are typically not part of the formal contract, but are considered part of the contractual agreement if offered in a side letter accompanying the contract. Which is more attractive? Which is more "binding?" Which is more important to the success of your book?

Competitive contract situations are a pleasant conundrum for authors and a challenge for publishers. Both authors and publishers want to end up with the best "deal" possible, but how that deal is defined varies according to what is most important to each. That calls for clarity and grace in communicating priorities.

If you negotiate a point with a press—whether it is an advance, a marketing plan, or some other element—and then do not accept the new offer, it is important to communicate why. It is not useful (or graceful) to negotiate one or myriad points with a press with which you would not choose to publish in any event.

Rarely, a competitive project will provoke a bidding war or go to auction, usually with the assistance of a book agent. Competitions at this level are usually more financially driven and less based on subjective factors like the relationship with an editor or the relative prestige of a press, but some of the same principles apply: Know, communicate, and stick with your priorities or you could end up with a financially attractive contract at a press that isn't right for your book or with an editor you can't work with happily.

Do You Need an Agent?

The prospect of a competitive project and contract negotiations is a major reason for engaging an agent. In general, academic authors do not need agents to successfully negotiate advantageous contracts for scholarly research monographs, textbooks, or midlist trade titles. If, however, an academic has made the leap to "public intellectual" status and is proposing a book with major trade potential, an agent may be a good idea.

Be aware that many agents require a referral by an established and successful author in the agent's stable in order to even consider an inquiry from an outside author, and an author can expect to pay an agent a significant sum either up front or as part of the ultimate royalty and advance arrangement. Some publishers decline to work with agents whereas others have good working relationships with key agents in certain fields.

An agent adds a third party to what is likely already a complex contract negotiation. The agent will expect to speak for the author in dealings with the publisher, so it is essential to clearly communicate publishing priorities to the agent from the outset of the relationship.

Bottom Line: What is Most Important in a Contract and How to Get It?

When it comes to scholarly publishing—a very tough business these days for authors and publishers alike—often the fact of a contract is more important than its substance. The fact of a contract is not enough, however, if it comes from an inappropriate press or an incompatible editor. Authors and publishers generally want the same things: a good book that reviews and sells well. Both authors and publishers prefer achieving these objectives in a relationship that flows readily—even enjoyably—through the ups and downs in any publishing relationship. The first indicator of that flow is the proposal and contract process. It is the foundation of a positive publishing partnership, and if the process gets off to a good start, a publishing experience in which everyone wins is more likely.

Recommended Resources

Derricourt, Robin. 1996. *An Author's Guide to Scholarly Publishing.* Princeton, NJ: Princeton University Press.

Germano, William. 2001. *Getting It Published: A Guide for Scholars and Anyone Else Serious about Serious Books.* Chicago: University of Chicago Press.

www.publaw.com. A Web resource offered by publishing legal expert Lloyd L. Rich of Denver, CO.

Note

*   This essay is not intended as legal advice and authors should consult an attorney if they have questions about any contract they are considering. Special thanks to L. Sandy Maisel and Dean Birkenkamp who provided helpful comments on an earlier draft of this chapter.

LEANNE ANDERSON, LYNNE RIENNER PUBLISHERS

THE ETIQUETTE OF PUBLISHING

15

When you've decided to write a book, finding a publisher can be a perplexing process, even for experienced authors. How do you find the right publisher? Once you've identified your top picks, how do you strike up a productive conversation with the right editor? Once you and your editor have established a relationship, how do you effectively respond to peer reviews, ask for concessions on a contract, or request changes in a cover design? When all is said and done, and your book has received rave reviews in *Perspectives on Politics*, how should you go about maintaining the relationship, or move on to another publisher without burning bridges?

The answers to such questions can be summed up under the rubric of publishing etiquette. Remember that publishing companies—even the large corporate conglomerates—are comprised of people, and as in any person-to-person exchange, understanding the "rules" of etiquette can help smooth out potentially sticky encounters. Additionally, establishing strong professional relationships with the publishing people you meet can be beneficial beyond the publication of a single book.

Just as you have a reputation among your academic peers, you will also develop a publishing reputation within a single company *and* among publishers. Your "in-house" publishing reputation will be important, because when an author is a pleasure to work with, people from all departments of the press will be more likely to go the extra mile in return. More broadly, just as you plan to have a long and productive career in political science, the editors you work with plan to have long and productive careers acquiring books in the same field—so they are likely to be part of your professional milieu for many years. Editors are known to "talk shop" with people at other presses, and also, like academics, to leave their presses for positions elsewhere; the editor you dismissed while she was at a press you weren't particularly interested in may wind up being the gatekeeper at a press with which you desperately want to publish.

FLIRTING, OR, EXPLORING YOUR PUBLISHING OPTIONS

Navigating the ins and outs of myriad publishing encounters will be infinitely easier once you have a sense of what your publisher expects throughout the course of your relationship. In the early stages, there are three important things to remember. First, talking to a publisher does not mean that either of you has made a commitment. Second, it is wise to keep an open mind about what you're looking for in a publisher. Finally, there are no rules about whether you or the publisher should take the lead when it comes to courting.

Publishers May Call You First

Editors need authors as much as aspiring authors need presses—and it is part of every editor's job to track trends in their fields and to identify exciting new scholars as well as new avenues in a familiar scholar's research plan. For these reasons, it is entirely possible that an editor may call you "out of the blue."

Help editors find you. As Beth Luey notes in chapter 1, pursuing the publication of journal articles related to your research agenda can be a good way to appear on editors' radar screens. Presenting papers at conferences can serve a similar purpose. Try to keep this in mind as you title your paper. If this particular piece is part of a larger project that you ultimately wish to publish as a book, incorporate keywords related to your broader questions into the paper's title.

When updating your CV to include your most recent paper presentations and articles accepted for publication, don't forget to post the most current version of the CV on your department web site. Alternatively or additionally, you might want to make a regular point of updating your profile on the department's faculty page. Editors are known to scour department web pages in search of such information, and mention of an interesting research agenda might prompt an editor to contact you.

It's okay to say no. If an editor contacts you after reading your article, spotting your paper in the conference program, or perusing your CV on the department web site, *and* you're ready to discuss a book project—great! But sometimes, this isn't the case. You may not have a fabulous new manuscript to discuss, or you simply may not be interested in this press for this project. How to respond?

It is always better to reply to an editor's queries than to ignore them altogether. As editors, we understand the concept of saying no. And there are a zillion ways of doing it: "Thanks so much for your interest, but I'm already working with a publisher." "No book project at present; I'll keep you in mind if/when that day arrives." "Articles are my current priority, but in about two years, I hope to be thinking about a book. Let's talk more then." Any of these quick replies will let the editor know that his query wasn't simply overlooked in the crush of a new semester/the holidays/the conference season *and* leaves open the possibility of working together on some future project.

Editors may propose book ideas. Sometimes an editor will have in mind a particular book that she wants to publish—and she may search out a prospective author to write it. If you aren't interested, or the timing isn't right, it is again perfectly acceptable to say no, or even to suggest a suitable colleague who may be interested. Taking that idea to an editor at another press, however, definitely qualifies as bad etiquette and constitutes burning bridges.

You Can Make the First Move

You don't have to wait for an editor to discover you. If you have a manuscript, or even an idea for a manuscript, and you want to figure out whether any publishers are interested, don't be shy about making the first move.

When should you approach a publisher? The simple answer is: whenever you're comfortable talking about a project. Some people prefer to wait until their manuscript is nearly complete before approaching a press, while others prefer to have editorial input early on. If you're one of the former, that's fine—just be aware that editors often have ideas for shaping projects to better meet the needs of a particular target audience. It is usually easier to work with these suggestions early-on in the life of a project, rather than after every page of prose has been polished to a golden sheen.

Which editors should you approach? You have likely heard this before: the presses who publish good books in your field will be excellent candidates for your project. (But don't automatically discount a press without an extensive list of books in your field *if* the editor has approached you or a colleague in your field first; the press may be expanding its publication focus and thus may give your book a little more attention than it would otherwise receive.) Other approaches include asking a colleague who has published with your ideal press to introduce you to his editor, or asking colleagues for their recommendations of editors and presses. Keep in mind that a formal introduction or reference is hardly essential for initiating a conversation with an editor—you should always feel free to contact your editor(s) of choice directly.

Conference book exhibits. The exhibit areas at annual and regional political science meetings can afford you an opportunity to assess a publisher's list (and to discuss with the attending staff what might be "in the hopper" but not yet in print), but editors' schedules are often very full during these conferences. To guarantee that you'll have a chance to talk, you should query the editor in advance of the conference (by phone, email, or snail mail) and ask for a meeting. In this kind of query, aim to summarize the main question driving your work and the significance of your findings in a few sentences or, at most, a few paragraphs. This allows an editor to ascertain quickly whether the project is appropriate for his list and either schedule a time to meet or direct you to another, more appropriate press. If at all possible, have a proposal ready to share with the editor when you meet.

If you haven't been able to send out advance queries, it is still worth stopping by the publisher's booth in the exhibit area. You may catch an editor between commitments, and/or the other staff members may be able to slip a meeting into his schedule. At a minimum, you will be able to find out who you need to contact about your proposal.

Meetings at conferences don't have to be lengthy. Even a five-minute conversation at a conference can tell you (and the editor) whether this relationship is worth pursuing. Bear in mind that book exhibits are rarely conveniently located to anything else in the conference hotel, lines for coffee are often long, and there is only so much coffee or tea a person can drink. This all means that it will likely be easiest to meet and talk in the near vicinity of the publisher's booth.

Discussing Your Project

Remember the job-search wisdom about preparing one-minute, five-minute, and forty-five-minute descriptions of your research? The same advice applies to discussing your project with publishers. You want to engage an editor in a conversation rather than lecture her, so start with the broad one-minute overview and let the exchange develop naturally. If she needs or wants detailed description of each chapter, she will ask.

In the course of your conversation, pay attention to the editor's questions. Editors usually pose questions in an effort to understand the scope of a project, its contributions, its audience, and how it might fit into their lists. This interchange can tell you a lot about the potential market for your book, as well as the specific kinds of information the editor will be looking for in your proposal—and may help you anticipate and prepare for similar questions from other publishers. These same principles apply anytime you are cold-calling an editor at a press.

As an aside, it is never a good idea to start a conversation by asking if an editor would like to publish your dissertation; the answer to that is invariably "no."[1]

Starting to Date, or, Submitting Your Proposal

In chapter 13, Alex Holzman discusses how to craft an engaging query letter and proposal, and following his advice will no doubt help your proposal stand out from the crowd. Nevertheless, there are a few points worth reiterating here. Spelling counts and grammar can make a strong impression. Take the time to address your initial query to a specific editor at the press—and, should you misspell an editor's name or the name of a company, at least misspell it consistently. If you're sending essentially the same query letter to a number of presses at the same time, double-check the individual letters to be sure that you're not telling Mr. Editor at Western Scholarly Press why your book will be a great fit with Eastern Scholarly Press's previous publications.

Submitting Query Letters and Proposals to Multiple Presses

The submission of query letters and proposals to several presses simultaneously is a common and widely accepted practice. (Allowing multiple presses to send your complete manuscript out for review at the same time, however, is another matter; more on this below.) Editors understand that when authors begin testing the publishing waters, they are often facing pressures ranging from a ticking tenure clock to time-sensitive research; submitting a proposal to one press at a time simply is not feasible. That said, remember that we do appreciate knowing as much as possible about your situation, including whether we're one of your top choices and what you'd ideally like from a publisher (an advance contract, a particular price-point for the book, etc.). Such information will help us quickly and honestly evaluate whether we are going to be able to meet your needs.

As a result of this process, you may find yourself in the lucky position of having multiple presses interested in your project. Whichever press you choose, let everyone know your decision—not just the lucky suitor! A forthright rejection is a much-appreciated courtesy, and can preserve your relationship with the losing editor(s): "Thanks very much for your consideration, but I've decided to move ahead with another publisher. I hope we'll be able to work together on a different book in the future." It is okay to name names here, and the other editors may appreciate knowing who their competition was.

Clear and Consistent Communication Is Key

After you have submitted your proposal (and for the duration of the publication process), it is valuable to maintain steady contact with the publisher. If you are curious to know what your editor thinks of your proposal, feel free to ask—but be judicious. Stalking her with weekly calls from the moment you submit the proposal is not likely to garner a positive response. Of course, communication is a two-way street; if she is not responding to your queries, it is entirely reasonable to turn your attention to a more responsive editor.

Once your proposal has been accepted, be sure to let your editor know if your anticipated manuscript completion date has changed. She needs to have a sense of which manuscripts she'll be receiving in the coming months, and she doesn't want to feel as though *she's* stalking *you* to figure this out.

MEETING THE PARENTS, OR, SURVIVING THE REVIEW PROCESS WITH YOUR DIGNITY INTACT

Multiple Submissions of Complete Manuscripts

The submission of complete manuscripts to multiple presses for simultaneous external peer review is rarely looked on favorably by publishers. You can always ask your editor if he is amenable to this, explaining the circumstances that might justify this course of action, but bear in mind that it is also okay—and the norm—for him to simply say no. Arranging for the external review of manuscripts requires a significant investment of resources, both financial and in terms of the editor's and the reviewers' time.

You should never submit your manuscript to multiple presses for simultaneous external peer review without telling the respective acquiring editors that you are doing so. There are a limited number of appropriate readers for any given manuscript, and your editor will be unpleasantly surprised to discover, upon contacting the perfect readers for your manuscript, that they are already reading it for another press. He will feel duped, and may officially retract any interest in the project rather than deal with an author he feels is not on the level.

Internal Reviews

A little secret of the publishing world is that, much as we acquisitions editors love the ideas and issues at the core of the books we publish, there simply aren't enough hours in the day to read every page of every manuscript that crosses our desks. (This is why it is rarely, if ever, effective to send your complete manuscript for our initial consideration in lieu of sending a well-crafted book proposal.) That said, editors will at a minimum skim the manuscript in the same way a prospective reader might. Unlike prospective readers, however, the right editor will be invested enough in your project to call you and discuss any problems or issues that she finds.

While it can be disappointing to have your editor tell you that she does not think your manuscript is ready for peer review, try to keep an open mind. If she has taken the time to offer such feedback, she is motivated by two desires: first, to increase the likelihood that your manuscript will receive strongly positive peer reviews, and second, to help you write the best book possible, meaning a book that reaches its target audience and that makes the largest impact possible. If you vigorously disagree with her comments, this may be the right time to conclude that the two of you have different visions for the work and should part ways.

Peer Reviews

You will no doubt be anxious to hear what the anonymous peer reviewers have said about your manuscript. So will your editor. Understand that peer review is the one part of the publishing process over which he has very little control. He can and will ask to receive comments within a set period of time, but because the reviewers are other scholars who have agreed to offer constructive feedback on your manuscript rather than people directly in the employ of the press, he cannot force them to adhere to his timeline. Calling your editor every day to ask whether the reviews have come in yet will not make them appear any faster; if your editor is on the phone obsessing with you about what the reviews *might* say, he is not on the phone finding out what the reviews actually *will* say (and when he can expect to receive written comments).

On the flip side, if you have agreed to review a manuscript for an editor, please remember that there is an anxious author waiting to hear how his masterpiece has been received. Sticking to your agreed-upon deadline for submitting comments is always appreciated! If circumstances change and you can't review the manuscript after all—a colleague quits, leaving you responsible for additional classes; you have to deal with an unexpected family issue; you realize halfway into the manuscript that you simply can't be objective—please get in touch with the editor right away. It is better for him to know as soon as possible that you are not able to write the review, and you'll feel better not having to avoid his calls and emails.

Responding to Reviews

The goal of any review process is to create a stronger piece of scholarship. It is a rare, rare thing to receive 100% glowingly positive comments. Bear these truths in mind when you receive your reviews.

Resist the urge to call your editor immediately after she sends you the reviews (unless of course you've been the privileged recipient of those glowing accolades). If you don't, whatever you tell her may be based on raw emotion rather than solid reason—and she may conclude that you're not taking the review process seriously. It is better to share your initial gut reactions with a friend who can unequivocally share your pain and support your indignation. Only after you have thoughtfully digested the reviewers' comments should you discuss them with your editor.

As with an internal review, you may not agree with everything an anonymous peer reviewer says, and may in fact have excellent reasons for not taking the advice. But if two or three reviewers raise similar questions or objections, at a minimum it means that you need to do a better job of explaining your point. In any event, it is always smart to ask for your editor's interpretation of the reviews. Because reading between the lines of reviews is a regular part of her job, she can help guide you through the critiques and point out anything that is especially important.

Finally, don't assume that your editor has selected wildly inappropriate reviewers or deliberately sabotaged your manuscript. While acquiring editors are by no means perfect, we are professionals at locating outside readers with the appropriate qualifications. It could well be that Dr. Eminent, who surely would have raved about your ideas, is in fact Reviewer A, who offered a lengthy critique of the flaws in the manuscript—and pages of suggestions on how to repair those flaws. Furthermore, editors are highly unlikely to send out a manuscript in the hopes that it will *not* pass review.

GETTING MARRIED, OR, ON THE SUBJECT OF CONTRACTS

Jennifer Knerr has provided an excellent detailed discussion of common publishing contract terms, and tips for negotiating them (chapter 14), so here I will simply reiterate her central point: when you sign a contract with a publisher, you are cementing a partnership. To ensure that it is a long and productive partnership, keep the bigger picture in mind when you start wrangling over contract details. A 1% difference in royalty rates may put an additional $200 in your pocket, but finding a press that will truly champion your project and an editor that you enjoy working with is priceless.

LEARNING TO LOVE THE IN-LAWS, OR, WORKING WITH THE PRESS AS A WHOLE

There are a number of people working for your publisher—beyond your editor—who want to help make your book a success. Learn to work with them, and you'll have a whole team of people eager to take care of you.

On the Design of Your Book

If you have a particular vision for the cover art or the design of your book, it is best to talk with your editor about this as soon as possible after your manuscript has been accepted for publication. He will be able to advocate more effectively on your behalf if he knows about your top concerns early on. But remember, publishers typically look at book covers as marketing tools and will likely have specific needs to meet.

If you find that an element of the design just doesn't feel right, realize that there is a real person at the press who created that design element. This does not mean you should say nothing. Rather, consider starting a conversation about the design flaw by asking questions: "I don't understand why you decided to. . . . Can you explain it to me?" If the answers you receive don't alleviate your concerns, be explicit about what you think is wrong. Telling your publisher that you "don't like X" is much less effective than offering constructive criticisms and specific suggestions to solve the problem: "X suggests that the book is about war, not peace. Could we replace it with Y instead?"

On the Marketing of Your Book

Be prompt when responding to the marketing department's calls and queries. This will help them to most effectively promote your book! In some instances—for example, if a publicist calls about a possible TV or radio interview—a delay of even 24 hours in responding can mean that the promotional opportunity has passed.

Remember that, when you've written a book, you have created a product that has value—one that you want people to buy and read. Your publisher's marketing department will do everything in their power to help spread the word about your project, but it is also entirely reasonable to engage in a bit of self-promotion, whether that means participating in an author-meets-critics session at a conference or arranging a talk and book signing at your local bookstore. If you do arrange a special event, give the marketing team as much advance notice as possible. There are often many details to coordinate, from the production of order forms and fliers to the negotiation of special discounts for the sale of books at the event itself, and the more time that marketing has to bring this all together, the better.

If you are curious to know how your book is selling, or whether there are any new reviews, feel free to ask—but as with your editor, be judicious about the timing of your calls. Your publisher simply won't know whether your book is "doing well" until several months or even a year has passed. Similarly, it can take at least six months before reviews of your book begin to appear (and it is not unusual to see reviews of books five or more years after publication). And much as we wish it were otherwise, marketing departments cannot *make* anyone review—or buy—your book.

Finally, remember that in the world of academic publishing, some books have a market of 400 while others have a market 50 times larger. If your book falls into the former category, it generally doesn't mean that you wrote a bad book, or that your marketing team didn't do its job.

LIVING HAPPILY EVER AFTER, OR, WHAT HAPPENS WHEN YOUR NEW BOOK IS OLD NEWS?

Barring unexpected circumstances, neither your editor nor your publishing house will disappear after your book has been published. If you have time while attending conferences, keep an eye out for your editor or other representatives of the press. Introduce yourself to whoever is working the booth (it could be the marketing assistant, who, impressed with your engaging personality and generous nature, will return to the office determined to help your book sell out its first printing). Check in periodically with the marketing contacts you've made, and/or call the editor to try out an idea for a new book. Even if you don't plan to write another book, or to work with the same press again, you may have grad students who will soon be in search of a publisher, and it is always good to keep your publishing contacts strong. At the end of the day, the etiquette of publishing comes down to just a few core principles: it is always okay to ask questions; honesty is still the best policy; and the Golden Rule (do unto others . . .) is always a safe bet.

REFERENCES

Holzman, Alex. 2008. "The Query Letter and Proposal as Sales Tools." In In *Publishing Political Science: The APSA Guide to Writing and Publishing*, ed. Stephen Yoder. Washington, D.C.: American Political Science Association, 213–20.

Knerr, Jennifer. 2008. "Negotiating a Book Contract with Grace, Finesse, and Success." In *Publishing Political Science: The APSA Guide to Writing and Publishing*, ed. Stephen Yoder. Washington, D.C.: American Political Science Association, 221–40.

Germano, William. 2001. *Getting It Published: A Guide for Scholars and Anyone Else Serious about Serious Books*. Chicago: University of Chicago Press.

———. 2005. *From Dissertation to Book*. Chicago: University of Chicago Press.

Luey, Beth. 2008. "Sharing What You Know." In *Publishing Political Science: The APSA Guide to Writing and Publishing*, ed. Stephen Yoder. Washington, D.C.: American Political Science Association, 11–20.

Thatcher, Sanford G. 2008. "Scholarly Book Publishing in Political Science: A Hazardous Business." In In *Publishing Political Science: The APSA Guide to Writing and Publishing*, ed. Stephen Yoder. Washington, D.C.: American Political Science Association, 35–51.

NOTE

For more detailed discussion of the difference between a dissertation and a book, see
  Beth Luey's *Revising Your Dissertation* or William Germano's *From Dissertation to
  Book* or *Getting It Published*. For more on the changing marketplace for published
  dissertations, see Sandy Thatcher's contribution in chapter 3.

CONTRIBUTORS

LEANNE ANDERSON is executive editor at Lynne Rienner Publishers, where she acquires books on U.S. politics and public policy, and has acquired in the areas of Asian studies, criminology, and sociology. Previously, she has held positions with a New York City literary agency, with a small, Seattle-based trade publisher, and with the Tattered Cover, one of the country's premier independent bookstores. She is a graduate of the University of Denver Publishing Institute.

THOMAS E. CRONIN is McHugh Professor of American Institutions and Leadership at Colorado College and president emeritus of Whitman College (1993–2005). He is author of nearly 200 scholarly and public affairs articles, and author, co-author, or editor of a dozen books including *The Paradoxes of the American Presidency* (Oxford University Press, 2004) and *On the Presidency* (Paradigm Publishers, 2008). He can be reached at tom.cronin@coloradocollege.edu.

DANIEL W. DREZNER is associate professor of international politics at the Fletcher School of Law and Diplomacy at Tufts University. Prior to Fletcher, he taught at the University of Chicago and the University of Colorado at Boulder. He is the author, most recently, of *All Politics is Global: Explaining International Regulatory Regimes* (Princeton University Press, 2007), which explores how and when regulatory standards are coordinated across borders in an era of globalization. His previous books include *U.S. Trade Strategy* (Council on Foreign Relations, 2006), *Locating the Proper Authorities* (University of Michigan Press, 2003), and *The Sanctions Paradox* (Cambridge University Press, 1999). Drezner has published articles in numerous scholarly journals as well as in the *New York Times, Wall Street Journal, Washington Post, Foreign Policy*, and *Foreign Affairs*.

DOUG GOLDENBERG-HART is an acquisitions editor for political/social science reference titles for CQ Press, Reference Division. He did graduate course work in government at the University of Texas at Austin, and spent six years teaching politics at Austin Community College. Among the multi-volume reference titles he has commissioned are *Polling America: An Encyclopedia of Public Opinion* and *Federalism in America: An Encyclopedia* (with Greenwood), and the forthcoming *Encyclopedia of U.S.-American Indian Policy and Law*, the *Encyclopedia of the First Amendment*, and the *International Encyclopedia of Political Science*.

JENNIFER L. HOCHSCHILD is the Henry LaBarre Jayne Professor of Government, Professor of African and African American Studies, and Harvard College Professor at Harvard University. She studies the intersection of American politics and political philosophy—particularly in the areas of race or ethnicity, immigration, education, public opinion, and political culture. Most recently, she is the co-author of *The American Dream and Public School* (Oxford University Press, 2003) and the author of *Facing Up to the American Dream: Race, Class, and the Soul of the Nation* (Princeton University Press, 1995), as well as various articles and book chapters. She was the founding editor of *Perspectives on Politics*. She is a Fellow of the American Academy of Arts and Sciences, and has been a vice-president of the American Political Science Association, vice-chair of the Board of Trustees of the Russell Sage Foundation, and member of the Board of Overseers of the General Social Survey.

ALEX HOLZMAN is director of Temple University Press. During a 30-year career in publishing he has worked in sales, editorial and administration, and in trade textbook and scholarly publishing, including books and journals. He also serves as political science editor at Temple, reprising the role he has filled during stints at Cambridge University Press, Ohio State University Press, and Charles Scribners Sons. During 2008–2009 he will serve as president of the Association of American University Presses.

RONALD J. HREBENAR is professor of political science, former chair of the department, and former director of the Hinckley Institute of Politics at the University of Utah. He is the author or editor of 14 books and author or co-author of more than 50 book chapters and political science journal articles. He received his Ph.D. from the University of Washington-Seattle in 1973. His most recent book is *Political Parties, Interest Groups, and Political Campaigns* (2008). In 2007–2008, Hrebenar was Fulbright Distinguished Professor of American Studies at the University of Vienna.

CHRISTOPHER J. KELAHER has been an acquiring editor at the Brookings Institution Press since 1999. Since the fall of 2004 he has also been marketing director. Previously he has held positions at Resource for the Future, the American University Press, and Chatham House Publishers (now part of CQ Press). His B.A. in political science is from the University of Dayton, and he holds an M.A. in political science from the University of Wisconsin-Madison.

JENNIFER KNERR is vice president and executive editor of Paradigm Publishers, a new independent, employee-owned press for the social sciences and humanities. She has negotiated hundreds of book contracts for publishers including Rowman & Littlefield, Westview Press, and Charles E. Merrill, and she looks forward to negotiating her first book contract as an author as soon as she finishes her thesis.

JEFFREY W. KNOPF is associate professor of national security affairs at the Naval Postgraduate School, Monterey, CA. He is the author of *Domestic Society and International Cooperation: The Impact of Protest on US Arms Control Policy* (Cambridge, UK: Cambridge University Press, 1998). His current research focuses on the role of deterrence in dealing with asymmetric threats in the aftermath of 9/11.

BETH LUEY, an editorial consultant in Fairhaven, Massachusetts, is the founding director emerita of the Scholarly Publishing Program at Arizona State University. She is author of *Handbook for Academic Authors* (Cambridge) and editor of *Revising Your Dissertation: Advice from Leading Editors* (California). She is a past president of the Association for Documentary Editing and of the Society for the History of Authorship, Reading and Publishing. She conducts workshops on publishing at campuses across the country.

IAIN MCMENAMIN is a senior lecturer in the School of Law and Government, Dublin City University. He has published on a range of topics in comparative politics in journals such as the *European Journal of Political Research, British Journal of Political Science*, and *Public Choice*. He is currently working on a book analyzing business financing of parties in parliamentary regimes.

MARK C. MILLER is associate professor and former chair of the department of government and international relations at Clark University, where he is also the director of the Law and Society Program. He received his Ph.D. from the Ohio State University and his law degree from George Washington University. He is author of *The High Priests of American Politics: The Role of Lawyers in American Political Institutions* (1995) and the co-editor of *Making Policy, Making Law: An Interbranch Perspective* (Georgetown University Press, 2004). During 2006–2007, he was a visiting scholar at the Centennial Center for Political Science and Public Affairs at the American Political Science Association. During the spring of 2008, he was the Thomas Jefferson Distinguished Chair, a Fulbright scholar to the American Studies Program and the history department at Leiden University in the Netherlands.

KAREN O'CONNOR is the Jonathan N. Helfat Distinguished Professor of Political Science in the School of Public Affairs at American University. She holds a J.D. and Ph.D. from SUNY Buffalo. She is the author of *American Government: Continuity and Change*, 9th edition (with Larry Sabato), as well as several other books on women and politics. She is past president of the Southern Political Science Association, National Capital Area Political Science Association, the APSA and SPSA's Women's Caucuses, the Women & Politics Organized Research Section of the APSA, as well as its Law and Courts Research Section.

ANDREA PEDOLSKY is chief of editorial acquisitions for CQ Press, Reference Division. In addition to overseeing the development of the company's list of award-winning reference works, she is involved in making strategic acquisitions and developing partnerships with outside organizations and companies. Prior to joining CQ Press, she ran her own literary agency for 10 years; prior to that she was an acquisitions editor for various publishers in New York City.

ANDREW J. POLSKY, professor of political science at Hunter College and the Graduate Center, CUNY, became the editor of *Polity* in 2005. His primary research interests lie in the field of American political development (APD), with a particular focus on the presidency, political parties and elections, and political economy. He is the author of *The Rise of the Therapeutic State* (Princeton University Press, 1991). In addition to *Polity*, his articles have appeared in *Studies in American Political Development, American Politics Research, Journal of Theoretical Politics*, and other journals.

MARC SEGERS is editorial acquisitions manager for new e-markets for CQ Press, Reference Division, creating new initiatives and products to reach beyond the traditional academic political science markets. Previously, he was an acquisitions editor for online and print reference at CQ Press, and developed a new product line of high-end, customized online editions. He has played a strategic role planning, researching, and overseeing the enhancement of all the online reference resources for CQ Press.

SANFORD G. THATCHER is director of Penn State University Press, where he has been since 1989. Previously he worked as an editor at Princeton University Press for 22 years, the last four as editor-in-chief. His articles about various aspects of scholarly communication have appeared in *Against the Grain, Chronicle of Higher Education, Learned Publishing*, and the *Journal of Scholarly Publishing*. An expert on copyright law, he serves on the copyright committees of the Association of American Publishers (AAP) and Association of American University Presses (AAUP) and also on the Board of Directors of the Copyright Clearance Center (CCC). In 2007–2008 he was AAUP's president.

CLIVE S. THOMAS is professor of political science at the University of Alaska-Juneau. Besides authoring and co-authoring books, chapters in books, and articles on U.S. national and state politics, and particularly interest groups in advanced, developing, and authoritarian societies, he has also edited/co-edited several books including: *Research Guide to U.S. and International Interest Groups* (2004), *Political Parties and Interest Groups* (2001), and four regional volumes on interest groups in the American states (with Ronald J. Hrebenar). He has received several grants and research awards, including four Fulbright Scholarships. In addition, he has served as a volunteer lobbyist and teaches seminars on how to lobby to various organizations.

STEPHEN YODER is a first-year doctoral student in the department of government and politics at the University of Maryland, College Park. His research interests include American state and local politics and political behavior. In academia, he earned an M.A. in history through the department of history and a certificate in scholarly publishing through the Scholarly Publishing Program at Arizona State University. In scholarly publishing, he has served as managing editor of *PS: Political Science and Politics*, as editorial assistant at *Documentary Editing* and at the book review section of the *Historian*, and as a freelance copy editor and proofreader for several books published by various academic presses.